A Floating World   Impermanence and Motion in Japanese Art

A Floating World

Impermanence and Motion
in Japanese Art

Stephan von der Schulenburg

Verlag der Buchhandlung Walther und Franz König

museum angewandtekunst

Cover image:

Aka-Raku chawan (cat. no. 13)
Earthenware, rust-red glaze with craquelure, gold lacquer repair (*kintsugi*)
Japan, Kyōto, Raku workshop, early Edo period, 17th c.

With kind support from

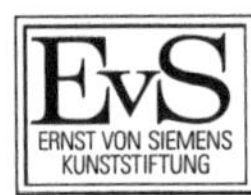

hessische
kultur
stiftung

EvS
ERNST VON SIEMENS
KUNSTSTIFTUNG

METZLER

Contents

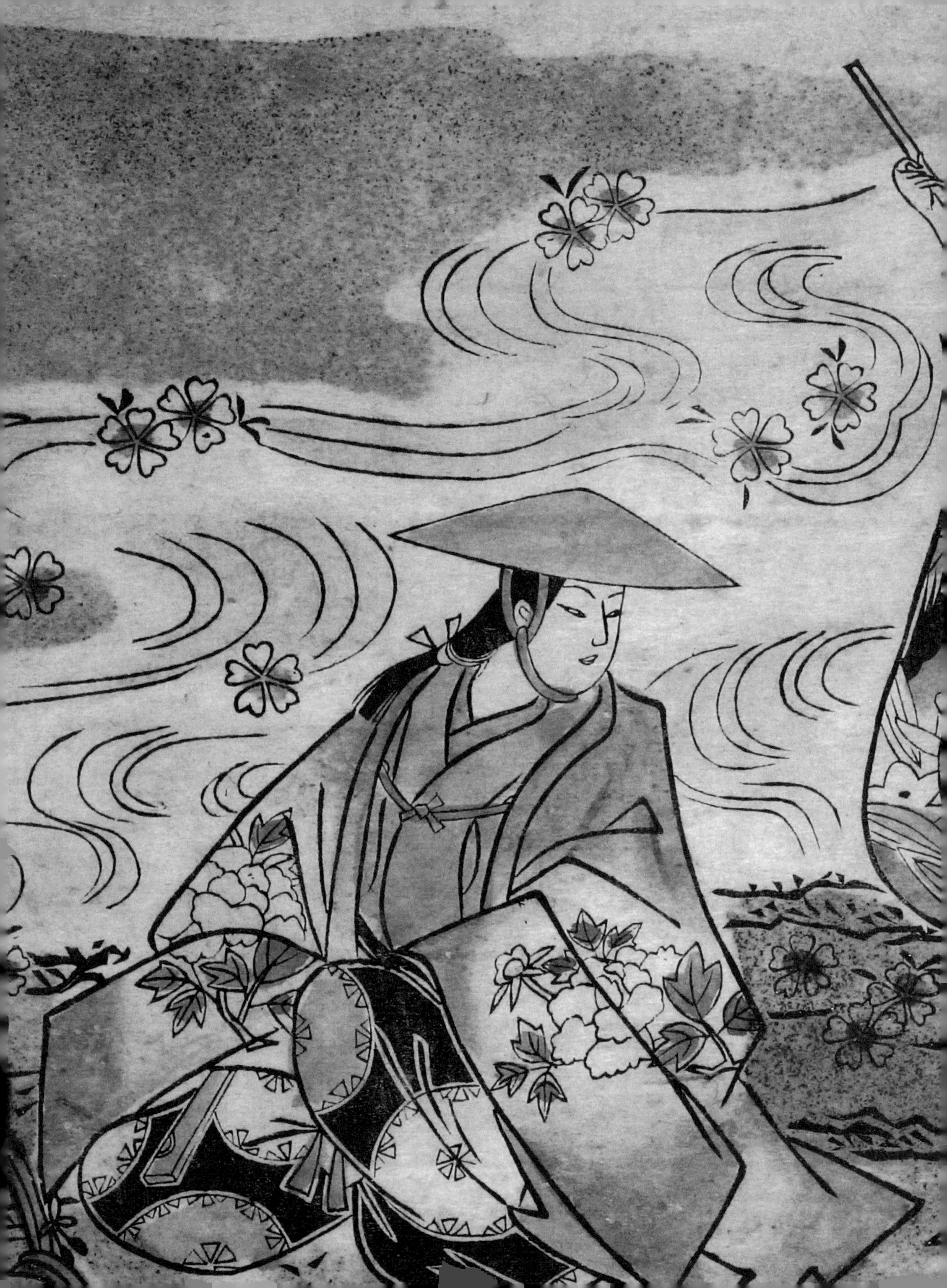

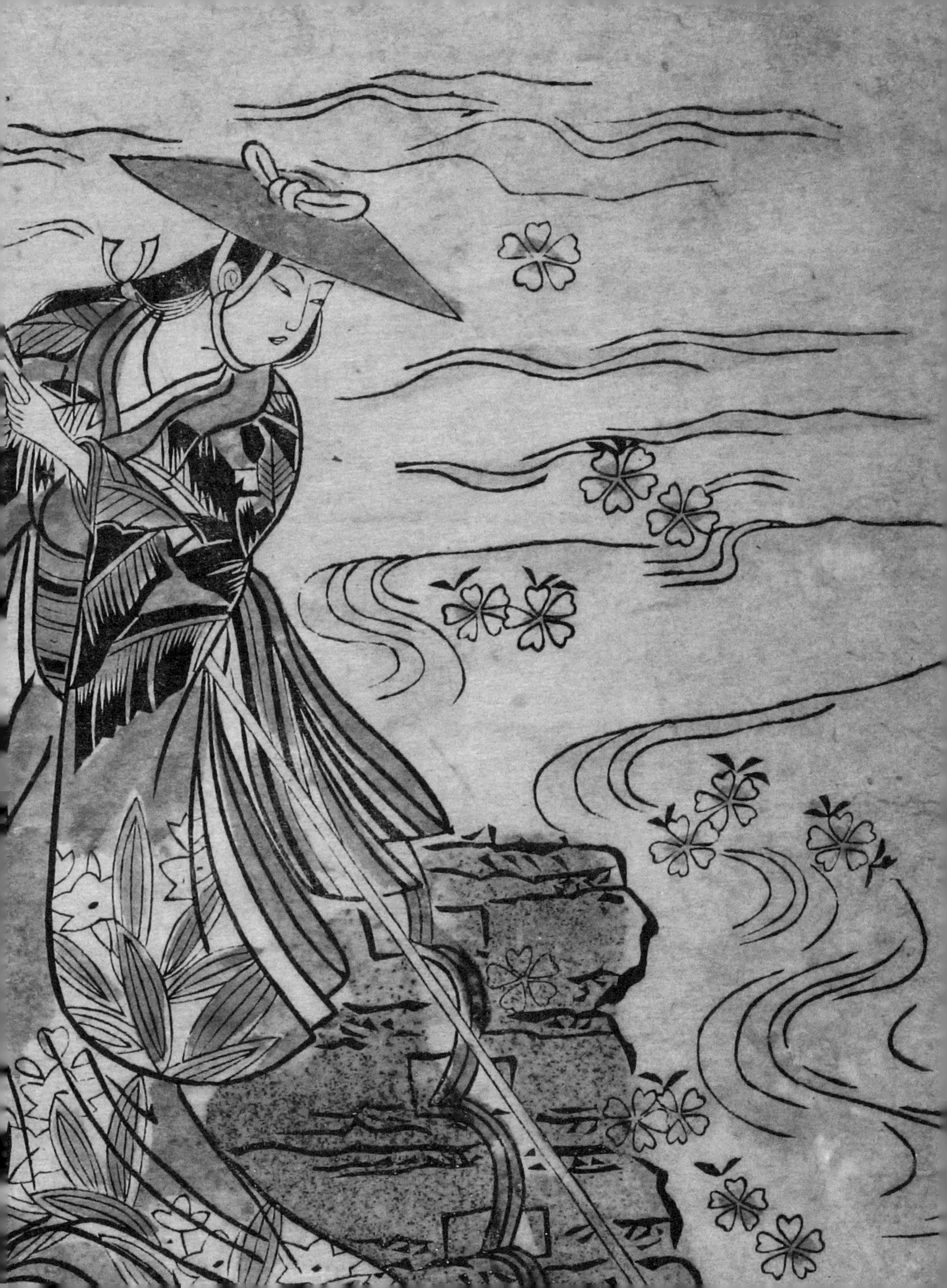

Preface

At first, mounting an exhibition on transience in a museum dedicated to holding works in perpetuity and preserving cultural artefacts and art might seem paradoxical. Yet the museum as an institution for heritage objects is vital precisely because it protects irreplaceable, fragile objects which would otherwise be lost to posterity.

The works on view in this exhibition demonstrate that artistic expression in Japan has long been concerned with transience, the ephemeral presence of life, fleeting nature of our existence, examining these ideas through a broad array of subjects. Moreover, these works offer insights into our museum's history of acquisitions, whose significance has grown since the late nineteenth century until today thanks to major purchases and bequests.

The genesis of our Japanese collection doubtless has its roots in the major world fairs Japan participated in between 1870 and 1910, after the country was forced to open itself to international trade in the late nineteenth century after almost 250 years of isolation. These exhibitions placed the local, national, and global in a productive tension. When Japan first took part, it created exhibition landscapes which could include gentle hills and artificial waterfalls with pavilions and temples.

Here, the country's cultural treasures were on display: its lacquerware, porcelain and ceramics, *ukiyo-e* woodblock prints, bronze works, and textiles. The Japanese perspective and aesthetic began to influence Western art and design, leading to a passionate desire among private collectors and institutions to acquire works. Two raku tea bowls (cat. no. 14, 15) purchased from the collection of Wilhelm Peter Metzler (1818–1904) in 1904 were among the museum's very first encounters with Japanese art. Metzler was one of the founders of the Mitteldeutscher Kunstgewerbeverein in Frankfurt am Main in 1877, and thus one of the founders of the Kunstgewerbemuseum (now the Museum Angewandte Kunst).

The ideas behind our exhibition and our choice of works will be covered in more detail over the subsequent pages. For now, we wish to note that we began planning a similar exhibition more than twenty years ago under the working title "Japanese Art in Space and Time". For various reasons, we were unable to realise it at the time. But when we bear in mind the aforementioned major additions to our Japanese collection in recent years, we can consider ourselves fortunate to only be mounting this exhibition now, as we have been able to draw on a far richer range of artefacts, to which the catalogue of works in the present volume testifies. The many pieces selected in our extensive collection of Japanese works now form the centre of *A Floating World*. Moreover, four new contributions unexpectedly bring it to life within the context of contemporary Japanese art.

Our thanks go first and foremost to Rikuo Ueda, Hide Nasu, Shiriagari Kotobuki, Peter Granser, and Mari Kashiwagi for their fascinating artistic contributions on movement and transience in contemporary Japanese art. Equally, we offer our thanks and respect to those masters (some quite elderly) whose mostly ceramic works have become part of our museum collection over recent decades and which we have selected for the present exhibition.

A special thanks goes to our lenders: Christa, Marcus, and Alexander Müller of the Frankfurt-based gallery Japan Art as well as the Kunstgewerbeverein in Frankfurt for their permanent loans to the museum. Moreover, we thank Mikiko Sato and her Hamburg-based gallery for her extensive support with the contribution from Rikuo Ueda.

It is a pleasure to once again work with Verlag der Buchhandlung Walther König, this time in cooperation with Thames & Hudson in London, who have published the English edition of this catalogue. We are especially grateful to Walther König himself as well as to Nicole Rankers for their editorial support.

Our Nara outpost headed by Wolfgang Höhn in cooperation with Mariko Sakai is vital to our work, and we thank them for their faultless professionalism and meticulous work in editing and translating from Japanese into German. Both the English and German versions of this publication were designed by Zarah Landes, whom we also wish to thank.

At the museum itself, we would like to offer our sincere thanks to all our colleagues who have aided our endeavour. First and foremost is our exhibition manager David Beikirch, who supported the project from the start with his usual professionalism. He realised a harmonious exhibition design in collaboration with Jasmin Kress, who was responsible for all graphic design elements.

Ute Kunze deserves a special thanks both for her background archival work and for most of the photographs of the objects in the exhibition. She was supported by photographer Franziska Krieg. Brigitte Sahler was kind enough to take responsibility for the online side of the project. Our thanks go to our press and PR colleagues Natali-Lina Pitzer, Lucy Rose Nixon, Janine Bartsch, and Katja Kummerfeldt. Equally, we would like to thank Simone Richter, Sonja Sikora, Dilan Alt, Nina Manes, and Elias Roth for their tailor-made outreach and education programme for the exhibition. We thank Sabine Huth for coordinating the exhibition events. Thanks go to Kathrin Röttger for her exemplary restoration work for the exhibition, to Isabelle Kollig for coordinating and administering loans, and to Natalie Graf-Schwab for carefully overseeing the finances. We are grateful to our administrative assistant Sandra Schwarz in the museum directorate and to Thomas Funk for his technical management. We thank Stanislav Yakushev and Alexander Schwarz for overseeing and maintaining the museum building.

We are grateful to the city of Frankfurt am Main and to Dr Ina Hartwig, head of the Department of Culture and Science, who represents all decision-makers.

Finally our heartfelt thanks go to three generous sponsors who were essential to the realisation of this project. The Hessische Kulturstiftung offered invaluable support and we are deeply grateful to director Eva Claudia Scholtz and the members of the board of trustees. We also give our sincere thanks to the Ernst von Siemens Kunststiftung, in particular Dr Martin Hoernes. And we are very grateful to Bankhaus Metzler, in particular Gerhard Wiesheu, whose support for the current exhibition contains a distant echo of the two aforementioned tea bowls from the collection of Wilhelm Peter Metzler, which already entered the museum collection some 120 years ago.

Matthias Wagner K
Director

Stephan von der Schulenburg
Exhibition curator

1   Specific additions to the collection that are particularly worth mentioning include *ukiyo-e* woodblock prints collected by Johann Georg Geyger (2001) and Utto Riese (2012), together comprising 240 outstanding prints; a diverse range of 150 works connected to Japan, gifted by Gabriele Günther (2012); and the H. collection of Japanese cloisonné, comprising around 440 objects, which belonged to a collector who wished to remain anonymous and were donated to the museum by his widow (2016). We also pay tribute to the acclaimed collector and patron Gisela Freudenberg (1923–2021), who bequeathed so many significant works of contemporary Japanese ceramics to the museum beginning in the 1990s. In doing so, she brought to life a further major part of our collection of works from Japan.

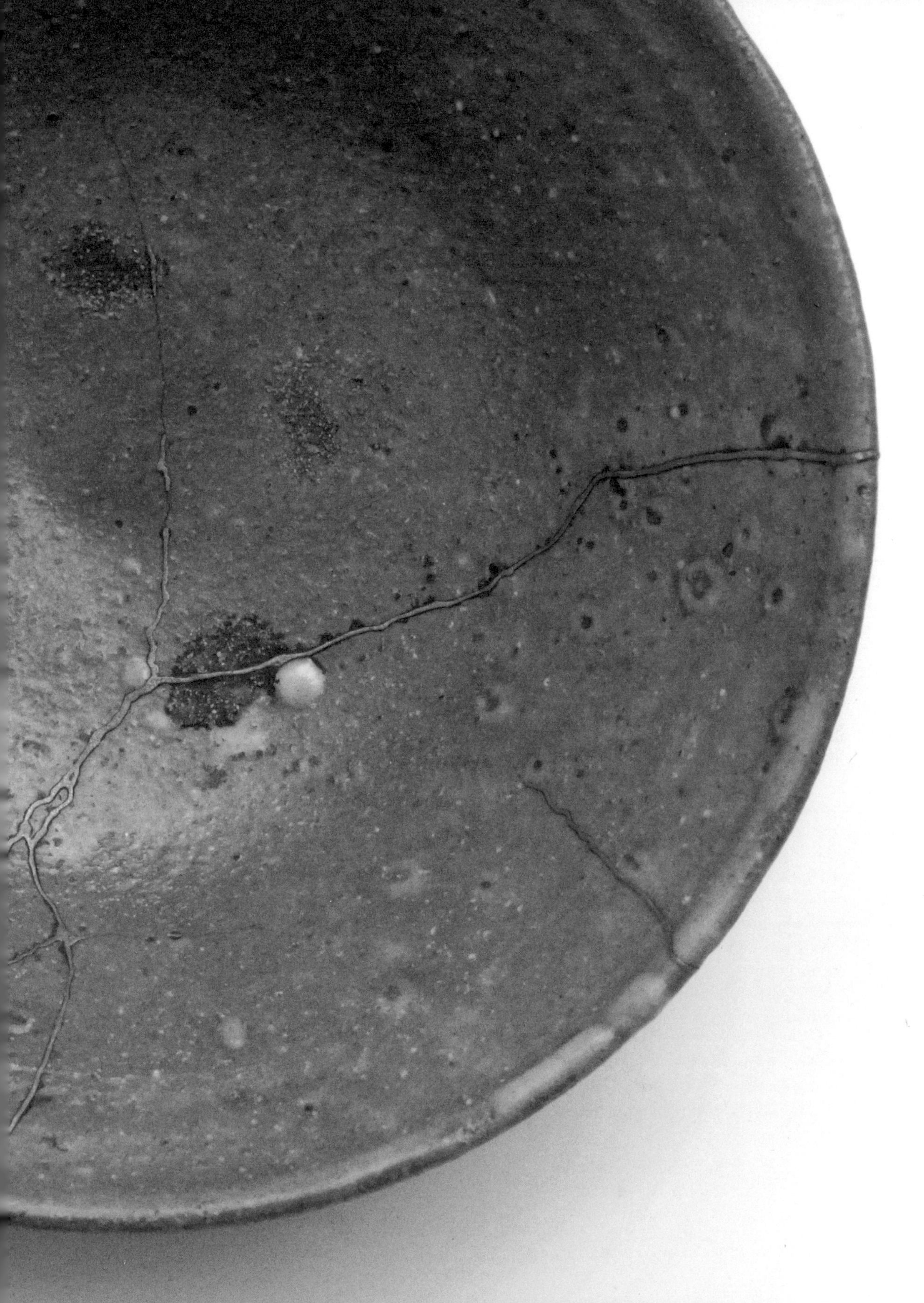

A Floating World

Impermanence and Motion
in Japanese Art

One of the most fundamental truths of human existence is our awareness that nothing in the world is permanent. Our lives are always subject to disruption and displacement, unavoidably exposed to an ever-changing universe. In other words, the only constant is this continual process of change, so it is no wonder that so many art forms have sought to explore this uncertain state of being. There is, of course, significant variation in the ways different cultures respond to this phenomenon. Rome is known as the "eternal city", a description which might appear to negate the idea of constant change. Despite the fact that the city on the Tiber has been perpetually transformed across the centuries, Rome's prominent landmarks such as the Colosseum, Castel Sant'Angelo or St Peter's Square, mean that it is often perceived as "eternal". Naturally, the city's ancient past and its historical and cultural significance are also factors. But the historic architecture does play an essential role, even though almost all of the city's classical buildings now only survive as ruins or in fragments.

Rome is not the only city to be defined by its idiosyncratic and historically significant buildings. Cologne Cathedral, the Taj Mahal in Agra, and the Forbidden City in Beijing fulfill similar roles. Similarly in Japan, the major temples can be seen in this context, such as the Tōdaiji in Nara, one of the world's largest wooden structures. Yet the fact that this temple, standing for over 1,200 years, was built not of durable stone but with the highly flammable material of wood indicates that Japan possesses a significantly different relationship to constructed permanence than many other parts of the world. Above all, the highly sophisticated use of wood in Japanese architecture is linked to the ever-present threat of earthquakes. From very early on, intricate column and support beam systems were developed as well as free-swinging wooden pillars in tall pagodas. As a result, these tower-like structures were able to withstand severe earthquakes without sustaining any significant damage. Wooden buildings such as temples, which were never intended to be demolished and replaced, constantly require sensitive repair and renewal.

One exception among major Japanese wooden structures is the 2,000 year-old shrine in Ise, which honours the sun goddess Amaterasu, the highest figure in Shintōism and the mythical ancestor of the Japanese emperor. Since the year 690, a new building has been erected every twenty years directly next to

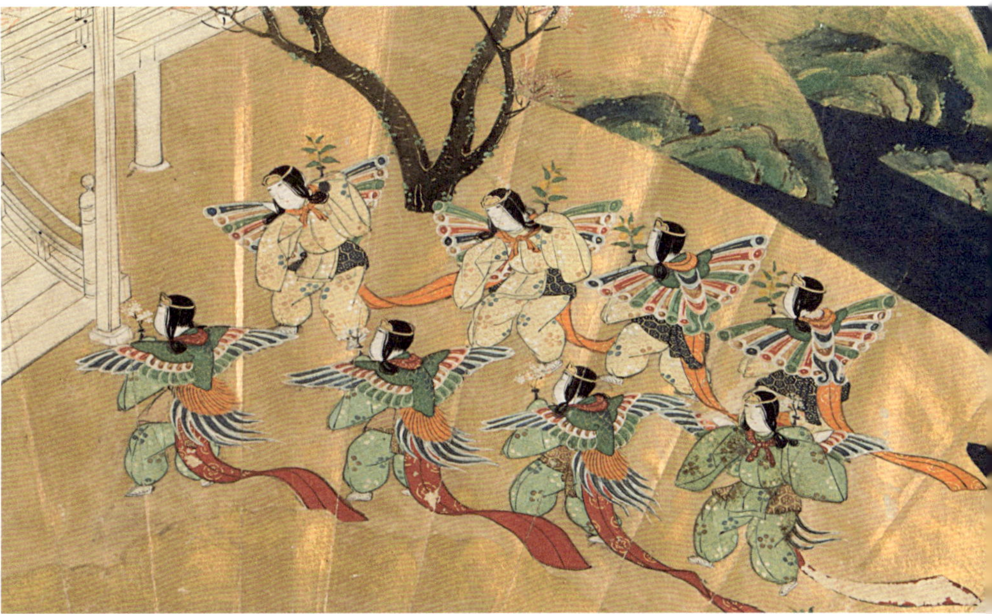

cat. no. 37 (detail)
The Butterfly Dance (*Genji monogatari*, cap 24. *Kochō*)
Japan, Momoyama period, late sixteenth century

the shrine's central sanctuary, a massive, wooden structure with a thatched roof that stands in a rectangular, fenced courtyard, after which the previous building is demolished. And so this shrine, a colossal, wooden structure inside a fenced, rectangular courtyard, is paradoxically both one of the oldest pieces of Japanese architecture and always a new building, with almost no signs of wear.

The history of the shrine's creation is also defined by a certain restlessness. The *Nihon shoki* ("Chronicle of Japan"), which dates to the early eighth century, narrates how Yamatohime-no-mikoto, daughter of Emperor Suinin, wandered for twenty years in search of a new home for the sun god. At that time the deity had always been worshipped at his home in the Emperor's palace in the region of Yamato, Japan's ancient heartland (near modern-day Nara).

The story explains that Amaterasu herself spoke to the Emperor's daughter, and told her that Ise was a secluded and pleasant place where the goddess deity wished to live in the future.

Even today, the expansive grounds of the Ise Shrine remain a place which its many pilgrims experience best on foot. Although the main shrine is fenced off and inaccessible, its location in picturesque, dense, hilly woodland filled with further shrines, offers visitors the chance to see many other religious buildings.

Shintō is an animist religion and was Japan's most important spiritual tradition well in advance of the adoption of Buddhism from the mainland. Its practices can also be experienced outside of Ise and other key shrines away from urban centres. Hiking along trails in the mountains, for example, it is common to see trees, rocks, and waterfalls marked by sacred lengths of rope (*shimenawa*) hung with strips of paper which indicate the gods' (*kami*) dwelling-places. Long before the first Shintō shrines were erected more than two thousand years ago, such methods of drawing attention to unique natural phenomena served as a physical expression of this spiritual tradition.

This ancient understanding of nature's spiritual dimension is clearly a significant antecedent to the way in which Japan later developed a distinctive sensibility for the integration of human life across nature as a whole, a philosophy also shaped by the influence of Buddhism and found throughout East Asia. Following a new wave of Chinese influences from the fourteenth and fifteenth centuries, landscapes as a cosmic all-encompassing image became a dominant trend in ink painting. Human figures are barely discernible or not at all present, swallowed up by the imposing mountainous or aquatic terrain.

Tea Culture and Ceramics in Japan

The tea ceremony is another major form of cultural expression which has had a significant impact on human coexistence as well as our relationship to the natural world. A specifically Japanese style emerged in the sixteenth century, most notably under Sen no Rikyū (1522–1591). He taught tea culture as both a meditative ritual and a *Gesamtkunstwerk* in which the architecture of the tea room, the surrounding garden's design, and a precisely defined sequence of movements combine to form a unique means of human communication.

The tea rooms designed by Sen no Rikyū are deliberately small, usually no larger than 4½ tatami mats.[1] This is because the master sought to encourage a heightened state of meditative focus. The emphasis is placed on the attentive and quiet manner in which host and guest interact, while the understated simplicity of these modest rooms transforms the tea ritual into a spiritual experience. Rikyū's most famous work is the Tai-an (待庵) tea room in the Myōkian temple in Kyōto, which is no larger than two tatami mats.

One key innovation is a shift in the relationship between the teahouse's interior and exterior. Initially tea rooms were entered via a wooden veranda typical of residential buildings.[2] However, Rikyū and his successors designed small tea huts in which a low entrance (*nijiri-guchi*) made it necessary to crawl into the teahouse interior, accessed directly via stepping stones along the outer wall. This created a direct counterpart between the garden as a microcosm of nature and the tea room.

Rikyū also took great pains over the utensils used when preparing tea. Eschewing the then-widespread fashion of displaying costly accessories imported from China during the tea ceremony, he chose to include simple objects, preferably produced locally, whose charm lay in their modesty and naturalness. Rikyū is said to have cut bamboo himself to make simple vessels holding *ikebana* arrangements prepared for his tea ceremonies. He also commissioned the roof tile maker Tanaka Chōjirō (died ca. 1589) in Kyōto to create tea bowls in a highly distinctive style termed Raku. These bowls continue to be made uninterrupted over fifteen generations to this day (see cat. nos. 13–16, 32 in the present volume), in a fashion that has spawned many imitators beyond the original Raku workshop.

1   A tatami mat is approximately 1.6 m² in size.

2   The low entrance places everyone in the tea room on an equal footing, making it not just a tranquil, spiritual space in which to step away from the hectic outside world, but also a place where even the most distinguished guest could only enter with a clear gesture of humility, and certainly not with their head held high.

This technique involves shaping bowls freely by hand (they were not thrown on a wheel), then glazing and firing the vessels at a lower temperature. The bowls are typically glazed black (*Kuro Raku*) or red (*Aka Raku*). They protrude more or less horizontally over a short stand before bending to form an almost-vertical wall.

A special feature of Raku ceramics is the fact that they are removed from the kiln when still hot and cool down rapidly. Moreover, the bowls are fired in muffle furnaces fired by wood or charcoal, producing random effects. This often results in attractive "landscapes" (*keshiki*) on the vessels' surfaces that are highly prized by ceramic collectors. Some famous tea bowls were also given poetic names such as *seppō* 雪峰 (snow-covered mountain) or *shigure* 時雨 (autumn rain), in references to their shape and particular glaze effects.[3]

Just like the mostly irregular shape and the sometimes scarred surface of a Raku bowl, names such as "autumn rain" also reflect the melancholy mood of tea culture, as developed by Sen no Rikyū. Japanese aesthetics uses the terms *wabi* 侘 and *sabi* 寂, concepts which are difficult to translate and which also characterise other important aspects of Japanese culture. *Wabi* describes a feeling of loneliness and forlornness, but also in a positive sense suggests the joy of silence, simplicity and austerity. The term *sabi* stands for age and maturity, as well as signifying the subtle beauty of these themes' visible manifestation on the patina. The term *wabi* in particular traces its origins to Buddhism and its philosophy of the world's fleeting and transient nature. *Wabi-cha* 侘茶 ("*wabi* tea") is a term that emerged in the Edo period (1603–1868) to describe the tea culture characterised by Sen no Rikyū with its penchant for simplicity, naturalness and appreciating the beauty of the ephemeral.

3   A red and a black Raku bowl, both by Hon'ami Kōetsu (1558–1637), see Hayashiya 1974, figs. 66, 68.

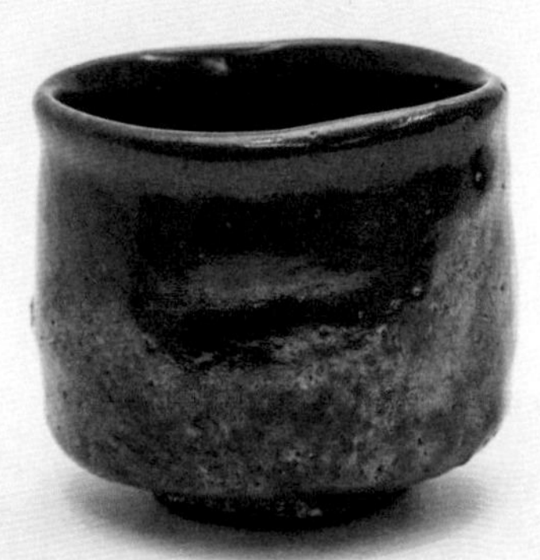

cat. no. 32
Tsujimura Shirō, winter tea bowl (*tsutsu chawan*)
Stoneware, black Raku glaze
Japan, Nara, circa 1990s/early 2000s

A Floating World presents a collection of tea-related ceramics (cat. nos. 8–11, 13, 15, 16) which, in addition to their often irregular shapes and worn surfaces, display another stylistic device characteristic of Japanese aesthetics: the repair of broken sections of the ceramics with gold lacquer (*kintsugi*). This unusual technique uses gilded lacquer to turn defects into thoughtfully highlighted symbols of transience.

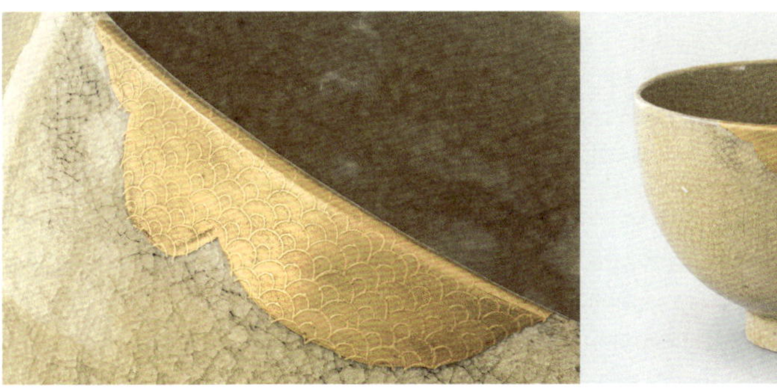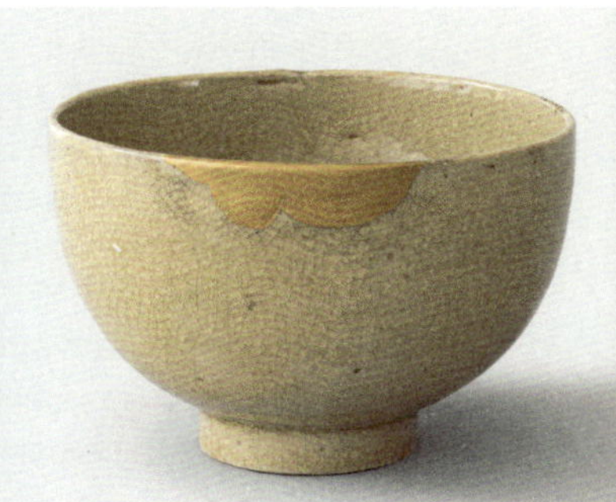

cat. no. 11
Tea bowl, light grey stoneware, celadon glaze with delicate craquelure, gold lacquer repair (*kintsugi*)
Japan, Karatsu, probably Shiinomine-gama workshop 椎の峰窯, mid-Edo period, 18th c.

Ceramics that in other parts of the world would perhaps have been thrown away as damaged, or have their broken sections perfectly restored, are instead accepted as damaged objects due to this gold lacquer repair; indeed, the repair itself lends a new aesthetic quality to the piece. In this way the fragility and the vulnerability of the piece is emphasised, reminding the viewer or user in a quiet, respectful way that all nature is transitory. In the example of a Karatsu tea bowl shown in our exhibition (cat. no. 11), the gold lacquer repair is even stylised into an ornament through a uniform wave pattern. The restored Chinese and Korean bowls (cat. nos. 8, 9) from the Song and Joseon dynasties are also likely to have come from a Japanese collection and may have been used as highly prized antique import items for special occasions in the tea ceremony.

In contrast to almost all forms of Chinese pottery, Japanese ceramics shows a remarkable tendency towards unevenness, deformation, and irregular features, regardless of such refinements of damaged sections. This applies to the Raku bowls described above, which were made especially for the tea ceremony, as well as to early *yama chawan* ("mountain tea bowls", cat. no. 10) produced from the Heian to the Muromachi periods (ninth to sixteenth centuries) using rural kilns in Japan, especially in the area around present-day Nagoya (Aichi and Gifu Prefectures). These were simple, everyday items primarily intended for local use. They were turned quickly using a wheel and without particular care, often severely deformed when fired in a wood-fired kiln, with an uneven ash glaze across their rough surfaces. Nevertheless, the tea culture's preference for these coarse, natural qualities meant that such bowls became coveted collector's items as early as the sixteenth century.

The term *rokkoyō* (Six Ancient Kilns), coined by Koyama Fujio in the mid-twentieth century, was central to the appreciation of ancient ceramics from remote, rural production centres: the pottery towns of Seto, Tokoname, Shigaraki, Tanba, Echizen and Bizen. Some of these kilns had existed since the Heian period (794–1185) and had already been discovered by Sen no Rikyū and the founding fathers of the Japanese tea ceremony in the sixteenth century, much like the *yama chawan* described above. However, these rural settlements experienced a significant decline in the course of Japan's dramatic upheaval during the Meiji period (1868–1912). It was only after the Second World War that a revival of traditional firing techniques and efforts to find new forms of expression for old ceramic objects, in keeping with the aesthetic principles of tea culture, led to a new heyday for the Six Ancient Kilns.

In several works by the ceramicist Takahara Shōji (1941–2000), active in Bizen[4] since 1969, our exhibition presents striking examples from this ceramics renaissance (cat. nos. 22–25). The majority are ceramics designed for the tea ceremony, which was the focal point of Takahara's work. As is typical with Bizen ware, the body is beige in colour, heavily discoloured in places due to natural ash accumulation in the wood kiln, and covered with an encrusted glaze. On the tea bowl and the square bowl, it is also possible to see the red traces created during the firing process, from the straw strings which are used to wrap Bizen ceramics before they are placed in the kiln. These marks are particularly notable in the round centre of the large bowl, where they create a sophisticated ornament that attractively contrasts with the silvery-black to mustard-coloured ash glaze in the outer areas. With their primeval shapes and rough, weathered-looking surfaces, each of Takahara's displayed works symbolises the particular sense of beauty that is integral to Japanese tea culture, focusing on simplicity, naturalness and an awareness of transience.

Tanba (Hyōgo Prefecture), another of the Six Ancient Kilns, is represented by Ichino Shinsui (1932–1997). His collection of work, in which tea ceramics are a major component, is characterised by a calm, clear sense of form. One memorable piece is his large round bowl (cat. no. 28), distinctive for its body fired in the dark red-brown colour typical of Tanba. In this piece the dark brown shade fades to a mustard-coloured ash glaze which runs down the inside of the bowl, merging to form a pool of colour in the centre, a visual, solidified representation of time itself.

4   The town is located in Okayama Prefecture on the Inland Sea, west of Ōsaka.

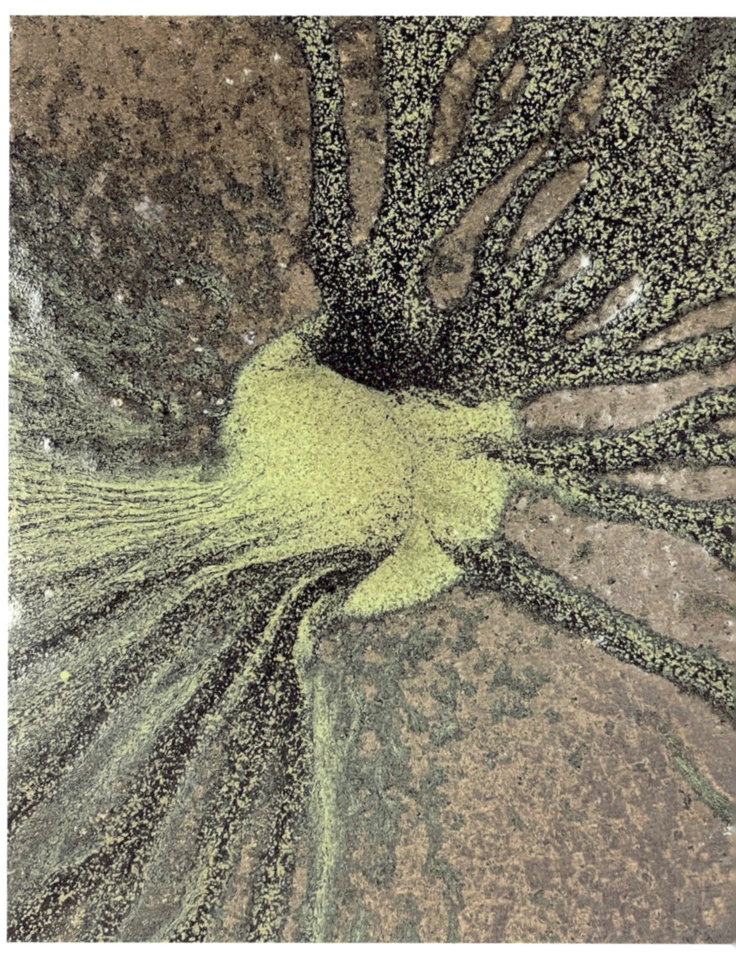

cat. no. 28 (detail)
Ichino Shinsui, (1932–1997), large dish (*ōzara*)
Red-brown stoneware, partial ash glaze
Japan, Tanba, Hyōgo Prefecture, circa 1986

In addition to the masters who are more strongly rooted in the local traditions of the Six Ancient Kilns, the exhibition also features modern ceramicists who have forged unique artistic paths. One of these is Tsujimura Shirō, born in 1947, who does not come from a traditional family of ceramicists but taught himself the craft of pottery. After studying painting in Tōkyō and spending several years in a Zen monastery in Nara, he built a workshop with a teahouse by hand outside the city before founding seven more kilns. His tea bowls, which are highly coveted by collectors, are based on the styles of different kilns. The "shoe-shaped" bowl (cat. no. 30) is made from reddish firing Shigaraki clay with small quartz inclusions. The porous black glaze of the winter tea bowl (cat. no. 32) is reminiscent of Raku ware from Kyōto.

However, none of these pieces imitate former styles; on the contrary, Tsujimura's unique hand is always clearly recognisable. Each of his bowls display a surprisingly modern artistic style. The Zen-trained ceramicist seems to imbue his works with a special spiritual power.

The two bowls by Mizuno Hanjirō (cat. nos. 20, 21) represent a markedly different aesthetic movement in modern Japanese ceramics. Born in 1926, the master ceramicist came from a family of potters in Seto, another of the Six Ancient Kilns. However, it was the *mingei* ("folk art") movement, which had been developing since the 1920s and which he encountered in the writings of its founder Yanagi Sōetsu (1889–1961), that influenced him more than the ceramic tradition of his home town. *Mingei* focussed on the beauty of simple, cheap, everyday objects produced by anonymous craftsmen.[5] Tea ceramics were typically rejected by the *mingei* movement as too elitist; but ceramics such as those made by Mizuno, who was influenced by this style, were never cheap, popular products. In the context of our exhibition, the sense of spontaneity and movement in these ceramics is of particular interest, expressed through the colourful splashes of green and light brown on the two bowls on display. These tones, combined with the underlying playfulness of the bowls' unplanned decorative features, reference the three-colour glazes on ceramics from the Tang dynasty. However, these loosely applied traces of colour are even more reminiscent of Jackson Pollock's drippings from the early post-war years than of those historical models from China.

5   See also one of the most influential volumes by Yanagi Sōetsu, *The Unknown Craftsman: A Japanese Insight into Beauty* (Tōkyō et al., 2013); first published in English in 1972.

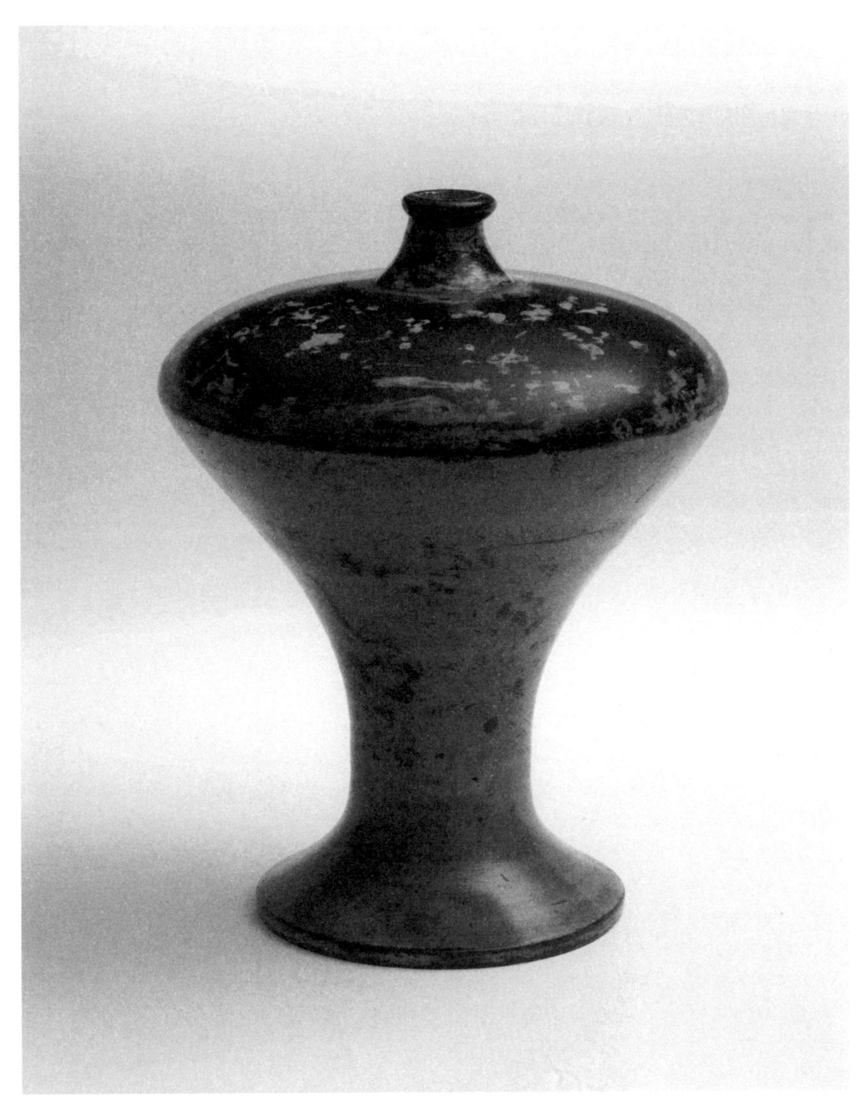

A Floating World in Japanese Lacquer Art

Alongside a wide range of ceramics, our exhibition also features several Japanese lacquer works in which the theme of transience manifests itself in a special way. The first item presented here is a sake bottle (cat. no. 2), considered to be among the masterpieces of the Frankfurt museum's collection. Dating from the Muromachi period (fifteenth to sixteenth centuries), it is also the oldest Japanese lacquer work in the Museum Angewandte Kunst. The shape of this relatively large bottle, with a broad shoulder and narrow neck, is an adaptation of the *meiping* form ("plum [branch]" vase shape). It emerged in the Tang dynasty (618–907) and enjoyed great popularity in Chinese ceramics from the Song dynasty (960–1279) onwards. In contrast to the Chinese *meiping* model, however, this elegantly shaped bottle stands on a comparatively wide foot, which is initially compressed to form a narrow "waist" in the lower part of the body before bulging out broadly towards the shoulder. Its surface looks as if it has been marked by the traces of time, lending it its special aesthetic quality: the areas of red lacquer applied onto black lacquer were partially rubbed off during production, an effect probably intensified by the bottle's many years of use. A delicate line drawing which presumably once showed cherry blossom branches has largely been rubbed away. This effect is at least partly deliberate, representing the Japanese *wabi-sabi* aesthetic described above. The piece has a time-worn patina which has been highly valued in Japan since the sixteenth century, particularly in tea culture.

These surface effects on lacquer are known as *Negoro-nuri* and refer to lacquer works said to have originated in Negoro-ji Monastery in Wakayama Province, where simple lacquer objects were produced for monastic use. Overlapping layers of red or black lacquer gradually rubbed off through constant use, creating irregular, multi-coloured surface effects. This appearance was highly valued as making visible the simple, modest life of the monastery and soon was deliberately emphasised when producing these lacquers. A bowl on a high foot made around 1993 by Kado Isaburō (1940–2006) with a rubbed *Negoro-nuri* surface on the inside (cat. no. 4) is impressive proof that this particular form of patination still has a place as a stylistic device among modern lacquer masters.

A special mention should also be made of a five-tiered stacking box (cat. no. 5). Like the sake bottle described above (cat. no. 2), it comes from the collection of the diplomat Dr Ernst Arthur Voretzsch (1868–1965).[6] The piece likely dates from the later Muromachi period (sixteenth century), and is an exceptional example of the *Kamakura-bori* carving technique.

6   Dr Voretzsch was the German ambassador in Tōkyō from 1928 until his retirement in 1933, following consular posts in Hong Kong, Shanghai, and other places. He was a dedicated collector of Asian art and published several specialist studies on the subject. In 1937, he presented his collection in an Asian Art Museum in Bamberg, which he founded himself. After its closure, a large part of the collection was acquired in 1959 by the Museum für Kunsthandwerk Frankfurt am Main, now the Museum Angewandte Kunst. See also Schulenburg 2023.

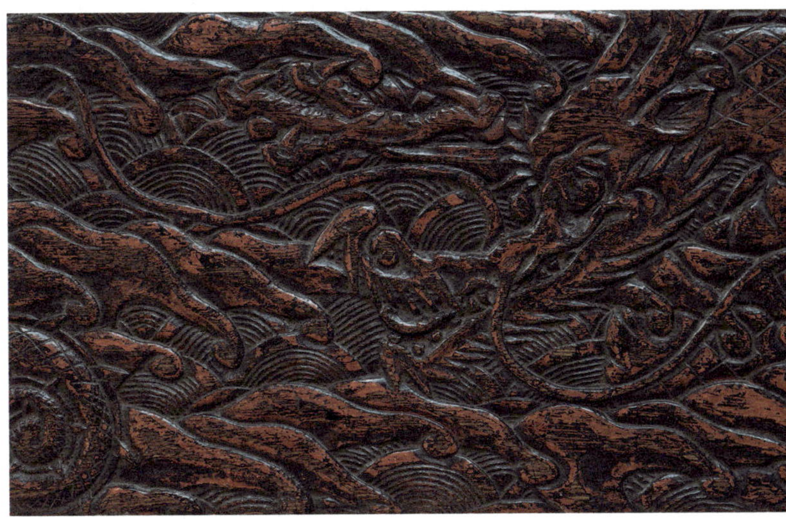

From the Kamakura period (1180–1336) onwards, lacquer workshops in what was then the capital city were established around Buddhist temples, initially to produce objects for ritual use in temples. They were inspired by Chinese carved lacquer imported to Kamakura, in which three-dimensional decorations are cut into a thick layer of lacquer. In *Kamakura-bori*, by contrast, the decoration is carved completely into the wooden core, then covered with only a few layers of lacquer. The decoration of the Frankfurt box covers the outer surface and the top of the lid, showing two dragons in dramatically moving waves. In this style, the sides would likely all have been carved in one piece (with the exception of the lid), then separated horizontally to form the box's individual compartments. The clearly aged surface shows that the wooden core was first covered with a layer of black, followed by a layer of red lacquer. In the lacquer workshop, part of the surface would be rubbed off during polishing to imbue the piece with a timeworn character, as in *Negoro-nuri*. This effect was intensified through use over time, so that even the wood beneath the layers of lacquer is partially visible. The piece is just as impressive for its lively relief drawing as it is for the elegant patina of its visibly aged surfaces. The box with its dragons set against waves quite literally conveys a floating world.

"Floating Worlds" in Japanese Painting

The following section focuses on traces of movement and transience in Japanese painting, book art and woodblock prints. In contrast to the previous section, the focus will be less on the traces of age and patina, but rather on the different illustrated subjects, which offer varied depictions of a world in flux.

An unusual hanging scroll (cat. no. 40) bears the signature of an outstanding painter of the late Edo period, Watanabe Kazan (1793–1841). The painting, possibly no more than a sketch, shows a goldfish in a small glass sphere, presumably a common type of "packaging" in which such decorative fish could be purchased in Japan in the early nineteenth century.

The naturalistic depiction of both the animal and its glass sphere reveals Kazan's mastery of *ranga*, the Dutch-inspired painting of his time. At the same time, the painting seems like a metaphor for the general atmosphere of the late phase of *sakoku*, namely the country's self-isolation as enforced by the Shōgun government. Kazan himself, who was repeatedly arrested, sentenced to death, then pardoned and exiled from Edo due to his critical stance towards the ruling leaders of his time, finally committed suicide to spare his feudal lord from further difficulties.

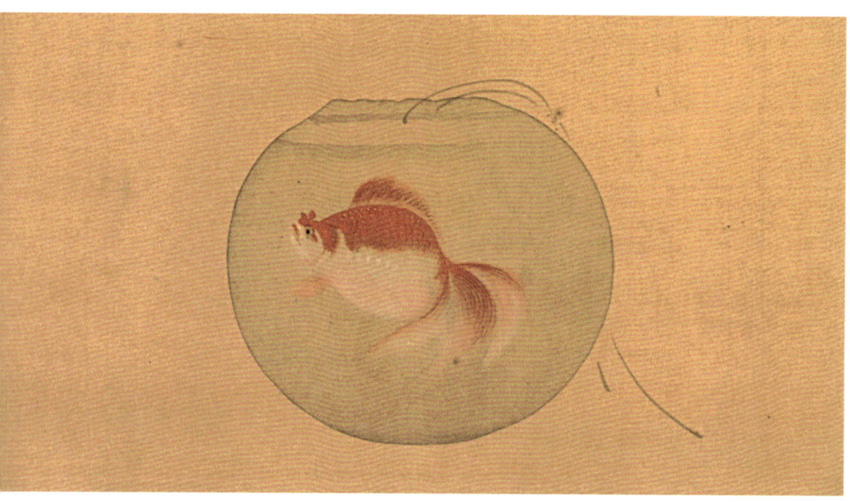

cat. no. 40 (detail)
Attributed to Watanabe Kazan (1793–1841), Goldfish in Basin
Hanging scroll, ink and paint on silk
Japan, Edo period, first half of the nineteenth century.

No less astonishing is a scroll painting (cat. no. 41) by Yokoyama Seiki (1793–1865). The painter, who worked in Kyōto and belonged to the Shijō school, was a pupil of Matsumura Keibun (1779–1843), the youngest brother of Matsumura Goshun (1752–1811), the founder of this school. The subject of the painting is *Yōrō no taki* 養老の滝, literally the "refreshment of the old-age waterfall" in Gifu Prefecture. It is said to have received its name from the Empress Genshō (r. 715–724). The title refers to the "fountain of youth" effect attributed to its waters, which were said to smooth the skin, blacken the hair, and improve eyesight. In its radical simplicity, Seiki's 1862 painting already anticipates aspects of modern abstract art in a striking way: the narrow, tall pictorial space is largely empty. Only in the top right-hand corner do a few bold traces of ink hint at the waterfall. The inscription on the picture notes that the work was created "in the face of the refreshment of the old age waterfall" by the "seventy-year-old man Seiki".[7] The composition itself can be seen as a metaphor for the life phase of the "old man" who died three years later: the end is already in sight, so to speak, with his life now only occupying a narrow strip at the very edge of the overall picture. The subdued mounting, dating from the time the work was created, is also remarkable. In its soft colours, predominantly grey-blue and brown to beige, as well as in its grained and striped surface, it forms a harmonious unit with the painting itself. Taken as a whole, the scroll painting is an elegant, accomplished *memento mori* without pathos, radiating serenity in defiance of its own transience.

A wholly different rendition of the floating world appears in a magnificent six-part folding screen depicting a spring landscape during cherry blossom season (cat. no. 38, see image on the following page). This unsigned work from the seventeenth century possibly originates from Kyōto, probably from a workshop of city painters (*machi-eshi*) who worked for merchants and other wealthy citizens. It might depict the picturesque region of Arashiyama on the River Hōzu at the western edge of Kyōto, which remains a popular tourist destination to this day, especially during cherry blossom season. Alternatively, it could depict the cherry blossom show in Yoshino in Nara Prefecture, a more common subject used by painters.

A samurai with his entourage crosses the bridge at the bottom left and approaches a group that has settled down on a platform for a cherry blossom viewing party. The white colour of the cherry blossoms fills the entire pictorial space and so defines the underlying theme of transience. The brief and extraordinary period of time when these trees bloom in spring has always been an important celebration in Japan, expressing the joy of the approaching warm season. At the same time, however, the falling cherry blossoms are a long-established symbol of transience, a reminder that nothing in the world is permanent.

7   In Japan, an additional year is traditionally added for the period of partum life when a person gives their age. By this reckoning, the artist, who was born in 1793, was already seventy years old in 1862.

By contrast to this interpretation, the vibrant colours of this spring painting suggest a seemingly carefree joy. A variety of genre scenes break up the composition, interspersed with clouds of gold; they include a group of swimmers on the far left, raftsmen, fishermen and rice farmers at work in the bottom centre and three men contemplating a waterfall in the top right.

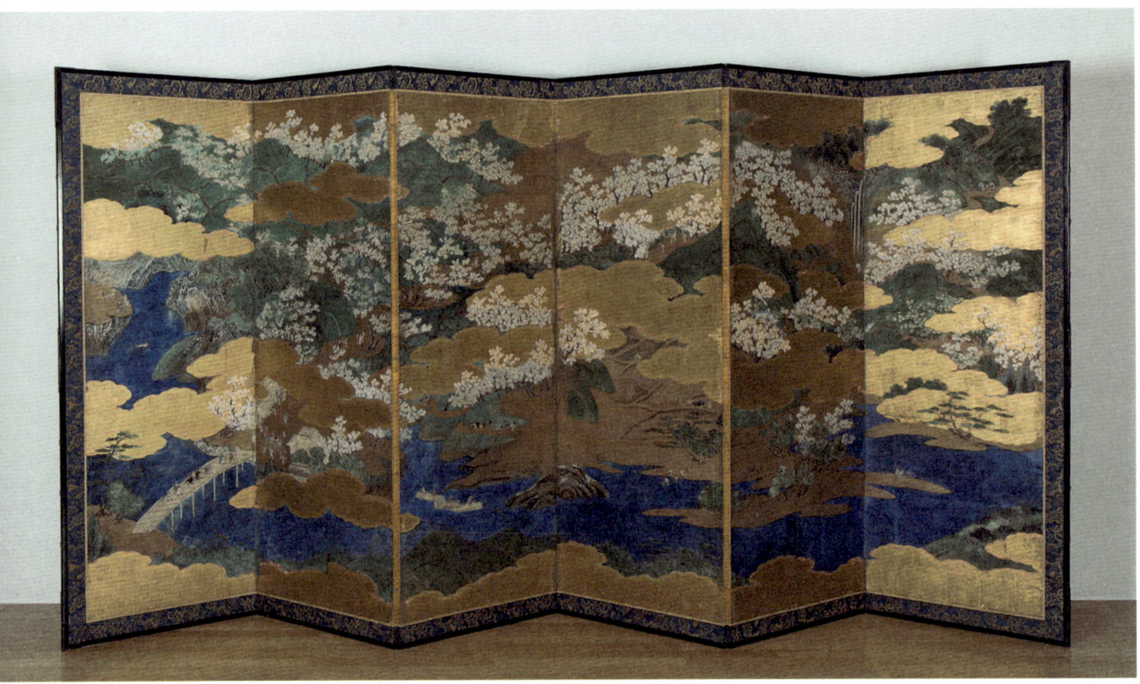

cat. no. 38
Spring landscape with cherry blossom festival
Folding screen, ink and paint on paper, leaf gold and gold paint
Japan, early Edo period, 17th c.

The message conveyed by this work expresses a simple truth: life is short-lived, like the splendour of cherry blossoms. In the spirit of the motto *carpe diem*, one should savour this incomparable moment of beauty and earthly pleasures to the full.

Nara ehon

Another chapter of the exhibition shows illustrated manuscripts from a group of 26 individual titles of *Nara ehon* 奈良絵本 ("Nara picture books") from the sixteenth to eighteenth centuries in the Museum Angewandte Kunst, which principally represent popular short stories from the Muromachi period (1336–1573), the so-called *otogizōshi* 御伽草子. Mainly written in syllable script, with only a few Chinese characters, alongside rich illustrations, they were also popular among the less literate classes. They also served as dowry gifts for a bride, among other things.

The chosen illustrations take as their subject the theme of movement in space. These are often travel scenes or pictures in which dramatic, moving events dominate the pictorial narrative. The manuscript *Kumano no honji* ("The Prehistory of the Gods of Kumano", cat. no. 42) is based on a Buddhist legend. In this story, an Indian prince, disgusted by the murder of his mother by jealous concubines, flees to Japan with his father and his spiritual teacher in a celestial chariot. Here, they settle as the three deities of the Kumano shrine on the Kii Peninsula south of Kyōto and Nara. The illustration shows the flying vehicle of the Mahārāja amid vigorously rippling white and bluish clouds, with the chariot obscuring the figures of the three characters. As is customary in *Nara ehon*, the actual picture segments are additionally framed by horizontal bands of clouds at the top and bottom. The manuscript shown here is one of the extremely rare *Nara ehon* and has a signature appended at the end of the book. However, this was probably added later, at least not by Tosa Mitsumoto (1530–1569) himself. Features of its style suggest it is a particularly early manuscript, likely produced in the second half of the sixteenth century.

Another aerial journey can be found in an illustration of the *Shaka no honji* manuscript ("The Legend of the Buddha", cat. no. 43). In it, Prince Siddhārtha, the later Buddha, rises on his horse into moving, multi-coloured clouds floating in the air with the help of the kings of heaven.

However, *Nara ehon* illustrations showing secular travelling companions are much more common than such fantastic celestial journeys. The exhibition presents two illustrations on this topic taken from multi-volume editions of the manuscript *Bunshō no sōshi* ("The Salt Merchant Bunshō", cat. nos. 44, 45).

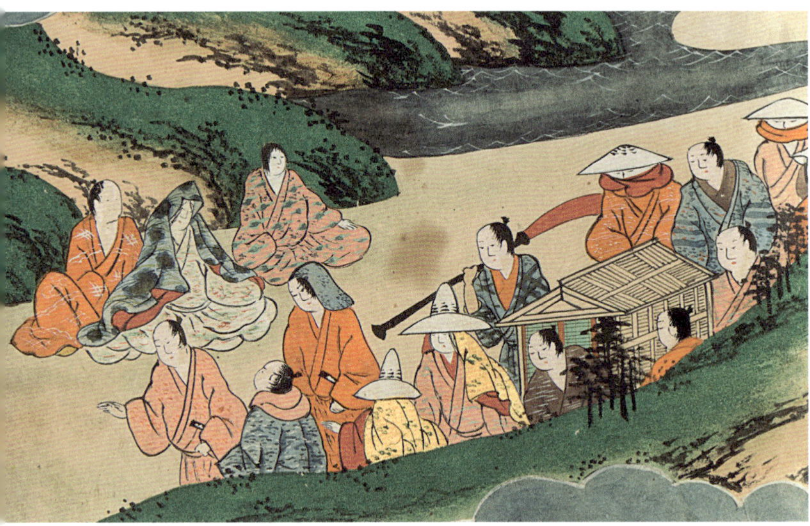

cat. no. 44 (detail)
The Salt Merchant Bunshō (*Bunshō no sōshi*)
Nara ehon, ink and paint on paper
Japan, Edo period, prob. Genroku era to Hōei era (1688–1711)

This tale exemplifies the social changes of the Edo period (1603–1868) when merchants originally at the bottom of the social hierarchy became the most powerful class in economic terms as major warfare became rare. Bunshō is a simple salt-boiler whose diligence gradually leads to his success as a wealthy salt merchant. Moreover, his two daughters' beauty attracts a great deal of attention. Eventually, a high-ranking courtier from Kyōto travels to the distant coastal town where the Bunshōs live and immediately falls in love with the elder daughter. With her father's consent, he takes her as his wife and returns to Kyōto with her. There, the emperor himself takes a liking to the younger of the two beautiful daughters and makes her his concubine. Bunshō is then appointed the prime minister in the capital.

This fantastic "rags to riches" tale, which originated in the Muromachi period, became one of the most popular texts in *Nara ehon*.[8] As an auspicious story of success, it was particularly popular as a reading to mark the New Year. Such manuscripts were also a common gift as part of a bride's dowry.

Our exhibition shows two travel scenes presented in two different *Bunshō* variants, which first deal with the courtier's bridal journey to the provinces and then, accompanied by his bride, his return to the capital. The first of the manuscripts (cat. no. 44) shows an unusual style in its illustrations, which can be described as reminiscent of naïve folk-art – as well as being rather peculiar. The outward journey scene shows a courtier meeting an old man, a recurring motif in *Nara ehon* illustrations.

8   The twenty-six *Nara ehon* in the Frankfurt collection include no fewer than seven *Bunshō* manuscripts (cf. Schulenburg/Jesse 2000, cat. nos. I–12 - I–18).

As in the scene depicting the return journey, the miniaturisation of the trees along the way is remarkable, contrasting as it does to the human protagonists in the plot. The travelling party returning to Kyōto is shown in a particularly colourful and lively manner, moving dynamically through the pictorial space from the back right to the front left.

In comparison, the same scenes from the second manuscript (cat. no. 45) appear rather stiff and far more conventional. Nevertheless, the illustrator has taken more care with the figures' faces. In principle, they follow the *hikime kagihana* 引目鉤鼻 style ("line-eye-hook-nose" style) of old Japanese *yamato-e* painting.[9] On closer inspection, the faces are surprisingly individualised in their expression. Details include the varied positions of the figures' heads, lips accentuated by red tones, and almost predatory facial features, with high eyebrows, diagonal eye shapes, as well as moustaches and dimples beside grimacing, downturned mouths.

Five other manuscripts on display are also concerned with the theme of travelling across a landscape. Yorimitsu and his warriors are depicted ascending to the palace of the monster in an illustration for *Shuten dōji* (cat. no. 47). In cat. no. 49, Sayohime encounters salt boilers by the sea near Mount Fuji on his way to the sacrificial altar.

9   The term *yamato-e* refers to a style of painting with strong colours, a rather flat composition and "line-eyed, hooked-nosed" faces without individual expression, which developed in the Heian period (794–1185) and was largely isolated from continental influences. It is fundamentally differentiated from the diverse Chinese stylistic elements summarised under *kara-e* 唐絵 ("Chinese [actually "Tang"] painting"), which went on to influence Japanese painting at various times.

cat. no. 47 (detail)
Drinking with the Man-eater (*Shuten-dōji*)
Nara ehon, ink and paint on paper
Japan, Edo period, second half of seventeenth century

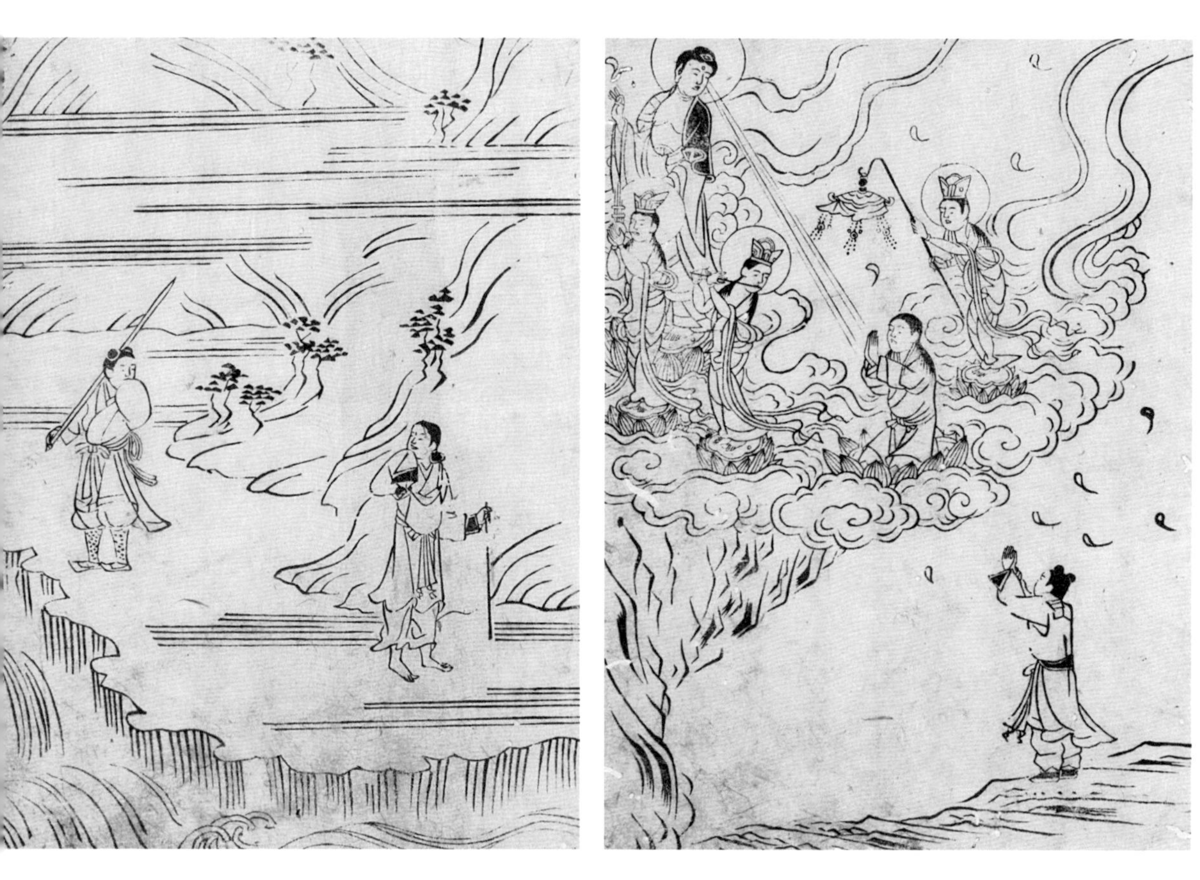

An illustration for *Shinkyoku* (cat. no. 51) is similar to two images found in the *Bunshō* books (cat. nos. 44, 45) in which a travelling group meets an old man. In *Hōmyō dōji,* a woodblock print book, the young Hōmyō has a similar encounter on his way to his sacrificial table (cat. no. 48). Finally, in the manuscript *Sagamigawa* (cat. no. 50), a journey by water is poetically depicted with a boat holding six passengers positioned diagonally in the picture frame.

Travel images are merely a prelude to far more dramatic events in the majority of the scenes referenced here. The *Shuten dōji* book, for example, culminates in a scene in which the hero Yorimitsu decapitates a man-eating monster that has long caused fear and terror by abducting, enslaving, and then eating young girls (see image on previous page). In the dramatic climax depicted, the monster's severed head snaps at Yorimitsu's head, which is fortunately protected by a helmet.

Hōmyō dōji and *Sayohime* are two essentially similar dramas with happy endings. Both glorify the virtues of self-sacrifice and Buddhist piety. In them, the boy Hōmyō forfeits his potential to become a rich son and makes himself a human sacrifice to a dragon in exchange for money (which he gives to his impoverished mother). The dragon is then transformed into a peaceful youth following the boy's fervent prayers. In the scene shown (cat. no. 48), the Buddhas have descended from heaven to save Hōmyō in his distress. Sayohime has also sacrificed herself to pay for the funeral mass for her deceased father, finally reciting the Lotus Sutra on the offering table (cat. no. 49). The evil snake then transforms back into a young girl and gives Sayohime a wishing pearl in return.

The ending of Hata no Takebun in *Shinkyoku* ("New Play", cat. no. 51) is less positive. This poignant scene shows Hata committing suicide alone on a small boat in the water, in the hope of being able to return as a ghost and free the kidnapped wife of his master, Prince Ichinomiya. His mistress is saved, but the faithful servant is left to die.

Images on left page:

Illustrations from cat. no. 48
The youth Hōmyō (*Hōmyō-dōji*): Hômyô on his way to the sacrificial table (left)
and his wonderful salvation thanks to a Buddha floating down from the heavens (right)
Nara ehon, woodblock prints
Japan, Edo period, dated Kanbun 8 (1668)

Travelling in Japan

The travel scenes presented above, which appear frequently in *Nara ehon* from the sixteenth to eighteenth centuries, may also reflect the significant increase in travelling within Japan from the beginning of the Edo period. This was initially due to an order issued by the Shōgunate in Edo, which instructed the feudal lords to maintain a residence in the capital while having their families live there as hostages of the Shōgun. The daimyō themselves were forced to travel back and forth between their province and the city of Edo at regular intervals, each time with a considerable entourage. In Japan, this arrangement was known as *sankin kōtai* 参勤交代 ("alternating attendance").

Stops were built at regular intervals along the trade routes where these travelling groups could spend the night and change horses. Due to the long period of peace under the Tokugawa shōguns, there was also a significant increase in trade and commerce along the long-distance roads. Another key economic factor is the popularity of pilgrimage at that time, which provided additional travelling activity.

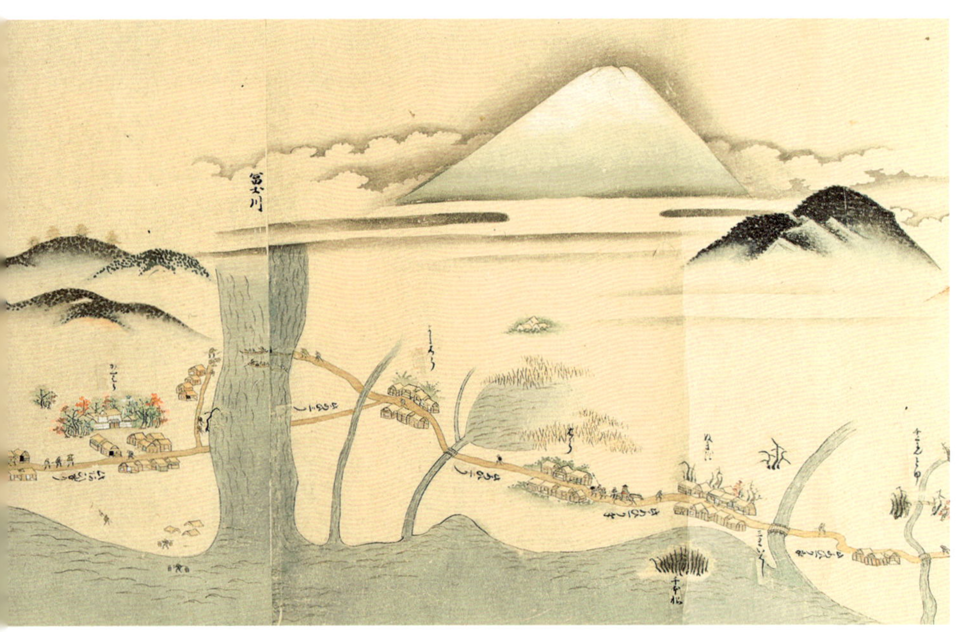

cat. no. 39 (detail)
The trade route from Edo to Nagasaki (depicted here: the trade route near Mount Fuji)
Scroll over, ink and paint on paper
Japan, Edo period, 18th/19th c.

An impressive document highlighting this new mobility is a more than handscroll more than seventeen metres long (cat. no. 39) which illustrates the trade
route by water and land from the capital Edo to the port city of Nagasaki in the
far west of Japan, a distance of more than 1200 kilometres. During the Edo period (1603–1868), Nagasaki was the country's only international harbour city, with
ships travelling between the settlement to Korea and China.

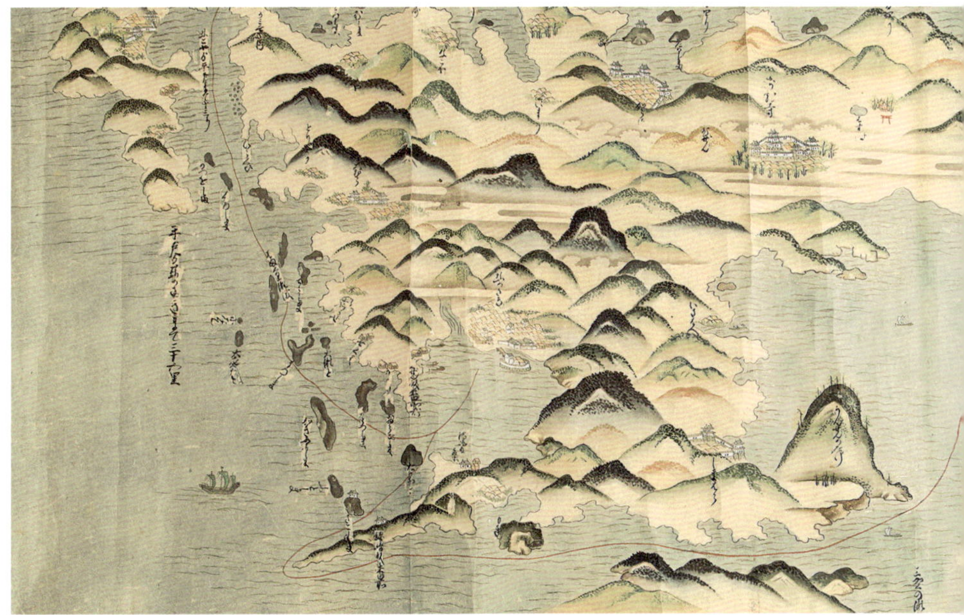

cat. no. 39 (detail)
The trade route from Edo to Nagasaki (depicted here: Nagasaki and surrounding areas)
Scroll over, ink and paint on paper
Japan, Edo period, 18th/19th c.

The trading post operated by the Dutch East India Company on the artificial
harbour island of Dejima was the only place in Japan where Europeans were
permitted to stay. Like the *daimyō*, the heads of the factories were expected to
pay their respects to the *Shōgun* in Edo at regular intervals, but without an obli-
gation to maintain a residence in the capital.

Ukiyo-e Woodblock Prints

The popular woodblock prints that emerged in the late seventeenth century provide a fascinating and incredibly diverse reflection of a new attitude towards life at the time. Soon after its inception this artform was given its name, which refers to the theme of our exhibition, the floating world, in a very literal sense: *ukiyo-e* 浮世絵 ("pictures of the floating world").[10] Here, *ukiyo* refers to the fleeting pleasures of theatres, brothels and street life, an ironic and blasphemous allusion to the Buddhist term *ukiyo* 憂き世 ("suffering world"). Although the sound is the same, the meaning is very different, referring to the painful cycle of rebirths from which Buddhists must endeavour to free themselves.

In the early *ukiyo-e* woodblock prints in particular, theatre and eroticism play a major role. This is illustrated by an outstanding print by Sugimura Jihei (active 1681–1704)[11], which shows a pair of lovers with a young "spy" (cat. no. 52). What is shown is more a matter of foreboding than anything visible; yet the undulating robes create almost more erotic tension than naked skin. Only one of the lover's feet and the phallic tip of his sword can be seen peeking out from under the fabric. Further frivolity is added by the figure of the boy, who has hidden under a thick, padded blanket and is watching the goings-on with relish. This print creates an astonishing tension between the almost abstract flatness of the composition and the dynamic movement of the action.

Another print by Sugimura Jihei (cat. no. 53) jumps across time by about eighty years in a very unusual way. The focus of this large-format print is the "love adventurer" and drifter Ukiyonosuke, hero of the novel *Kōshoku ichidai otoko* (The Life of an Amorous Man), published in 1682 by Ihara Saikaku (1642–1693). Here, he holds his umbrella above the *jōruri*[12] actor Kantō Koroku, who is taking on a female role here. His gesture and the intense eye contact between the two men might signal a homoerotic relationship. A diagonal bar running through the picture separates the gentlemen on the street from Miyako no Ōkuni (ca. 1572–1613), founder of the *kabuki* theatre[13] and her assistant.

On the surface, this diagonal line indicates the fact that the ladies have taken their seats on the upper floor (of a house of pleasure?). Metaphorically, however, it also represents the displacement between the period circa 1600 when the *kabuki* founder was alive and the lifetime of the novel's hero, published in 1682, which also corresponds to the time when this print was created.[14]

10   For the Johann Georg Geyger and Otto Riese collections in the Museum Angewandte Kunst, see http://ukipedia.de/ (accessed 21 June 2024).

11   Sugimura Jihei has gone down in history mainly as a master of erotic *shunga* woodblock prints.

12   *Jōruri* are ballads sung to the accompaniment of *shamisen*.

13   *Kabuki* ("the art of song and dance") is one of the most popular Japanese theatre forms to this day, comprising song, pantomime and dance to predominantly secular subjects.

14   According to another interpretation, all four figures labelled here with ribbons are actors in an unknown play, whereby the names of the actors also remain anonymous. See also the online entry for a further, hand-coloured print of this sheet at Art Institute Chicago: https://www.artic.edu/artworks/19052/on-the-yoshida-highway (accessed 04.10.2024).

The third woodblock print in the exhibition (cat. no. 54, see image on following page), which dates from the early phase of *ukiyo-e*, shows a lady in courtly travelling clothes on a raft on the left. While her companion slowly propels the raft

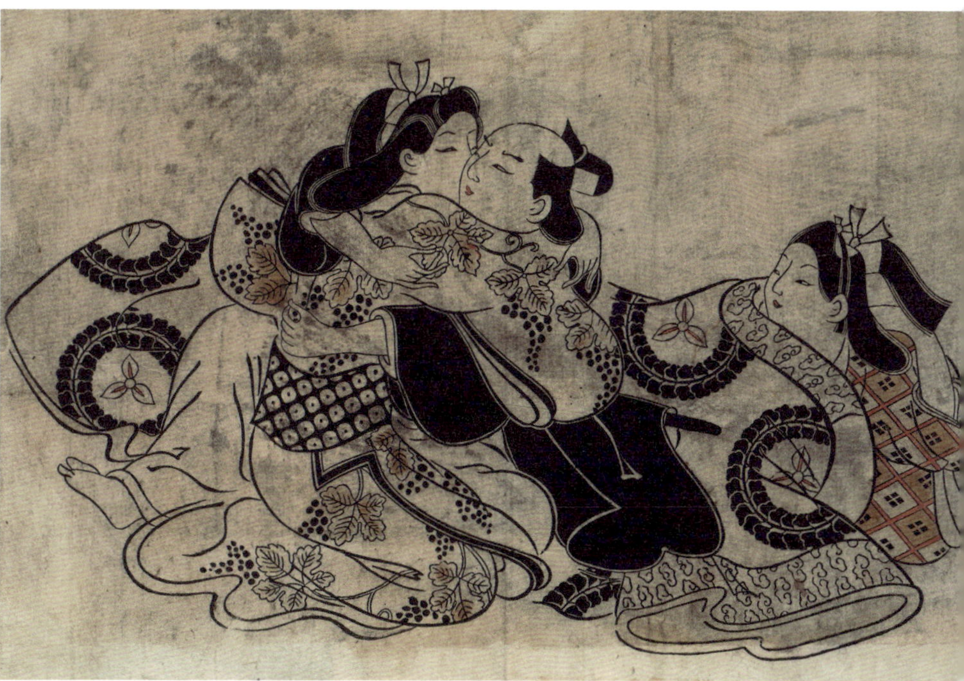

cat. no. 52
Sugimura Jihei (active 1681–1704), Couple with Voyeur
Hand-coloured woodblock print, *ōban* Japan, Edo period, circa 1685

with a long pole, the pair, lost in thought, gaze at the water covered with cherry blossoms. This leaf, delicately coloured by hand, very harmoniously conveys an atmosphere of gentle, even entirely aimless and purposeless gliding along. The seal names refer to the printing workshop; the master, who presumably belonged to the Torii school, remains anonymous, as does the literary model presumably illustrated by this leaf.

Towards the later phase of the *ukiyo-e* print, which began with the development of polychrome printing (with a block for each colour) in the mid-eighteenth century, the fixation on theatres, pleasure houses and street scenes noticeably and gradually diminished, with artists' preoccupations increasingly shifting to the subject of nature.

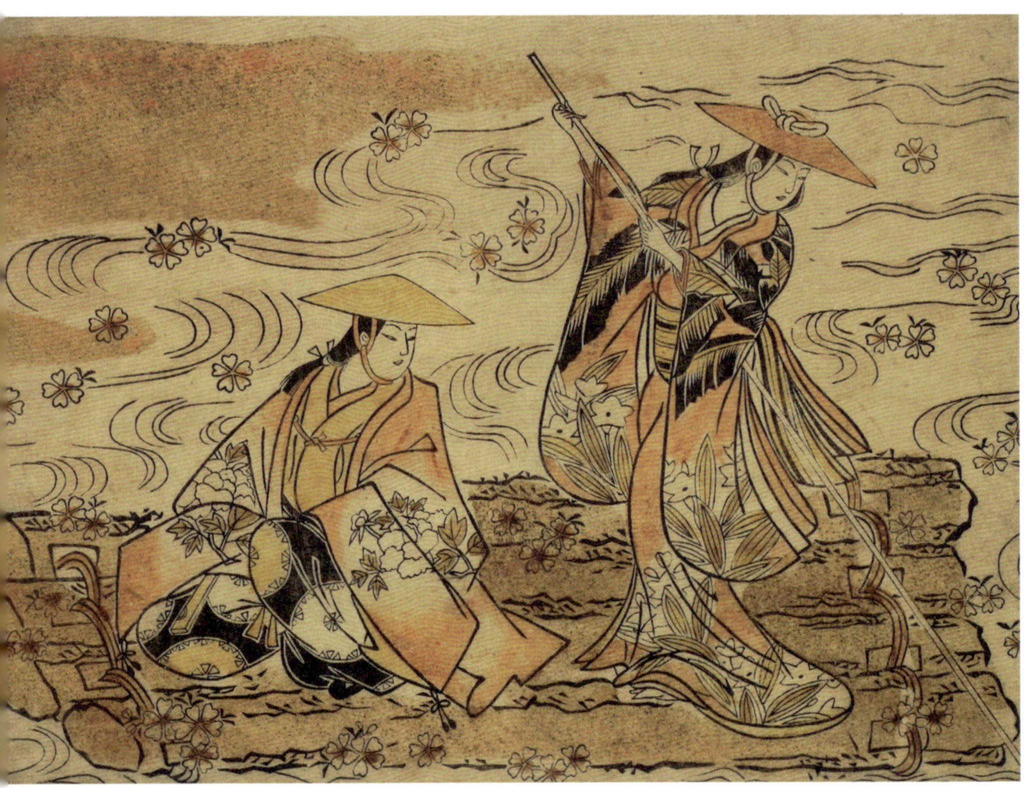

cat. no. 54
Early Torii master, Two Women on a Raft
Hand-coloured woodblock print, *ōban*
Japan, Edo period, ca. 1718–1720

In addition to portraits of actors and courtesans, the *ukiyo-e workshops* concentrate more on the increasing amount of travelling in Japan. Well-developed long-distance roads such as the Tōkaidō ("East Sea Road"), which criss-crossed the elongated country, already defined the routes in the seventeenth to nineteenth centuries, many of which still form the heart of Japan's transport infrastructure today with motorways and high-speed railway lines (cf. cat. no. 39).

Increasing demand for travel souvenirs led to a greater number of works depicting prominent places along the trade routes. In some cases, extensive series of motifs were also successful from a commercial point of view, as buyers and collectors sought to obtain complete collections, which helped to promote sales. To a certain extent, this desire also applied to the many Western collectors who discovered an enthusiasm for Japanese colour prints in the late nineteenth century.

For this exhibition, we have focussed on prints that depict rivers, waterfalls, the sea and heavy rain. Given the topography of the Japanese archipelago and its humid climate, it is hardly surprising that water, whether as a picturesque waterfall, a lazily flowing river, a heavy downpour or even a deadly tsunami wave, has always stimulated the imagination of Japan's inhabitants and inspired countless artists for centuries.

Katsushika Hokusai's (1760–1849) woodblock print "Behind the Great Wave (off the coast) of Kanagawa" (cat. no. 56) is presented in place of honour here. This iconic image, also known simply as the "Great Wave", is without doubt Japan's most famous and influential work of art, despite its modest commercial value at the time of its creation.[15] Hokusai's "Wave" can also be seen as a reflection of the Japanese psyche, mirroring like no other work the ambivalence of beauty and potentially fatal danger, a combination which dominates Japanese culture more than in any other country in the world. The powerful forces of nature depicted here arouse fascination and fear in equal measure. At the same time, this work is a paradox: the wave, just a few metres high, rises towering above Japan's highest mountain, the 3776-metre-high Mount Fuji. The brave rowers in the two speedboats, which are on their way to supply the large fish market in the capital Edo, seem to defy the elemental forces of this monster wave with contempt for death.

The viewer of this enduringly popular Japanese *ukiyo-e* print may be first drawn to the precise beauty of the waves, depicted in various shades of Prussian blue. On closer inspection, however, its spray looks more like the tentacles of a giant octopus, which in the next moment plunges down on the doomed men in the boats. It is precisely this relationship between an almost unearthly grace, impetuous power and deadly danger that immortalised Hokusai, who was already seventy at the time the leaf was created.

The print "Kajikazawa in Kōshū" (cat. no. 57), also from Hokusai's series of "Thirty-six Views of Mount Fuji", is not as famous, but is no less impressive as a work of art. This composition, in which the waves are again somewhat reminiscent of octopus rigs, is also dramatic. In this image they ripple underneath the narrow rock jutting out over the water, from the edge where a fisherman has cast his net. Fuji towers up to the upper edge of the picture, separated from the foreground by hazy shades of colour, its contour line appearing like an echo of the fishing net holding lines. The fisherman, located almost exactly in the centre of the picture, appears to be the master of the action, even if his position on the front edge of a cliff above the sea is quite precarious. Should a large fish be caught in his net, the figure would likely struggle to keep his balance and not plunge into the water.

A crouching figure behind him, bent over a basket and perhaps inspecting the catch he has already made, appears mysterious. While the standing fisherman is recognisable in profile, this secondary figure turns away from the viewer. Or is this figure, resting as it were in itself, an *alter ego* of the fisherman balancing exposed on the cliff top?

In comparison to these two masterpieces, four leaves from the series "Round Trip to the Waterfalls in the Provinces" (cat. nos. 59–62), also by Hokusai, appear rather cheerfully picturesque and genre-like.

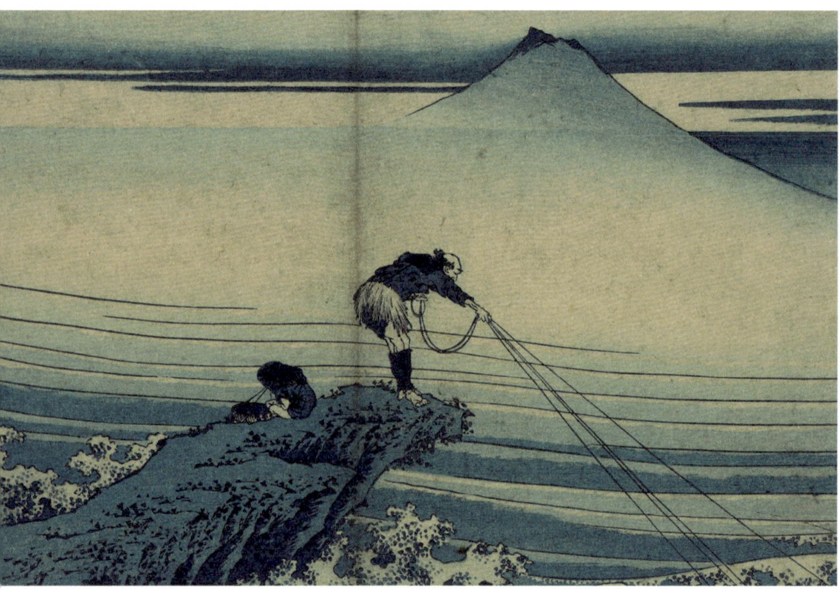

cat. no. 57 (detail)
Katsushika Hokusai (1760–1849), "Kajikazawa in Kōshū (Kai Province)"
Colour woodblock print, *ōban*, Japan, late Edo period, 1830

These are highly refined, surprising compositions, which gain additional charm through the "Berlin blue" (*beru-ai* –"Prussian blue") – new at the time in the early 1830s – as well as through effective use of contrasting colour. In any case, due to the medium of the colour print, this piece stands in contrast to the radically simplified Yōrō waterfall by Yokoyama Seiki (cat. no. 41), as discussed above. Hokusai's small series, consisting of a total of eight prints, is an impressive example of the veneration of natural phenomena in Shintō. Many of these places of natural beauty were also considered to be inhabited by Shintō deities (*kami*) and worthy of worship, with shrines erected in the nearby area.

Popular pilgrimages were taken for physical and spiritual purification. Bathing in the often ice-cold water of these mountain waters may also have been seen as a form of exercise, but it was primarily a religious act, as the print "The Rōben Waterfall in Ōyama in Sōshū" (cat. no. 59) charmingly demonstrates. Here, the bathers enter the water completely naked except for a loincloth, wearing elongated prayer boards. Works such as these prove that in Edo period Japan, as in many other world cultures, pilgrimage was a kind of precursor to tourism, and that there were art forms which lent it a visual language.

The second great master of the later *ukiyo-e* woodblock print is Utagawa Hiroshige (1797–1858), a notable master of the poetic landscape. Our exhibition shows one coastal and three river landscapes by him (cat. nos. 63–66).

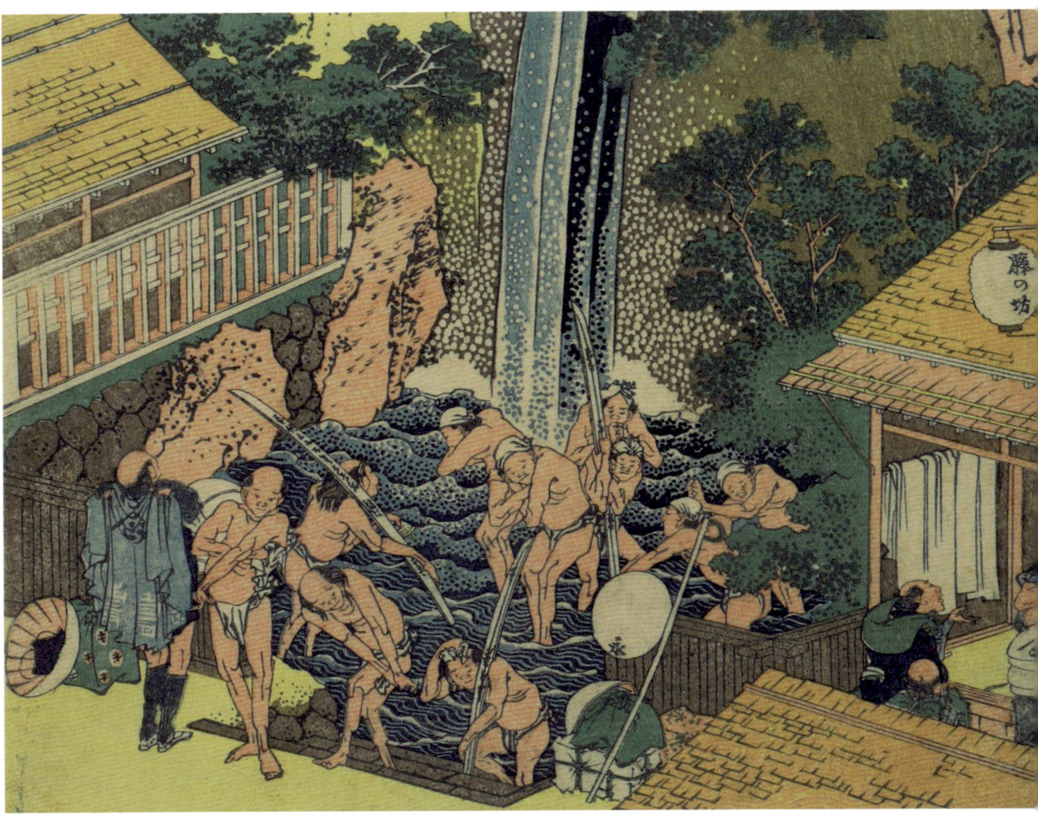

cat. no. 59 (detail)
Katsushika Hokusai (1760–1849), "The Rōben Waterfall in Ōyama in Sōshū" (Sagami Prefecture)
Colour woodblock print, *ōban*
Japan, late Edo era, 1834/35

The leaf "The Wakanoura Coast in the Province of Kii" (cat. no. 63), published in 1857, is particularly surprising both in terms of its composition and its vibrant colours. The viewer's attention is first drawn to the huge cranes flying high above in the foreground, which look as if they have been captured with a tele-photo lens from an aeroplane; it seems as if Hiroshige is playing with human-kind's enduring fantasy of flying. Since, according to Daoist ideas in East Asia, the immortals glide through the air on cranes, there is also a sense of a supra-mundane, metaphysical existence suggested through this landscape. At the same time, the early morning light in which the picturesque coastal landscape is bathed depicts a liminal state, perhaps a moment of hope at the beginning of a new day. A few years after the landing of the American Commodore Perry's "Black Ships", which ended more than two hundred years of self-isolation in Japan, it delivers a poignant message.

In the other three of Hiroshige's prints shown in this exhibition, a river domi-nates the scenes. The rafts floating on the water in each of the prints create an atmosphere of leisurely gliding. In "Evening Rainstorm over the Ōhashi Bridge near Atake" (cat. no. 66), however, this calm movement acts as a counterpoint to the force of the heavy rain, which is depicted in black and grey through closely spaced, almost vertical lines, causing the people on the bridge to hurry away.

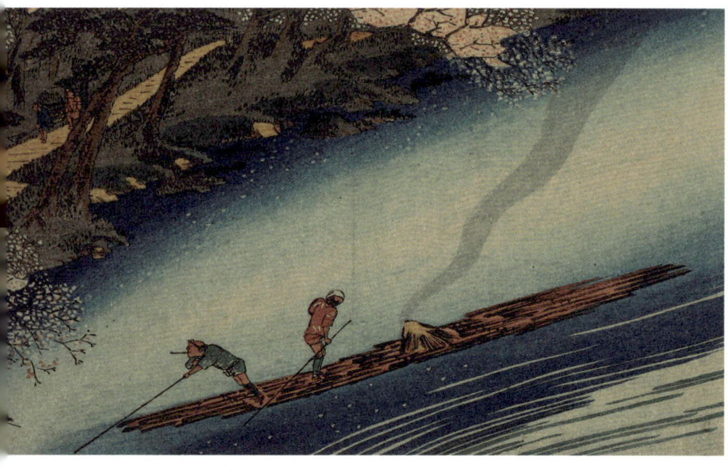

cat. no. 64 (detail)
"Arashiyama Cherry Blossoms in Full Bloom"
Colour woodblock print, *ōban*, Japan, late Edo era, 1834

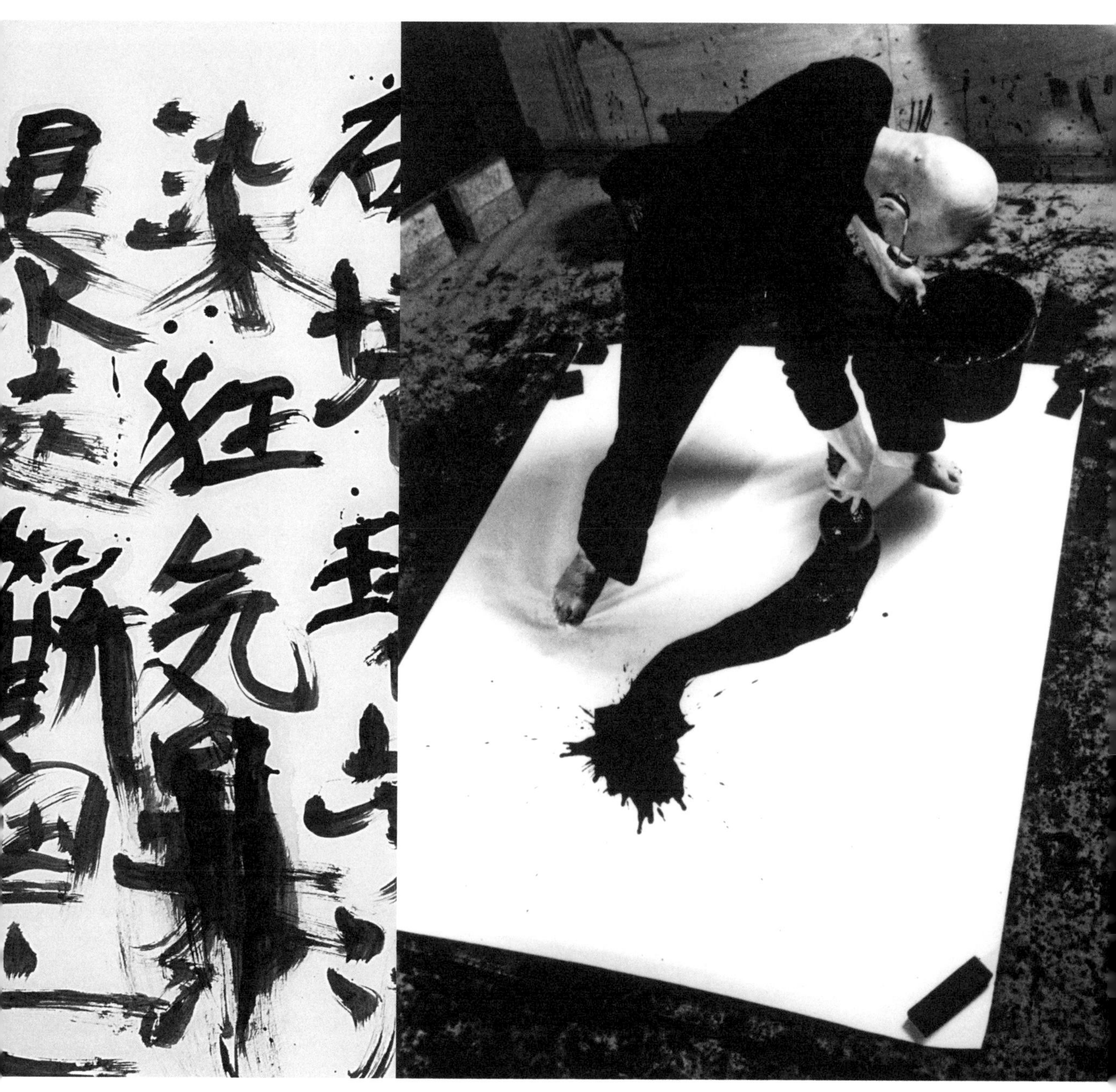

Inoue Yūichi

With a work of calligraphy by Inoue Yūichi (1916–1985), the modern Japan of the second half of the twentieth century bursts in with all its contradictions (cat. no. 68), a much more disturbing shift than the gradual evolution of the modern ceramics presented above, which all move within a canon of forms that have developed over centuries. Yūichi[16], who radically broke with all the aesthetic features that had characterised Japanese calligraphy up to the modern period, is one of the most important figures of the post–1945 avant-garde art of writing. The work *Economic Growth*[17] from 1978 may be regarded as one of his most political works, functioning as a cri de cœur against unbounded greed and the ruthless destruction of nature. Yūichi describes Japan's economic rise to become an industrial superpower as a rampage ("madness is raging") destroying the country. The theme of transience is addressed here with unsparing candour, as is the looming, primarily self-inflicted demise of Japan and the industrial-capitalist modern world as a whole.

The artist repeatedly formulated his counter-model to the destructive lifestyle of modern industrialised society, for example in a series on the character *hin* 貧 ("poverty")[18] that was developed over two and a half decades from 1954. For Yūichi, poverty was a way of life with the greatest possible absence of need. "Preserving poverty" (*shuhin* 守貧)[19] became his life motto. He remained a primary school teacher throughout his life and deliberately avoided contact with the elite circles of modern calligraphy in Japan.

Yūichi's style is raw and uncompromising, just as the form and writing style of his *Economic Growth* emphasises the ugliness of the message. The crude crossings-out in the text and the tumbling of the angular characters reflect the accusatory, even desperate tone of the text on a visual level.

16 In English-language literature, the artist is usually referred to by his first name, also as YU-ICHI.

17 In 1995, the work was given a prominent place in the triple exhibition on Inoue Yūichi in Frankfurt (at Schirn Kunsthalle, Galerie im Karmeliterkloster, Museum für Kunsthandwerk [today: Museum Angewandte Kunst]). While the Schirn show traced the character *hin* 貧 (poverty) in a series of monumental works of written art, and the Galerie im Karmeliterkloster commemorated the fiftieth anniversary of the bombing of Tōkyō (which led to more than one hundred thousand deaths), the show *Economic Growth* at Museum für Kunsthandwerk was dedicated to the dark side and effects of the emerging economic bubble in Japan.

18 Cf. Schulenburg/Unagami 1995. The exhibition presented thirty-two large-format works showing only the character 貧.

19 *Shuhin* 貧守 is the title of a work from 1981 (ink on paper, 63.5 x 91 cm, UNAC TOKYO, CRNo. 81046), see Schulenburg/Unagami 1995, p. 101.

"A Floating World" 2025

All of the works presented so far embody the ephemeral in Japanese art in one way or another. They span a wide range from the Kamakura period (1185–1333) to Inoue Yūichi in the 1970s. However, the viewer may be unjustified in asking: what of the floating world, the moving and ephemeral, in contemporary Japanese art so far in the twenty-first century?

In this exhibition, we present four perspectives that represent the ephemeral as a subject of contemporary art: Rikuo Ueda and Hide Nasu[20], both born in 1950, as well as Shiriagari Kotobuki (born 1958). The fourth analysis examines contemporary forms of expression of Japanese tea culture with Peter Granser and Mari Kashiwagi.

20   Both artists have produced many publications in Western languages, particularly in English. We follow the Western spelling of first name before surname that is common there.

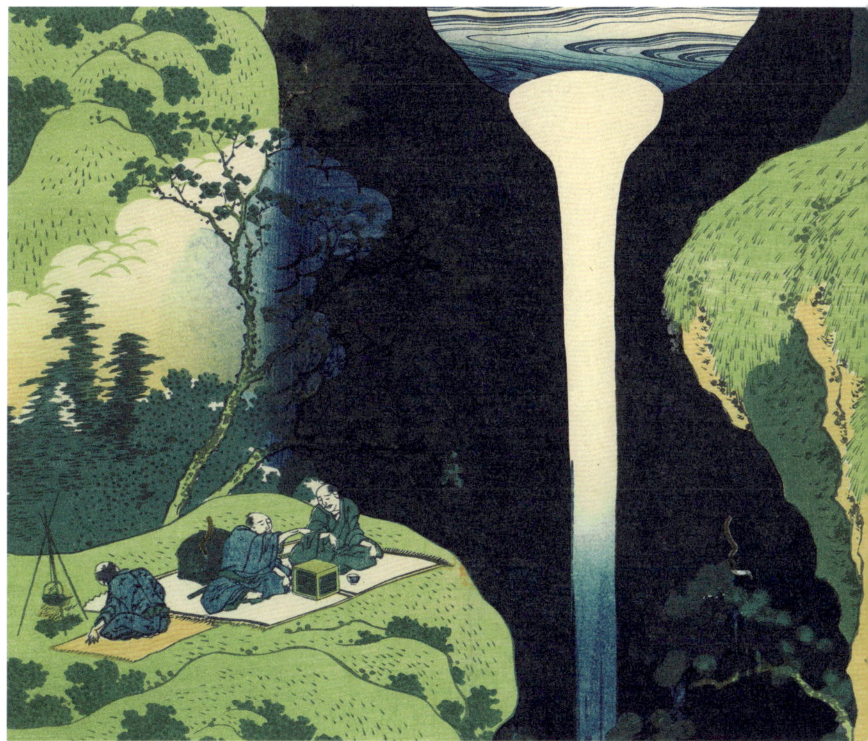

cat. no. 62 (Detail)
Shiriagari Kotobuki, 渇水 Drought, C-print in varying dimensions, 2024
Parody of Katsushika Hokusai's woodblock print "The Amida Waterfall at Kisokaidō" (cat. no. 62)

Rikuo Ueda

Rikuo Ueda lives and works in the old harbour town of Sakai, south of Ōsaka. He has set up his studio – he prefers the term "warehouse" – in a former back-yard business where knives[21] and later machine parts were manufactured for a long time. He has redesigned the "Hardware Factory" sign to read "Chaos Factory" (*konton seisakusho*) (illustration left).

Ueda emphasises with a mischievous smile that he is not actually an artist, but rather only helps the wind to create art. This idea has been at the centre of his work for many years. During a visit to Sakai in May 2024, two apparatuses were in operation directly in front of and in an attic of the

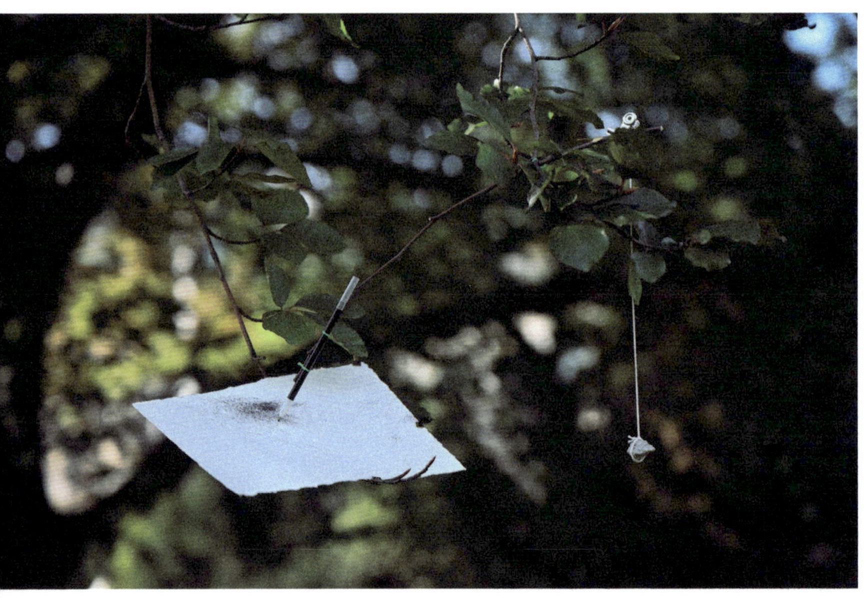

cat. no. 69
Rikuo Ueda, a wind drawing in progress

"Chaos Factory". In one, a sheet of paper floated on a raft-like form in a shallow pool of water. Above it, a metal tube was installed on a diagonal, high above the roof with a small stone attached to it with a string, which vibrated slightly in gusts of wind, causing a writing instrument attached to the lower end to make blue traces of colour on the paper floating in the water (centre/right). In a space below the gable of the "Chaos Factory", another "wind-painting machine" constructed by Ueda was at work. Its long arm was extended into a sail at the rear of the building, which set two writing instruments in motion over a piece of paper attached to the side of a wall (fig. below).

On other days, Ueda sets up a stick on a tree or bush, using the wind to draw with pencil on paper. Based on this principle, Ueda has created a large number of such arrangements all over the world, the working method of which is documented in numerous YouTube videos on the internet.[22]

The resulting abstract drawings, which are somewhat reminiscent of compositions by Wols (1913–1951) or Cy Twombly (1928–2011), are usually framed individually or grouped together in albums. In addition to a Wind House by Ueda (Cat.No. 69), the Frankfurt exhibition presents selected works from the Mikiko Sato Gallery in Hamburg, which has represented the artist for more than twenty years (see p. 198ff.). A wind-painting apparatus created by Rikuo Ueda especially for the Museum Angewandte Kunst is also being planned.

Ueda's artistic work has taken him outside Japan to the USA, Germany, Denmark, the Netherlands, Israel, China and Taiwan, among other places.[23]

22   One particularly spectacular, unusual project was "Letter", created in 2018 at the Kunststation Sankt Peter in Cologne. See https://www.youtube.com/watch?v=2bYhxpDSGLo (accessed 4 June 2024). In this performance, the flow of air from the church's organ pipes was all that set the wind apparatus into motion. However, the organist's hands and feet indirectly became the creator of the drawing on the paper during the musical performance, rather than the wind itself – unlike the majority of Ueda's projects.

23   See https://de.wikipedia.org/wiki/Rikuo_Ueda (accessed 4 June 2024).

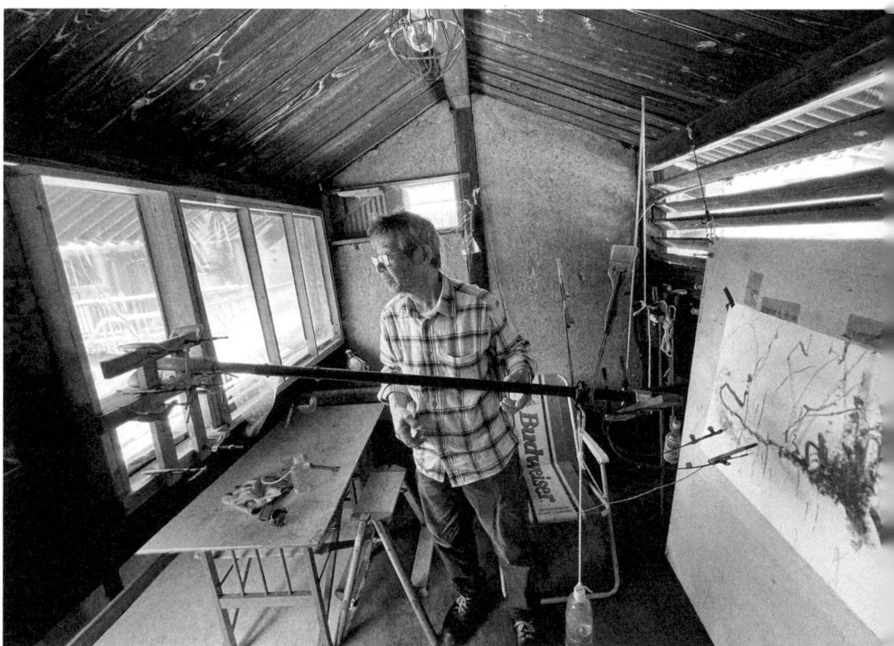
Rikuo Ueda and his "wind-writing machine" on the top floor of the "Chaos Factory" (May 2024)

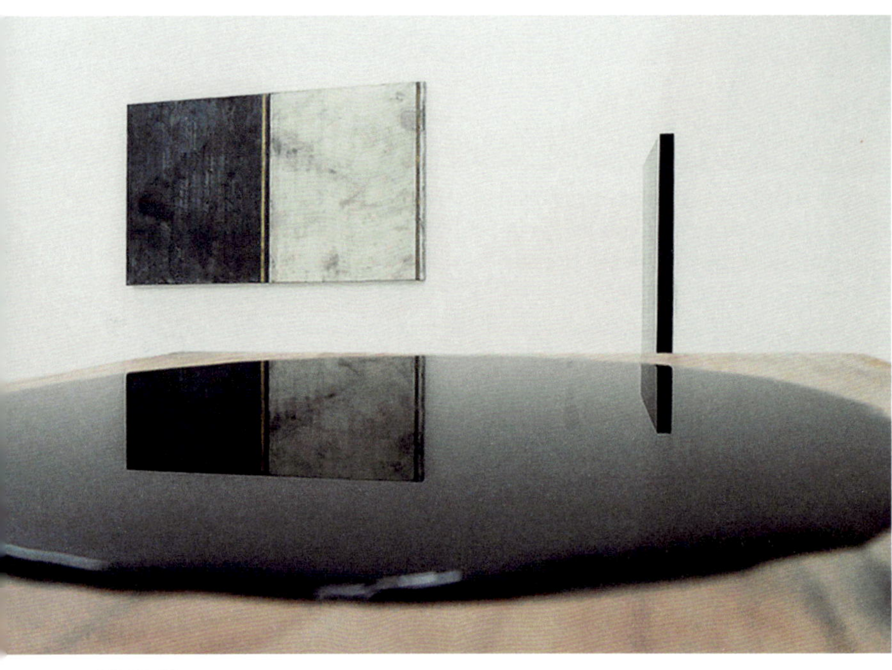

cat. no. 70
Hide Nasu, *Mizukagami* (mirror pond), ink, wax, wood, 30 x 30 x 3 cm
In the background: Untitled, 90 x 120 x 2 cm (two parts), Kaneko Art Gallery, Tōkyō, 2016

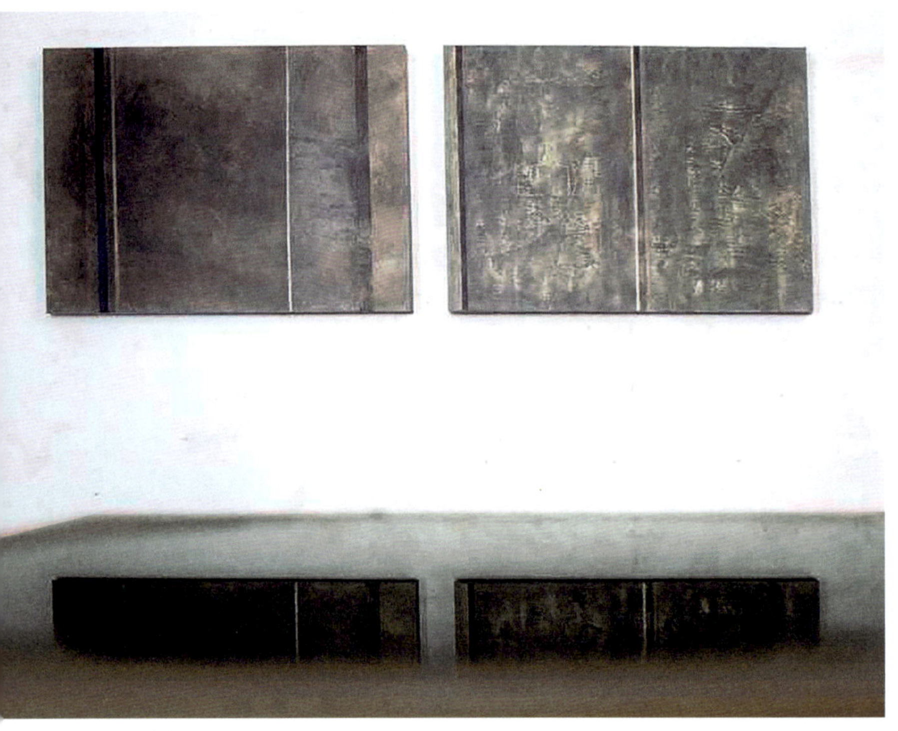

cat. no. 70
Hide Nasu, *Ma* 間 01 and 02, encaustic on wood, 60 x 90 x 4 cm each; and *Mizukagami* (mirror pond)
Atelier Hide Nasu, Frankfurt am Main, 2024

Hide Nasu

Like Rikuo Ueda, Hide Nasu was born in 1950. After studying art and art history in Tōkyō, he joined the Stuttgart Art Academy at the age of 27 and soon moved to the Städelschule in Frankfurt. He has lived in Frankfurt ever since while remaining in regular contact with the art and gallery scene in Japan.

For Hide Nasu, there is no such thing as a finished work of art. Rather, the work lives on day after day, long after it has left the studio. This idea is perhaps represented most impressively by a series of cubic wooden blocks with a milled round "mirror pond" (*mizukagami*) on the top. The wood is either coated with a light varnish or completely lacquered with Japanese *urushi* to create a glossy black surface. The mirror pond is then filled with water. The wooden block remains in place and the water gradually evaporates until it has almost vanished, leaving only deposits of lime or other initially invisible components in water. This process is repeated both by the artist himself and – or at least, this is Hide Nasu's wish – by the person who acquires his work. This experiment could be termed "art in use": it expands our conventional conception of art in a surprising way. Of course, this is not applied art in a literal sense as in a piece of furniture, a drinking bowl, or similar. Rather, the gradual process of change, or patina, becomes the actual theme and the specific character of the artwork. We are therefore dealing with much more than a block of wood with a hollow at the top. Rather, it is a metaphor for our human existence, or perhaps even for the passage of time itself. Changes take place everywhere and every day in nature, as well as within ourselves.

Hide Nasu's work also plays with the viewer's sense of perception: his largely monochrome painting, also shown in the exhibition, is not just a painting on the wall, a rectangular panel with non-representational surface structures. His creation also includes, perhaps to disrupt our typical way of viewing, the work's reflection. This appears usually in a square, black basin filled with water on the floor, in which the reflection of the painting on the wall and its surroundings appears, constantly changing with our own movement.

Shiriagari Kotobuki

Themes of the ephemeral, the quick and fleeting are presented very differently in the work of Shiriagari Kotobuki (born 1958). Alongside his early career as a commercial designer for the Kirin brewery, Kotobuki had already begun work as a comic artist. He developed an inimitable, rough and deliberately awkward style that clearly deviates from the mainstream of the Japanese manga industry.

For many years, Shiriagari Kotobuki has also repeatedly moved beyond the boundaries of *story manga*[24] in a more literal sense. In 2004 at the ASK? art space gallery in Tōkyō and in 2009 at the Museum für Angewandte Kunst Frankfurt am Main (image below), he showed the monumental and ephemeral work "My Kingdom" (*ore no ōkoku*). In this presentation, the visual language of manga was transformed into an expansive, walk-in installation. He considered this act to be a deliberate provocation, a way of ignoring the usual manga style, with no fixed picture narrative, no pages with framed text-image plots and no draft sketches as the basis for finished manga illustrations. "Ultimately," says the artist, "I refrain from commanding my hand with my brain to draw something specific."[25]

24   *Story manga* ストーリー漫画 refers to Japanese comics with long picture narratives that usually extend over several chapters.

25   Shiriagari Kotobuki: "My Kingdom has Traveled across the Ocean" – on a variant of the aforementioned installation in the ASK?/art space gallery in the Museum Angewandte Kunst Frankfurt am Main. Cf. Deutsches Filmmuseum/ Museum of Applied Arts 2008, p. 184.

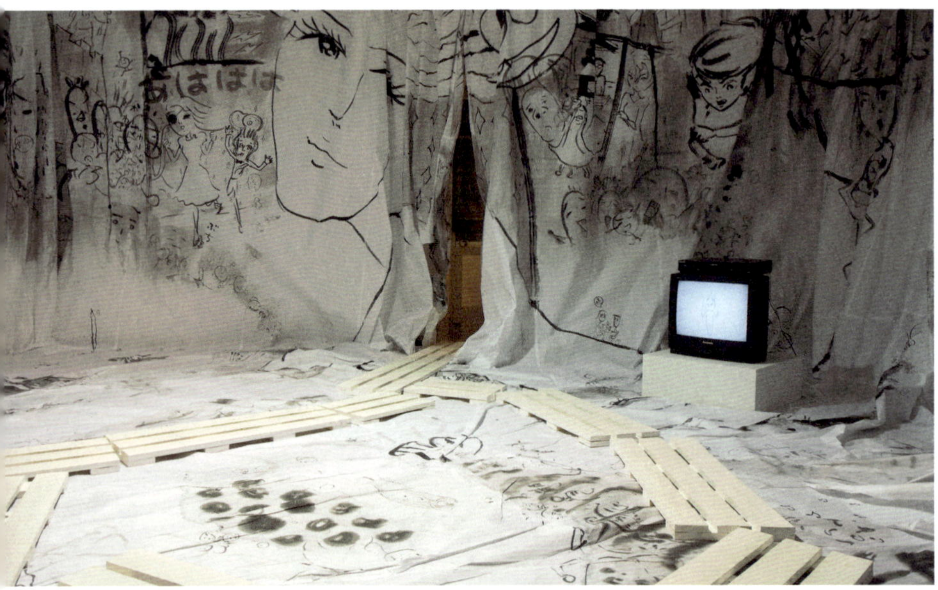

cat. no. 71
Shiriagari Kotobuki: "My Kingdom" (*ore no ōkoku*)
Installation, ink on paper, wood, tube TV set with cartoon film by the artist, approx. 6 x 6 x 3 m
Exhibition *Mangamania*, Museum für Angewandte Kunst, Frankfurt, 2008

In Shiriagari Kotobuki's work, the floating world can also be understood as an intellectual concept: movement, change and real provocation are expressed in his wildly expressive, politically subversive *story manga*, which are characterised by black humour. But the even greater significance of his oeuvre is his attempt to redefine what manga can be in the twenty-first century, perhaps even has to be: a satirical, grotesque visual language no longer expressed in comic books the size of telephone books, but through cinematically animated production in the form of anime. Kotobuki is constantly testing the limits of this form of popular art. Against the backdrop of AI and the rise of fake news on the internet, the forms of "manga-anime syndrome"[26] are once again in a phase of upheaval, which Shiriagari Kotobuki continues to articulate in his deliberately clumsy yet highly sophisticated way of working.

Alongside his work as a manga illustrator and artist, the mangaka has also long enjoyed a reputation as a critic and expert, as shown by his interview on the Berlin Hokusai exhibition at the Martin-Gropius-Bau in 2012[27] many years ago, as well as carrying out academic teaching and frequently participating in panel discussions, such as at the Art Gallery GEESEN 藝泉/Kyōto organised by his brother on 11 May 2024.[28]

Fifteen years after his "Manga Kingdom" was shown in our museum in 2009, Shiriagari Kotobuki presents a very personal homage to Katsushika Hokusai for the exhibition *A Floating World*. The master of the "Great Wave" appears in a completely new light in these subtle transformations of his woodblock prints.

26 See Stephan von der Schulenburg: "Manga und Japanische Gegenwartskunst", op. cit. pp. 176–183.

27 Cf. https://www. wochikochi.jp/english/topstory/2011/10/ hokusai-berlin.php (accessed 3 June 2024).

28 See, for example, his professorship at the School of Progressive Arts, Kōbe Design University (神戸芸術工科大学, Kōbe geijutsu kōka daigaku) since 2006; on the aforementioned panel discussion: Art Gallery GEESEN 藝泉, 1036–2 Katahara-chō, Kamigyō-kū, Kyōto https://www.instagram.com/geesen2024/ (accessed 19 June 2024).

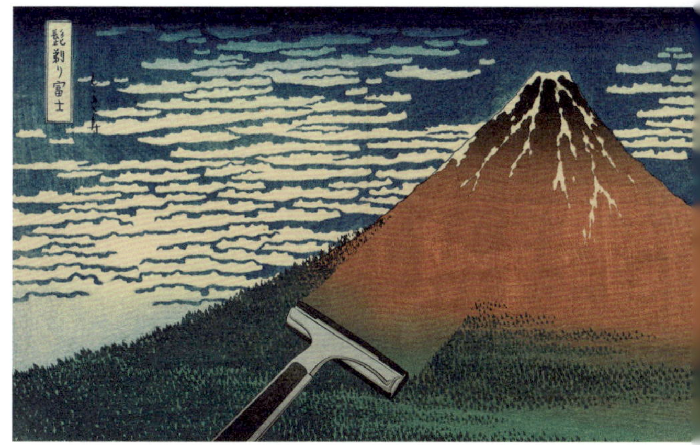

cat. no. 71:
Shiriagari Kotobuki: Hokusai Parody, Nr. 3: 髭剃り富士 Shaving Mount Fuji
C-print in variable dimensions, 2024

Japanese Tea Culture Today

The exhibition closes by examining another performative *Gesamtkunstwerk*, the Japanese tea ceremony, going beyond the use of historical artefacts.[29] Tea culture has experienced an unprecedented renaissance far beyond Japan in the twenty-first century. In Japan, the cultivation of this art in its centuries-old tradition is an integral part of aesthetic education, particularly in educated circles, and is practised by many people throughout their lives. Nevertheless, the practices have changed considerably in recent years, particularly in teahouse architecture. In Frankfurt, Kengo Kuma's mobile teahouse designed in 2008 for the outdoor area of our museum is an impressive testimony to this revival.[30] His house in the shape of a double igloo is made of a special plastic and illuminated from beneath. This example of conceptual architecture is an attempt to translate transience and ephemerality into a light, seemingly weightless building.[31]

29 For the beginnings and earlier history of the Japanese tea ceremony, see pp. 3-6 above.

30 See Fischer/Schneider 2008. Kengo Kuma, born in Yokohama in 1954, is one of the most important Japanese architects of the present day. An overview of his life's work can be found at https://en.wikipedia.org/wiki/Kengo_Kuma and https://de.wikipedia.org/wiki/Kengo Kuma (accessed 19 June 2024).

31 After its opening in the presence of the architect in 2008, Kengo Kuma's teahouse, for which a special foundation was constructed on a small hill opposite the EMMA METZLER museum restaurant, could only be used at this location a few times due to vandalism. In the future, fencing off Metzler Park may make it possible to restore and utilise the now-dilapidated foundation on a long-term basis.

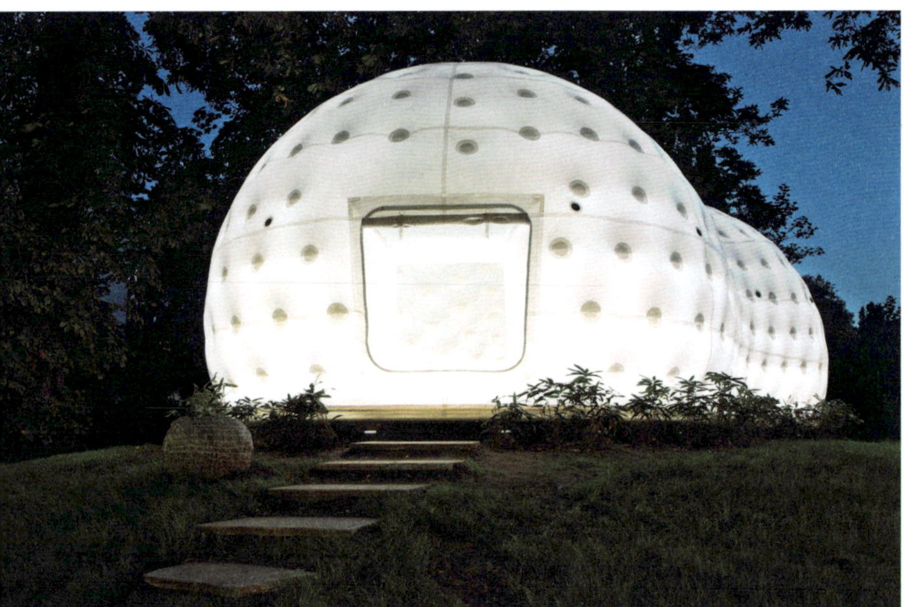

cat. no. 72
Kengo Kuma, Teahouse
Double layer of plastic (Tenara 3T40) held in shape through air pressure
Museum für Angewandte Kunst/Metzler-Park, Frankfurt am Main, 2007

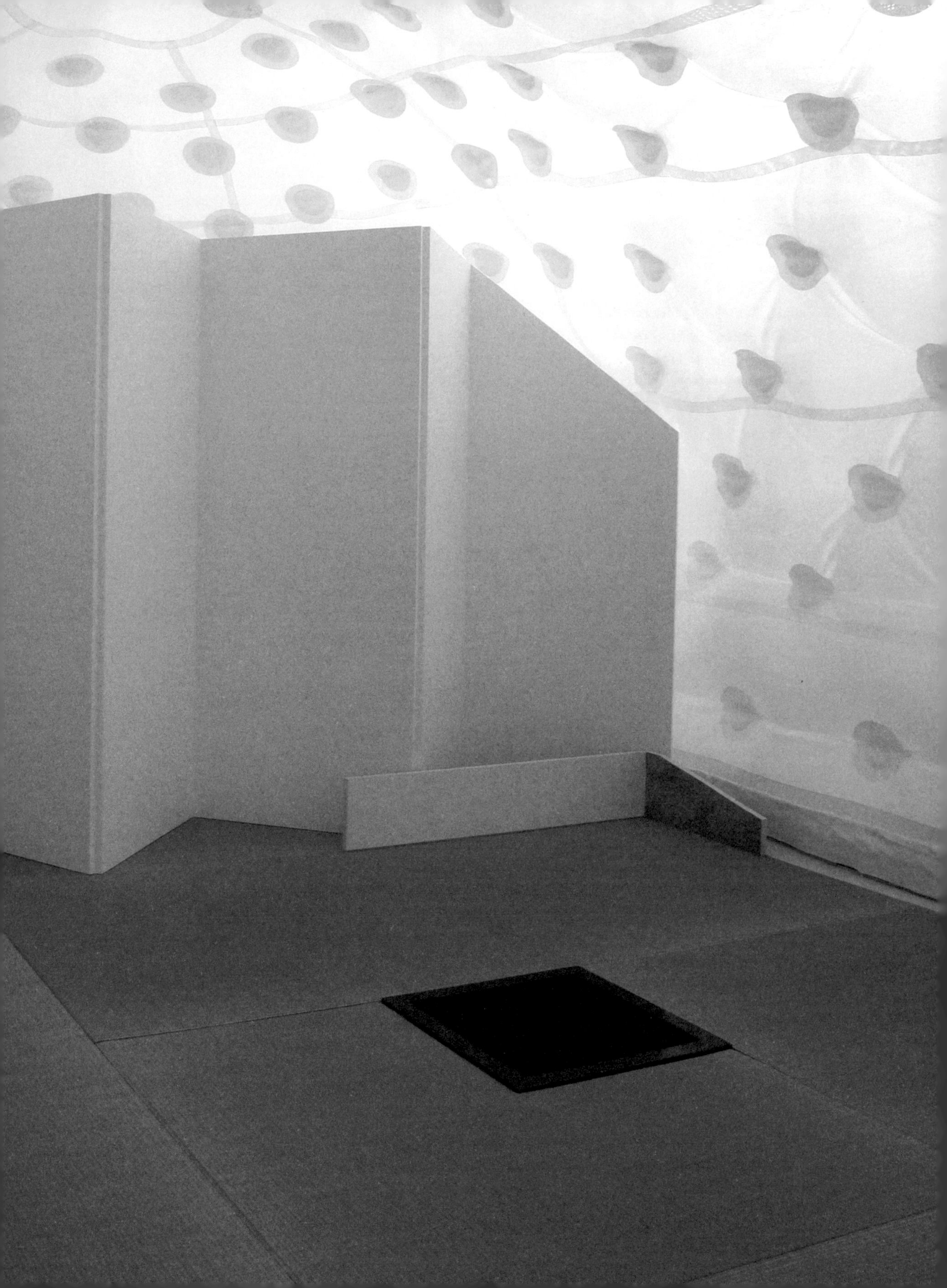

Peter Granser, in collaboration with Mari Kashiwagi:
The Manchurian Crane and the End of the World

Peter Granser (born 1971)[32] and his project *The Manchurian Crane and the End of the World* opens up an extraordinary contemporary tea room. Like an ensemble of Japanese folding screens, its interior walls are designed with large-scale photographs of steam clouds from a volcano which create a sense of rhythm. In this exhibition, these motifs are juxtaposed with almost-abstract black-and-white photographs of a group of cranes surrounded by snow (see image on p. 215).[33]

32   I would like to take this opportunity to thank Grit Weber, who drew my attention to Peter Granser's artistic work in the run-up to this exhibition.

33   See also Granser/Kashiwagi 2025.

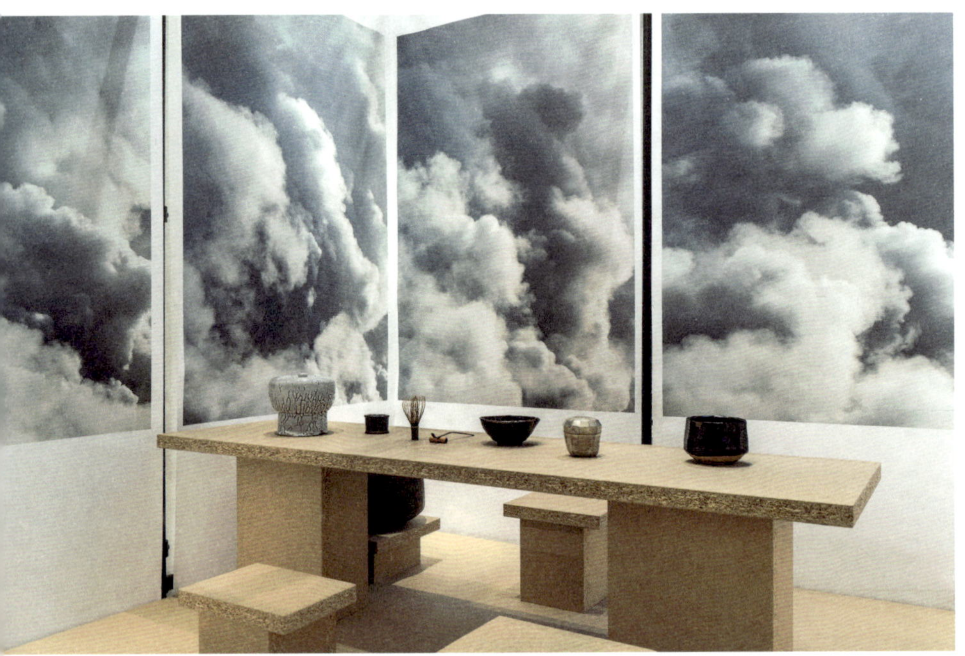

cat. no. 73
Peter Granser, The Manchurian Crane and the End of the World
Tea room installation
Stiftung Federkiel, Munich, 2020

Almost literally at the "end of the world", in the far north-east of Japan's remote northern island of Hokkaidō, a few hundred of these birds have managed to defy extinction. The pictorial programme of these photographic works draws on aesthetic principles of Japanese painting in their two-dimensional arrangements use of a simplified black and white colour palette in the crane pictures. As the mythical form of transport of the immortals, the crane in Japan – as in the whole of East Asia – is a symbol of long life present across all forms of artistic expression. At the same time, references to the precarious living conditions of these legendary birds today act as a warning to a world that is increasingly depriving itself of its own sources of life through human activity.

Together with Beatrice Theil, Peter Granser has been developing the ITO project space in Stuttgart-Bad Cannstatt since 2015. *Ito* 糸, the Japanese word for thread, stands for the linking of different aesthetic languages and practices. The art shown at this location brings together ideas of time, emptiness, nature, existence and consciousness. The viewer's perception of this art is linked to the ritual of the tea ceremony, as regularly presented by Peter Granser.

For the project *The Manchurian Crane and the End of the World*, Granser has invited the Japanese poet Mari Kashiwagi to participate as a literary figure. Her poems are often arranged in space, providing a literary counterpoint to the visual artworks and so completing the viewer's multi-sensory experience. They also reference the importance of poetry and calligraphy in the classical Japanese teahouse, for example in the form of scroll paintings hung in the *tokonoma*, the picture niche of the tea room, especially for a tea gathering. Born in Erlangen in 1970, Mari Kashiwagi was raised in Japan. In addition to her work as a poet, she is also an art historian with a subject focus on ceramics.

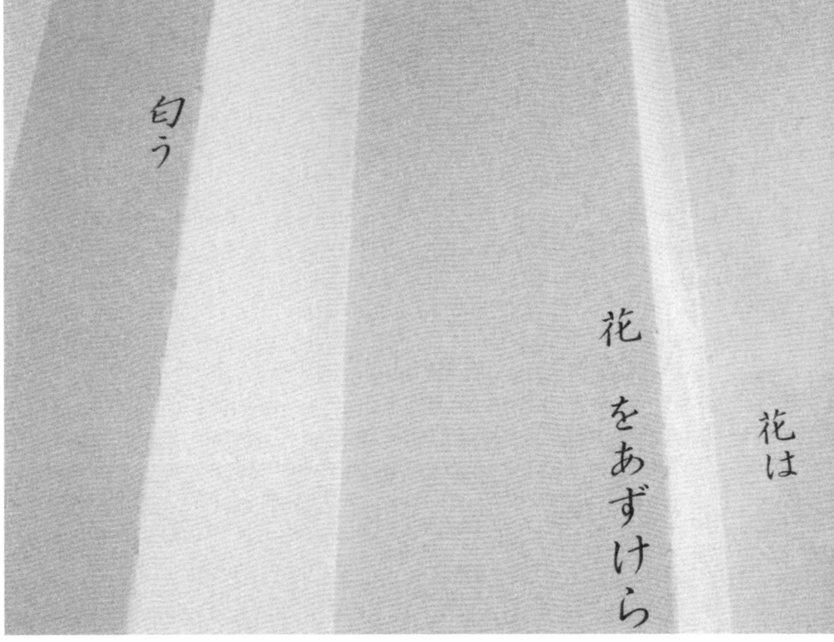

Mari Kashiwagi, poetry installation, 花は The Flowers…, 2024

Conclusion

The works presented here are drawn from a wide range of historical and aesthetic sources. They have been brought together in order to emphasise a recurring base note in Japanese art and convey the sense of a country which emphasises life's fragility and vulnerability at all times. Almost anyone who spends even a few months in Japan will experience the helplessness felt by the country's inhabitants, constantly at the mercy of unexpected forces of nature despite the otherwise perfect organisation of industrial society.

I will never forget waking up one night on the outskirts of Tōkyō to the nervous cries of birds, during my student days. A few moments, the earth shook – not dramatically, but enough that I could feel it. Another time, also at night, I was crossing a lantern-lit shrine district in Kyōto after a lively evening with friends. For a moment, I leaned against one of the mighty wooden pillars of the shrine gate and looked at the main shrine, which suddenly began to sway very slowly, almost like a ship; the lanterns swayed to the left and right. At first, I wondered if I had had a few too many glasses of beer. But then I realised that even Kyōto, which is considered a comparatively safe seismic zone within Japan, had once again been shaken by an earthquake.

These are innocent anecdotes – but if you think back to the great Tōhoku earthquake of 2011, for example, in which entire villages were swept into the sea and a serious accident occurred at the Fukushima nuclear power plant, it immediately becomes clear that even without human-caused wars and other atrocities, Japan is living atop a powder keg. And it is obvious that this state of affairs, which has always confronted the inhabitants of Japan, expresses itself in many different forms of artistic output.

A number of the works presented here express a unique attitude of humility. The simple, natural, rough, or even ugly have always been highly popular in Japan, existing in dialectical tension with highly artificial, refined, even perfected forms of artistic expression (which are not the subject of this exhibition). Unsteadiness, movement – a particular expression of dynamic change – is also one of the basic forms of aesthetics in Japan.

Matsuo Bashō (1644–1694)[34], one of Japan's greatest poets, wrote the maxim *fueki ryūkō* 不易流行, which literary scholars have labelled dialectical poetics. The poet is concerned with the tension between "immutability" (*fueki*) and "constantly changing fashions" (*ryūkō*) as a prerequisite for poetic creativity.

Bashō spent important parts of his life as a wanderer: the haiku cycle *Oku no hosomichi* ("On narrow paths into the hinterland") is one of his most important works. Wandering and (world) flight are two parts of the same concept of living, and this is of particular importance to Japanese art and culture. It is clear that this restless, dynamic principle also expresses a fundamental sense of the fleeting nature of earthly existence.

This awareness of precarious living conditions creates a certain melancholy in Japan. The difficult-to-translate Japanese term for this state (*mono no aware* 物の哀れ) indicates something akin to "the heartbreak of things" or "the gentle sensitivity of the impermanent". At the same time, Japanese art often seems to be a joyous celebration of transience, of living an almost-carefree life day by day, an Asian version of the ancient Greek and Roman concepts of *panta rhei* ("everything flows") and *carpe diem* ("seize the day, savour the moment"). In our exhibition, this idea is presented distinctively through the *ukiyo-e* woodblock prints which focus on the fleeting pleasures of nightlife as well as the beauty and diversity of the Japanese landscape. In a wholly different approach, this attitude to life is also expressed in bizarre, rough, dented ceramics as well as in gold lacquer repairs to broken tea bowls, which aesthetically exaggerate the traces of their breakage and in doing so create a unique kind of dialectical tension. Finally, Peter Granser's work makes it clear that "a floating world" is an artistic design principle that has left its mark far beyond Japan.

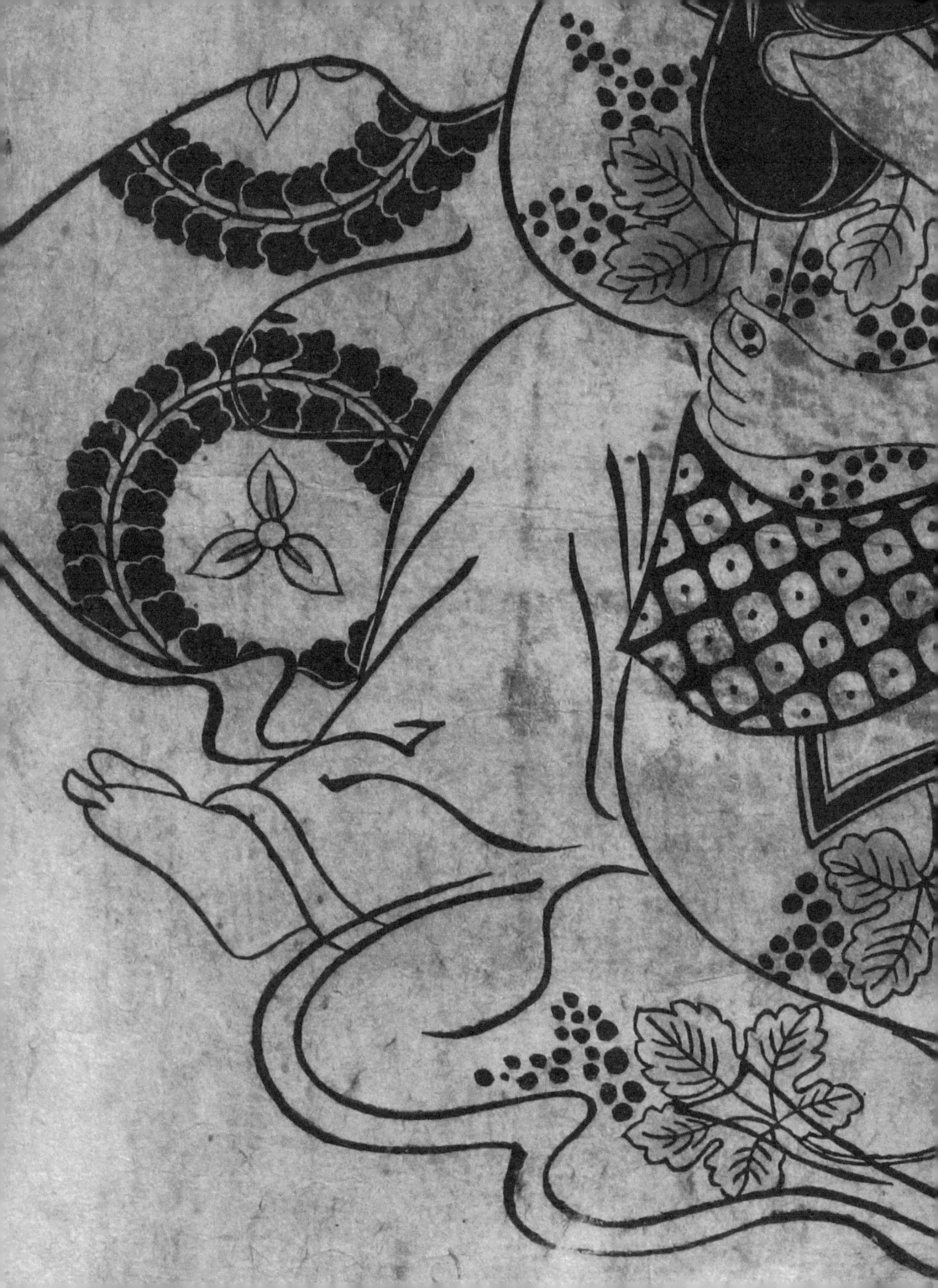

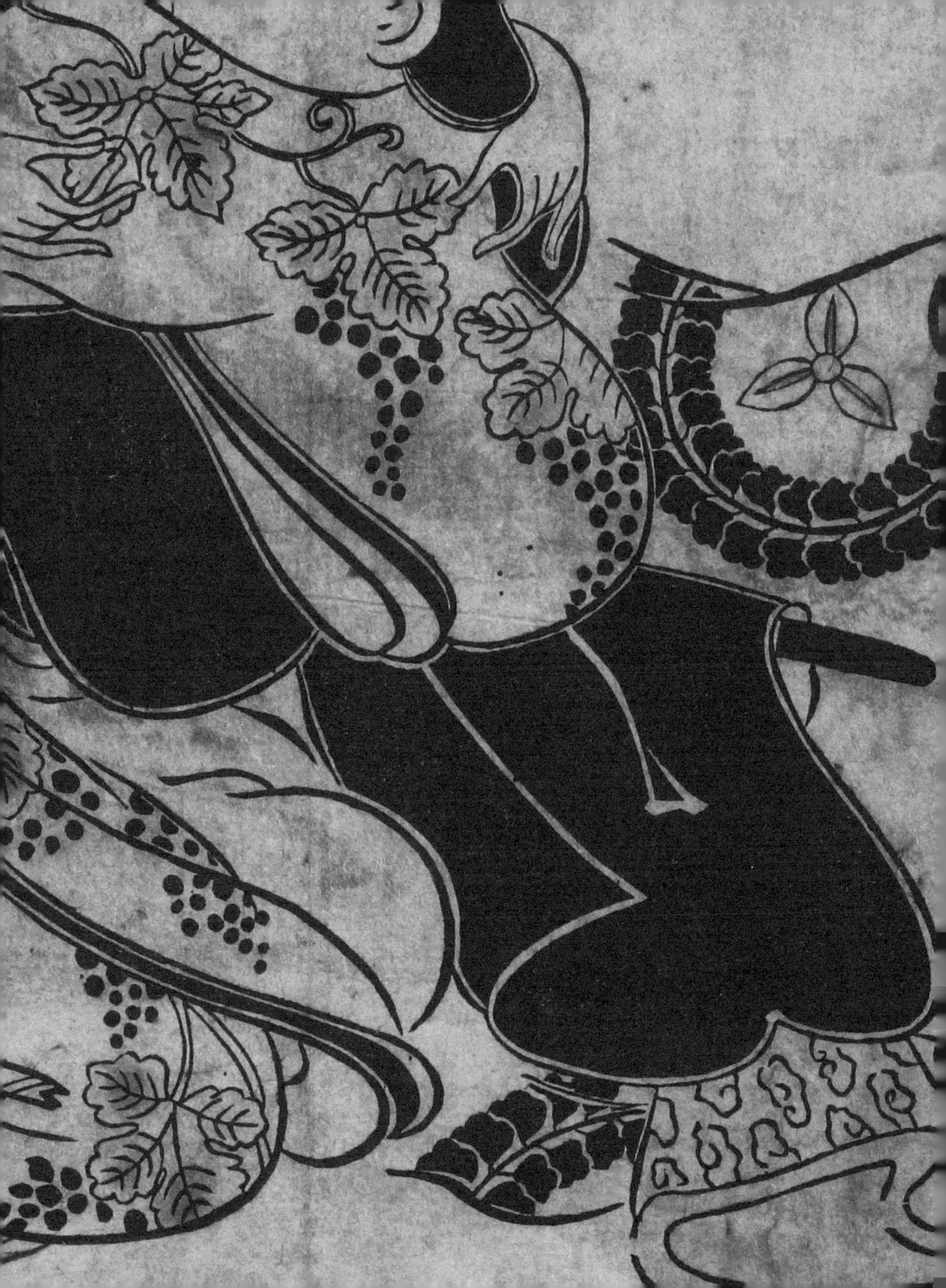

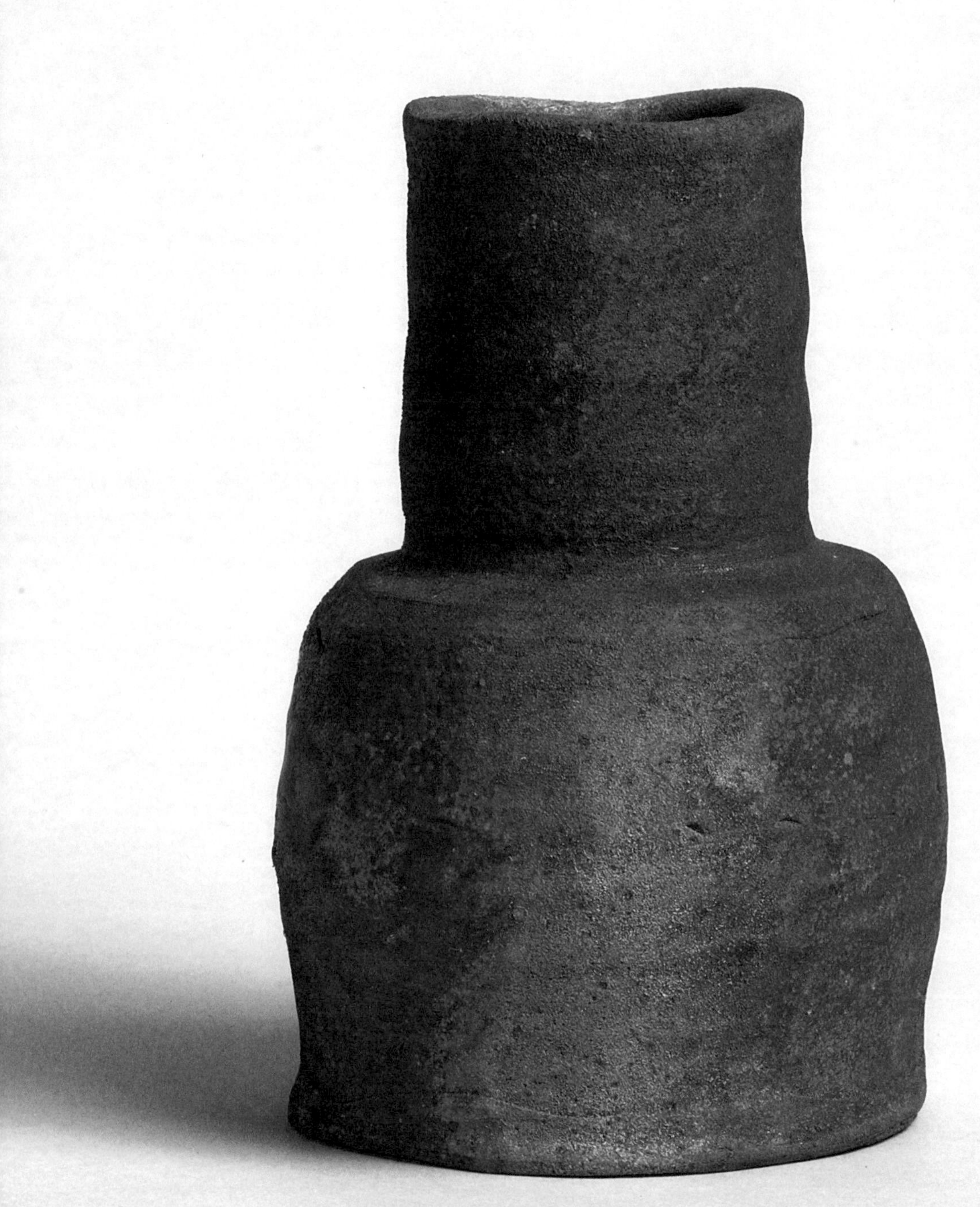

Catalogue

Pair of "lion dogs" (*Koma-inu*)
Hinoki burl (Japanese cypress) with traces of white primer and red paint on the underside
H 40 cm, L 42 cm (male animal) / H 39 cm, L 42 cm (female dog)
Japan, Kamakura era (1185–1333)

On loan from Japan Art, Frankfurt am Main

Koma-inu literally means "dogs" (Jap. *inu*) from the ancient
Korean kingdom Goguryeo (Jap. *Koma*). In Japan, they act as
symbolic guards flanking the entrance to Buddhist temples
and Shintō shrines. Ultimately, the idea of powerful lion watch-
dogs protecting the Buddhist sphere derives from India, where
actual lions can be found. In contrast, lions are not native to
China, Korea, or Japan, and thus these figures more closely
resemble dogs.

In keeping with the Chinese concept of yin and yang, the male
animal with his mouth open represents "a", the first letter in
the Sanskrit alphabet, whereas the female animal with her
mouth closed represents "un", the final letter in the same alphabet, with the two representing the Buddhist concept of the
beginning and end of all things. Since the Nara era (710–794),
koma-inu were common in Japan and throughout Asia, usually
made from wood, although they were also sometimes made
from metal during the Heian era (794–1185).

The sculptures shown here are made from *hinoki* (Japanese
cypress), which retains a light fragrance even after centuries.
They become even more expressive with their visible patina
and the severe woodworm affecting the animals' faces.

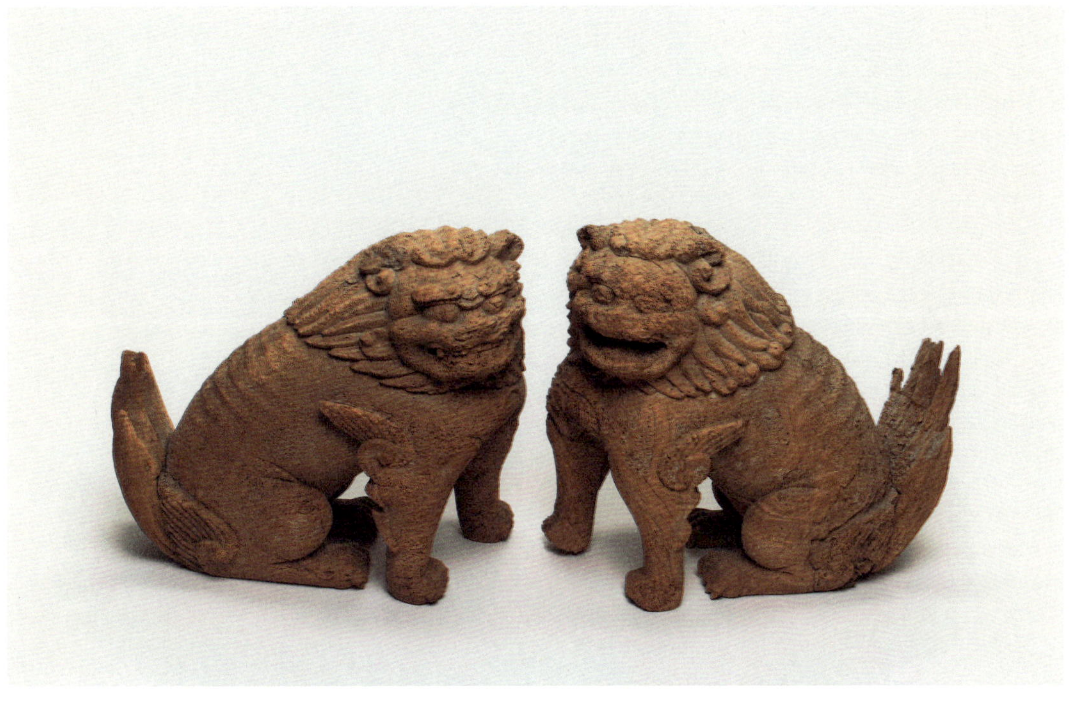

1

Sake bottle
black and red lacquer on wooden base (*Negoro-nuri*)
H 36, Dia 26 cm
Japan, Muromachi period (15th/16th c.)

12935, Ernst Arthur Voretzsch Collection, acquired 1959

The camphor wooden base is clad in a cotton layer over which
black lacquer and a partially eroded layer of red lacquer have
been applied. The red lacquer shows traces of a painting made
in deep red. The interior and the lower part of the base are
painted in black lacquer. This shape may be traced to a type
of vase used to hold a plum branch (Chin. *meiping*) popular
during the Song dynasty in China (960–1279). Such lacquered
bottles were used in royal and Shinto ceremonies in Japan.

This type of deliberate patina has its roots in the Negoro-ji
Temple located in the Wakayama Prefecture. It represents the
respect, even joy with which old and used everyday objects
were regarded, acting as a metaphor for the humility of
monastic life. With its elegant, balanced form and lively yet
mysterious surface design, this piece may be regarded as an
early *Negoro-nuri* masterpiece.

The flask forms part of the collection assembled by diplomat
Dr. Ernst Arthur Voretzsch, which was acquired by Museum
für Kunsthandwerk in 1959. Voretzsch's collection of works
from East Asia are among the most significant in our museum
collection. To learn more about his life, see the preface (p. 7,
note 6).

Lit.: Gabbert 1978, no. 92

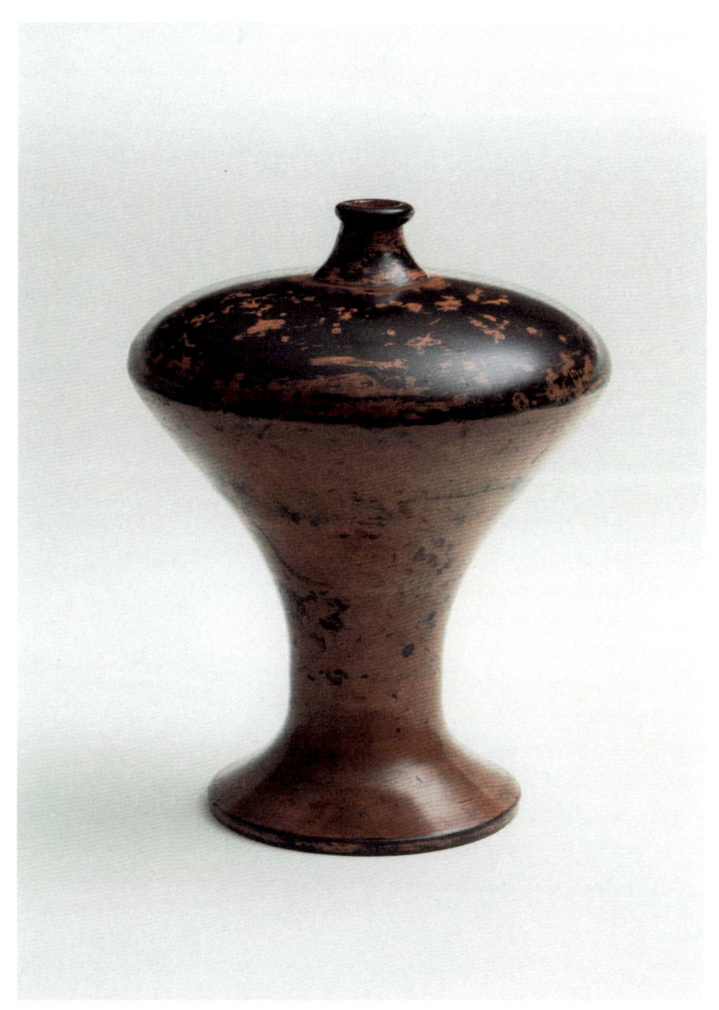

2

Three bowls (*Hidehira-wan*)
Black and red lacquer on wooden base with traces of *kirikane* decoration
H 9.1/5.5/3.7 cm, Dia 14.1/13.2/12.4 cm
Japan, early Edo period, 17th c.

12933a,b; 12934, Ernst Arthur Voretzsch Collection, acquired 1959

Wooden base with a thin layer of black lacquer on the exterior
and below the foot rim and a red lacquered interior. Painting
on the exterior in red lacquer and decoration in cut gold
leaf (*kirikane*). On the base is the sign *kichi* 吉 (happiness),
thought to be the name of a workshop. The interior reveals
traces of use and there are small signs of damage.

Three bowls. The largest sits on a high, conical foot rim,
curving outwards then rising in an almost straight line. The
middle-sized bowl has a shorter yet similarly conical foot rim
and a broadly curved wall. The smallest bowl has a modest
foot rim with a broadly curved wall. The bowl interiors are
coated with red lacquer. The exterior has been coated in such
a thin layer of black lacquer that the wood grain beneath it
is still visible. Exterior decoration on the rim: stylised clouds
(similar to lambrequin shapes) including trapezoid and zigzag
shapes in *kirikane*. Beneath these forms are apricot blossoms
with leaves and crab apple blossoms.

These bowls were likely made for everyday use, with their
clarity of form and the rapidly applied, spontaneous decoration
adding a special touch. They may be used individually as well
as in combination, and the smaller bowls may each be used as
a lid for the next-larger bowl.

Lit.: Gabbert 1978, no. 121

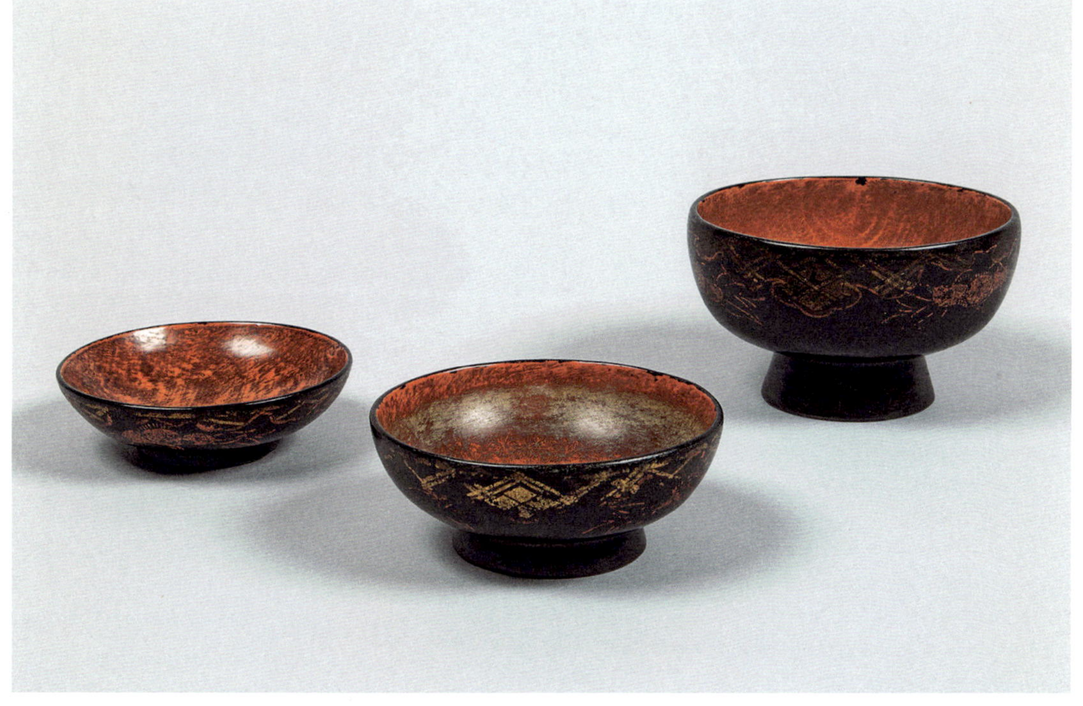

Kado Isaburō (1949–2006)
Bowl on a high base (*uchi Negoro wan*)
Black and red lacquer on wooden base
H 10.8, Dia 13.8 cm
Japan, ca. 1993

15782, acquired from Galerie Fred Jahn/Munich 1994

The core of this bowl on a high foot rim is formed from turned
keyaki wood (Japanese zelkove wood). The exterior has a relatively thick layer of black lacquer which nevertheless shows
the wood grain. In the interior, layers of red shimmer through
the black lacquer in the *Negoro-nuri* manner (c.f. cat. no. 2).
The artist's geometric workshop stamp is visible on the base,
painted in red lacquer.

Kado was the son of two lacquer masters, born in Wajima on
the Noto peninsula north of Kanazawa, a secluded town known
for its long history of lacquer workshops. Over a long period
of time, he experimented with modern means of expression
through lacquer, yet in his later years, he increasingly returned
to the clear forms of applied art objects. His lacquers from the
1980s and 1990s are distinguished by their powerful and fresh
shapes which simultaneously emphasise the archaic and the
simple. Kado never denied his ties to the Japanese art of lacquer, yet he also closely engaged with the lacquer traditions
of other Asian art centres in China, Korea, Thailand, Myanmar,
and Bhutan. Kado died relatively young. This master's work
has been recognised widely on an international scale and he
is regarded as one of Japan's most important twentieth-century lacquerwork artists.

Museum Angewandte Kunst presented Kado Isaburō's work in
a solo exhibition in 1994/95 (Weinmayr 1994) and acquired a
number of his works for its collection.

Lit.: Weinmayr 1994, p.78f.

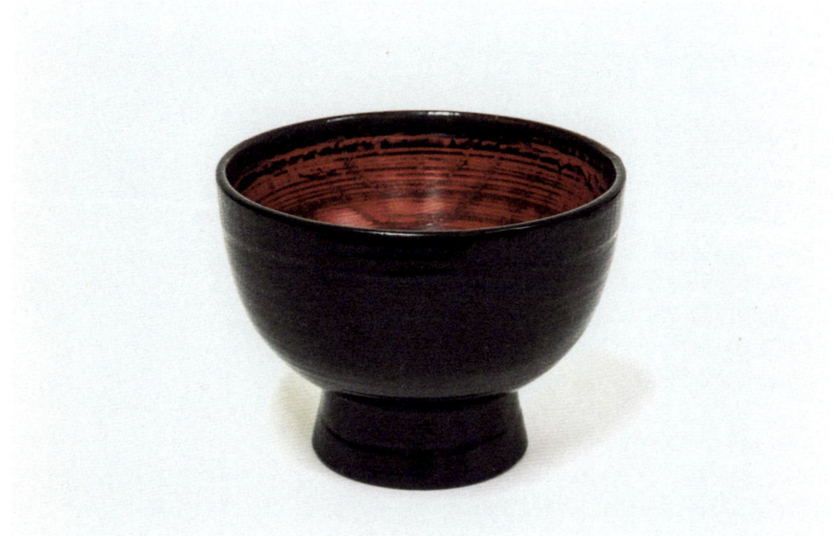

Five-layer stacking box with lid
Carved wood, red and black lacquer (*Kamakura-bori*)
H 23.9, W 34.8, D 21 cm
Japan, later Muromachi period, 16th c.

12936, Ernst Arthur Voretzsch collection, acquired 1959

Carved wood covered in layers of red lacquer over black
lacquer without the use of a textile gauze typical in traditional
lacquerwork. Much as with *Negoro-nuri* works (cat. no. 2, 4),
both layers of lacquer have been partially worn away revealing
parts of the wood support. The deeply engraved decoration
shows a dragon in powerful waves on the lid and on the front
side.

This technique is thought to have been developed during the
Kamakura period (1185–1333) near the ancient capital city
of Kamakura. It was first used to create Buddhist sculptures
and associated objects for the altar. The relatively simple
procedure may be seen as an imitation of the more laborious
craft of Chinese carved lacquer in which a number of layers
are applied to form a several-millimetre-thick lacquer coating
before being decoratively and deeply engraved.

The stacking boxes shown here are thought to have held five
servings of a meal assembled for five diners. This unusual
object speaks to the exhibition theme of *A Floating World* both
through its *Negoro-nuri*-esque surface patina and through the
dramatic motif of dragons in moving waves on the sides and
lid.

Lit.: Gabbert 1978, no. 93

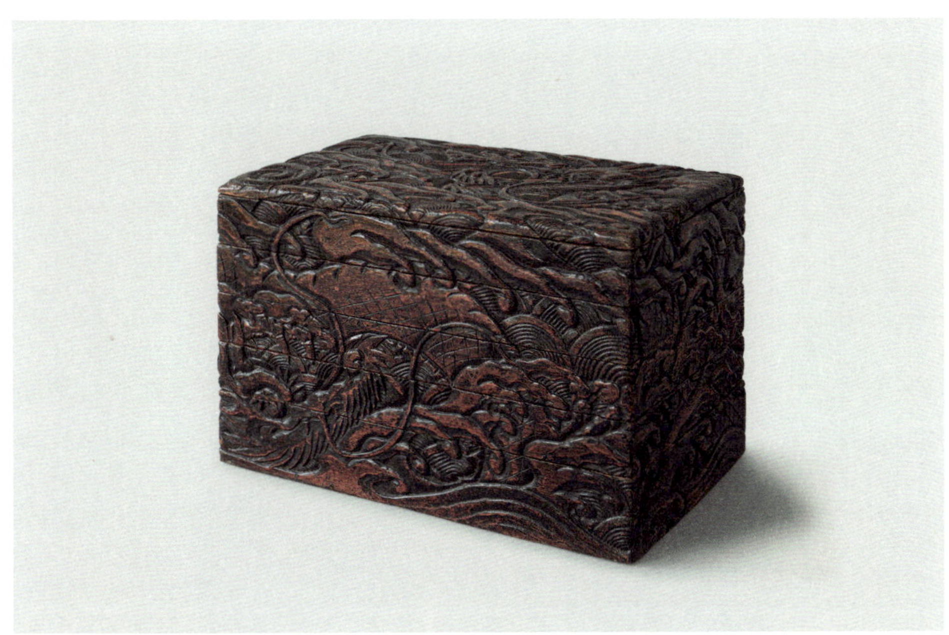

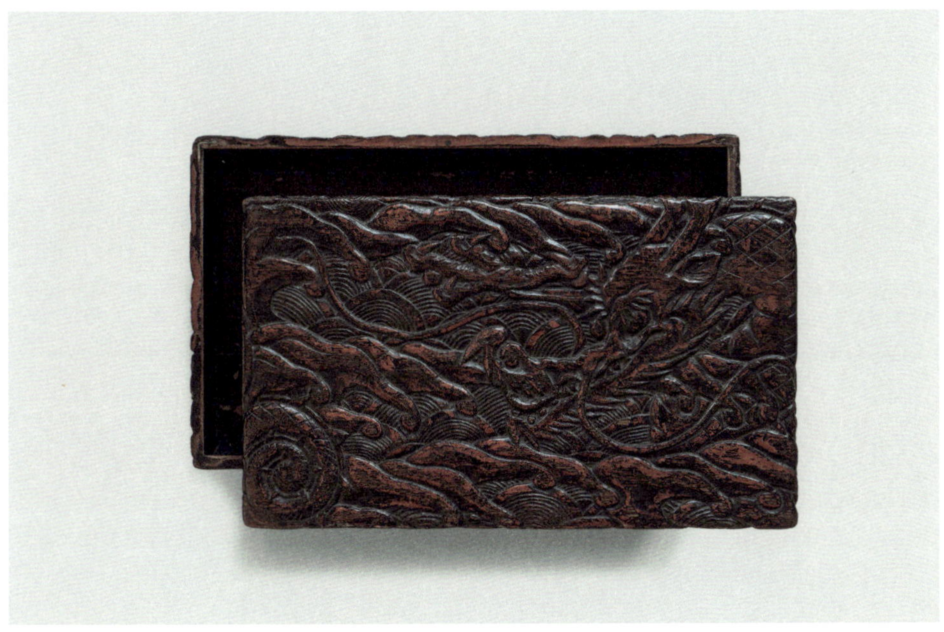

5

Kofuku **tea bowl**

Dark stoneware, red-brown glaze with flecks of black evoking clouds or wisps of fog on the exterior
Written on the exterior of the wooden box: *Rikyū Seto* 利休セト and *Kofuku* 小服,
on the lid interior: *Rikyū Seto* 利休瀬戸 and *Enshū jidai* 遠州時代, signed: *Hoshi* 星 and *kakihan*
H 8.4, Dia 10.0 cm
Seto, Edo period (at latest 17th/18th c.) or earlier

17249, Gabriele Günther bequest, 2012

The small bowl sits on a foot rim with its walls rising in a
conical curve and shaped with delicate horizontal rills. Apart
from the base and the area immediately above the foot rim,
the bowl is coated in a rust-red glaze touched on the exterior
wall in places with dark shadows. This effect might evoke a
landscape in fog, a frequent theme in East Asian ink drawing.

Kofuku tea bowls (小服) are intended for communal tea
drinking outdoors. They are usually made in a smaller size
than the bowls intended for use in tea rooms, so that they can
be transported in baskets, together with other tea parapher-
nalia. Moreover, they are often designed more freely and more
closely resemble ceramics intended for everyday use.

The inscription on the lid interior of the wooden box made
at a later date (the signature of *Hoshi* 星 cannot be verified)
attributes the bowl to *Rikyū Seto* 利休セと, i.e. Seto ware
after tea master Sen no Rikyū (1522–1591). Located in the Aichi
Prefecture, Seto is one of the six ancient kilns which produced
ceramics from the 1300s and later took on a prominent role
within tea ceremonies. The same inscription offers a date in
the era of the garden architect and tea master Kobori Enshū 小
堀遠州 (1579–1647), but a later date to the middle of the Edo
period is not unlikely.

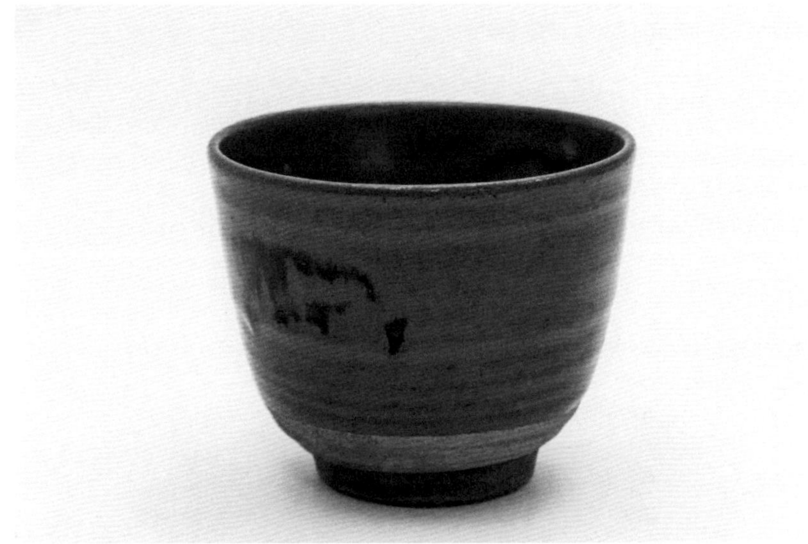

6

Large sake bottle
Stoneware
H 20.5 cm, Dia 14.9 cm
Japan, Edo period, 18th/19th c.

V.230, on permanent loan from Kunstgewerbeverein in Frankfurt am Main, acquired by Fa. Loeb/Brussels, 1965

The body is largely cylindrical over a flat base and curves
inwards at the rim, narrowing towards the short neck in the
rounded shoulder area. The mouth is cup-shaped with a
diagonal lip on the outside. The solid beige-coloured body
has been fired dark grey on the base. Traces of throwing on
the potter's wheel can be seen on both the base and the wall.
The russet-brown glaze, translucent black in places, has been
applied with sweeping black brushstrokes in a gestural style,
especially in the shoulder area. The glaze has generally been
applied quickly and with little precision, leaving parts of the
beige-coloured body visible beneath it.

The spontaneously and carelessly applied glaze contrasts with
the bottle's bulky, stout body. With its dark, earthy tones, pores,
cracks and possibly deliberately imperfect glaze, the bottle has
a patina effect, but also evokes a carefreeness reminiscent of
folk art.

Lit.: Bauer 1998, p.252f.

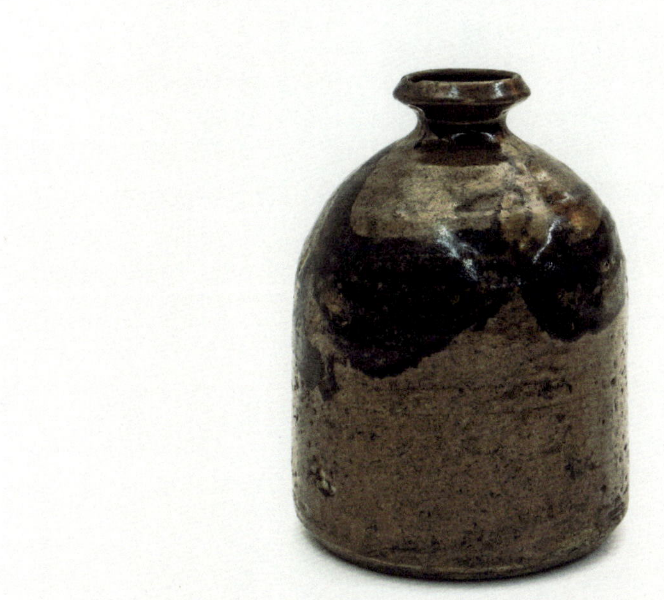

7

Bowl

Reddish fired stoneware with faint red shimmer and olive-green celadon glaze, gold lacquer repair (*kintsugi*)
H 5.8, Dia 13.2 cm
Longquan kiln, China, Zhejiang province, southern Song dynasty, 1127–1279

14175, Maria Gräfin Lanckoronska bequest, 1978

The bowl opens outwards in the shape of a stylised lotus flow-
er from a small, narrow base, unglazed only on the bottom, and
then curves inwards again just before the rim, in the shape
of a begging bowl. The elegantly shaped, thin-walled vessel
also has a subtle colour scheme of rust red and an olive-green
celadon shade. A very fine craquelure evenly covers the entire
surface.

In the context of our exhibition, particular attention is paid
to a fine crack, possibly caused by firing, which presumably
a Japanese collector had repaired with gold lacquer. This
emphasises the intactness of the precious object as a special
aesthetic quality.

Maria Gräfin Lanckoronska (1896–1978), who bequeathed
her small but exquisite collection of Asian artefacts to our
museum, came from the Jewish Wertheimber banking family
based in Frankfurt. Due to her marriage to Count Leo Graf
Lanckoronski in 1923, she seems to have been somewhat
protected after 1933. It is not known how and where she
survived the Nazi era. As a young woman, she worked as a
librarian at the Rothschild Library. Together with her husband,
whom the Nazis had forced into early retirement in 1937 due to
his marriage with her, she wrote works on art and literature as
well as translations from English, French and Italian. She also
dedicated a study to the Linel book art collection in the former
Kunstgewerbemuseum Frankfurt am Main, now the Museum
Angewandte Kunst.

Lit.: Schulenburg/Simon 2002, no. 231

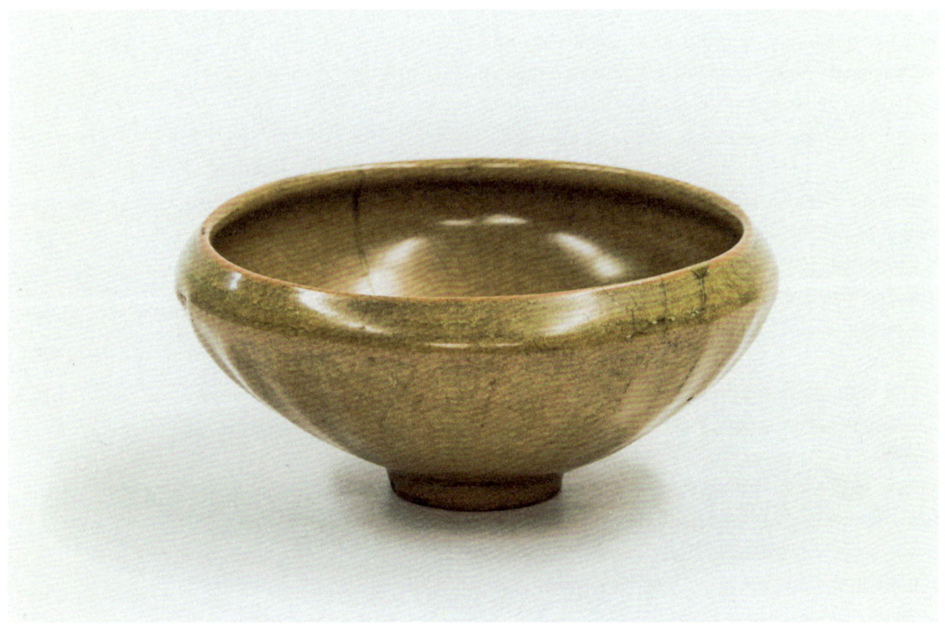

8

Tea bowl
Stoneware, transparent glaze, gold lacquer repair (*kintsugi*)
H 5.8, Dia 15.8 cm
Korea, Joseon dynasty, prob. 16th c.

4444, Johann August Parrot bequest, 1908

The simple bowl is made from thin-walled, brownish stoneware and is free of decoration. The wall rises from the wide,
flat foot rim, curving slightly at first, then extending diagonally, only to rise again slightly vertically just before the rim.
Underneath, inside the foot rim, there are swirl-like throwing
marks which recall the Korean gogok or Japanese magatama
(a comma-shaped jewellery pendant). Traces of throwing on
the potter's wheel can be seen in the horizontal grooves on
the wall. The body with fine quartz inclusions is completely
covered with a brownish, salmon-coloured glossy glaze
which shines whitish in a few droplets that protrude from the
surface. Only five traces of firing supports in the centre and on
the foot rim remain unglazed.

Around a third of the bowl was broken off when damaged and
then skilfully repaired with gold lacquer – a clear indication
that the bowl must have formed part of a Japanese collection of tea ceramics. As Sen no Rikyū (1522–1591) developed
an aesthetic of simplicity and modesty in the Japanese tea
ceremony, the interest in importing precious foreign tea
ceramics in Japan shifted from Chinese ceramics of the Song
dynasty (960–1279), to simpler, less perfectly crafted but highly
expressive Korean tea bowls. Japanese terms were created for
the different types of Korean ceramics. The piece shown here
corresponds to the Toyota type which, alongside the Ido type,
was particularly popular among tea masters.

Lit.: Vos/Stiller 2011, no. 44

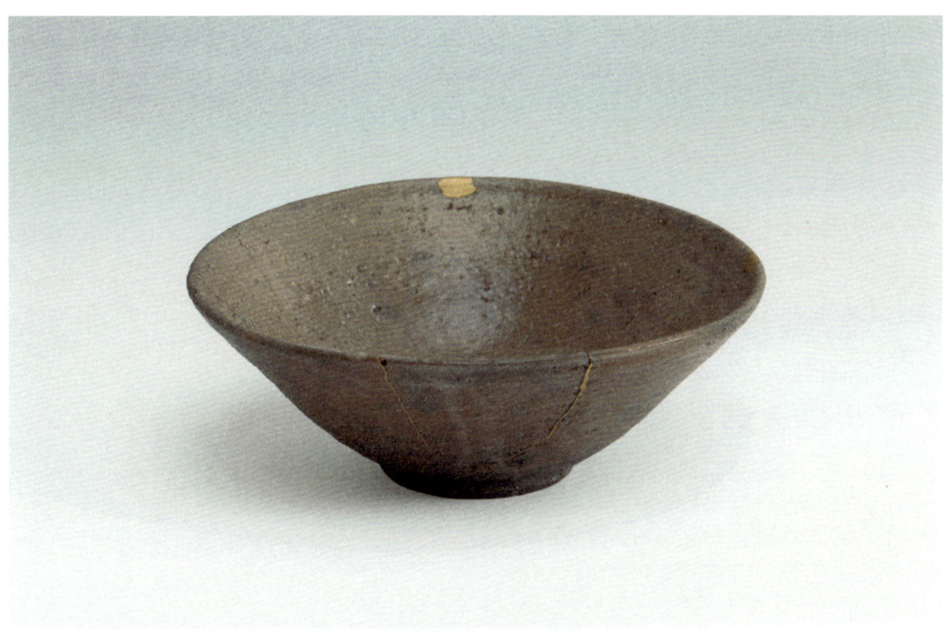

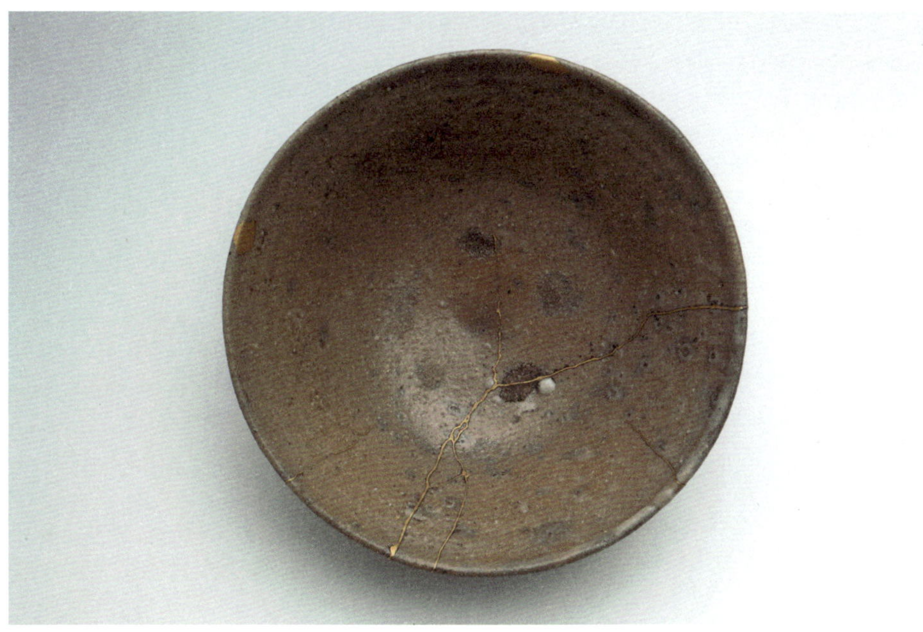

9

Yama chawan
Pale stoneware, wheel-thrown, ash glaze, gold lacquer repair (*kintsugi*)
H 5, Dia 12.5 cm
Japan, probably Aichi or Gifu Prefecture, Kamakura/Muromachi period (14th/15th c.)

17244, Gabriele Günther bequest, 2012, acquired from Japan Art/Frankfurt am Main

The body has been roughly thrown, with visible traces on the
flat base. The piece has a conical wall and a cracked section
towards the rim has been reattached with gold lacquer. The
light celadon-coloured glossy transparent glaze over the light
grey body is the result of flying ash during wood firing.

Yama-chawan 山茶碗 ('mountain tea bowls') are ceramics that
were produced in rural kilns from the Heian (794–1185) to the
Muromachi (1392–1573) periods, primarily in the mountainous
region north of Nagoya (in the Aichi and Gifu Prefectures).
They are simple, everyday utensils that served as eating,
drinking and storage bowls. They were created at a time when
the tea ceremony had not yet been developed. However, much
like simple Korean bowls for mundane everyday use, they
became a central feature of tea culture from the late sixteenth
century onwards. Bowls like the piece presented here were
produced quickly and carelessly, which is why their shape is
often imperfect and firing errors were accepted. It is precisely
this authenticity, its rustic and modest appearance, that made
pieces such as this one a sought-after find for tea ceramics
enthusiasts. Any damage caused during their varied use was
carefully repaired with gold lacquer, as can be seen in this
piece.

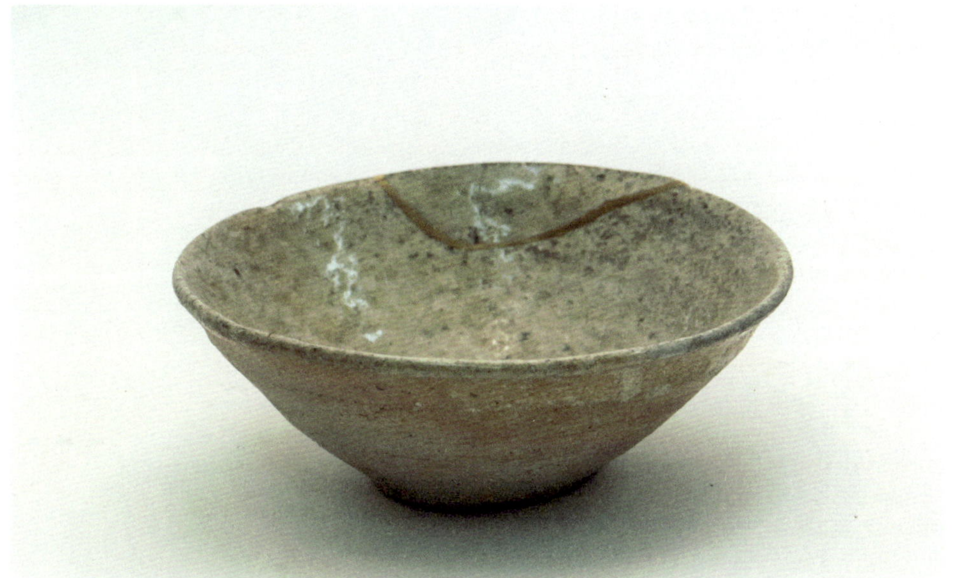

10

Tea bowl
Light grey stoneware, celadon glaze with delicate craquelure, gold lacquer repair (*kintsugi*)
H 7.3, Dia 11.0 cm
Japan, Karatsu, probably Shiinomine-gama workshop 椎の峰窯, mid-Edo period, 18th c.

17242, Gabriele Günther bequest, 2012, acquired from Japan Art/Frankfurt am Main

A nearly hemispherical wall over a vertically ascending
foot. Thin-walled earthenware, only the base ring unglazed.
Transparent glaze with even, finely reticulated craquelure. On
the lip is a larger section with gold lacquer repair, inscribed
with a fine pattern of waves. Opposite, another very small spot
of gold lacquer.

Karatsu, located in the far west of Japan, opposite the Korean
peninsula on Kyūshū in the Saga Prefecture, became an
important centre of ceramic production from the Momoyama
period (1573–1603) onwards. New technical developments in
Karatsu were originated by Korean craftsmen deported under
Hideyoshi. Although the central focus was the production
of ceramics for everyday use, this bowl is an example of the
highly developed tea ceramics made in Karatsu, highly valued
by connoisseurs.

The modern wooden storage box attributes the bowl to the
Shiinomine-gama 椎の峰窯 workshop and is labelled as *muji
Karatsu chawan* 無地唐津茶碗 (literally "unpatterned karatsu
tea bowl"). This clearly distinguishes the piece from the more
common *e-karatsu* 絵唐津 (picture karatsu) ceramics, which
feature decoration – often floral – painted under the transparent glaze.

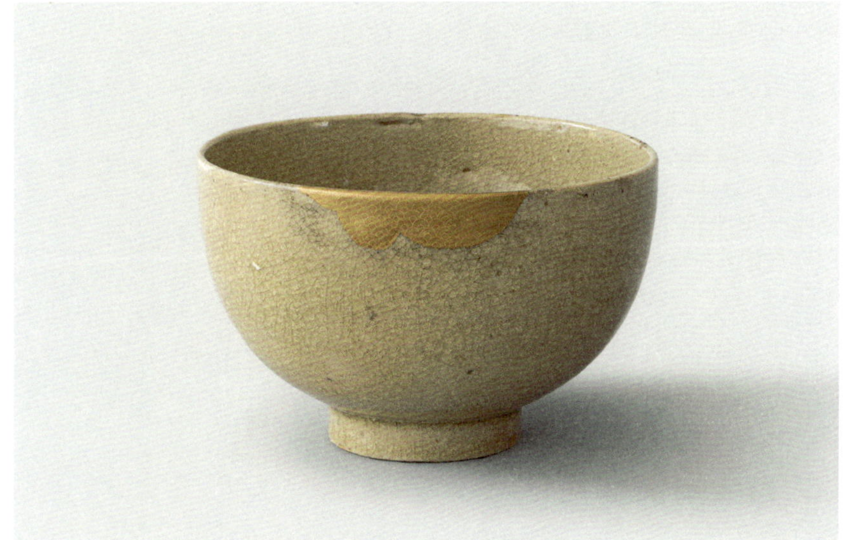

11

Chawan
Dark brown fired and porous stoneware, thick glaze
H 7.5, Dia 13.8 cm
Japan, Karatsu, Edo or Meiji period, mid-/late 19th c.

17243, Gabriele Günther bequest, 2012, acquired from Japan Art/Frankfurt am Main

Slightly flared at the lip, the wall of the bowl extends outward
over a short, neatly moulded base ring. This shape may
ultimately be based on Korean models. Influences of this kind
are characteristic of works produced in Karatsu, a centre of
ceramic production in Kyūshū, on Japan's western coast.

Particularly appealing is the viscous glaze, dripping downwards and seemingly applied multiple times. On the upper
portion of the outer wall, it is light grey to bluish in appearance; the earthenware's brownish tone shines through toward
the lip. A dark brown underdrawing at the foot creates a lively,
jagged colour change reminiscent of Chinese hare's fur glazes.

Fine craquelure to interior. The multiple applications of the
glaze, dripping down from the lip like cloud formations, create
a lively mixture of thinner and thicker layers of glaze, varying
in colour between a light bluish-grey and celadon.

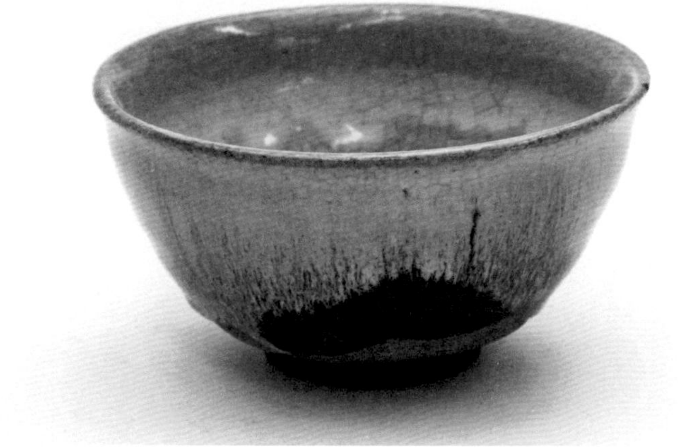

Aka-Raku chawan
Earthenware, rust-red glaze with craquelure, gold lacquer repair (*kintsugi*)
H 8.8, Dia 11.8 cm
Japan, Kyōto, Raku workshop, early Edo period, 17th c.

17250, Gabriele Günther bequest, 2012, acquired from Japan Art/Frankfurt am Main

As is customary with Raku ware, the bowl has been moulded
by hand without a potter's wheel and stands upon a short,
slender foot with a wide rim. Above it, the wall begins to move
outwards, almost horizontally, before extending to form a
relatively even vertical wall ending in a slightly wavy lip. The
rust-red glaze shows delicate traces of craquelure, the surface
broken up by clouds of milky, darkly spotted engobe.

An unusual effect is created by the opposing cracked and
chipped zones, which have been repaired in a fine line with
gold lacquer and further secured with black clips made of
shakudō, a copper-gold alloy. This technique, then rare in East
Asia, was far more common in European ceramic and porcelain
collections until the nineteenth century.

This *Aka-Raku* bowl ('red Raku') is a rare example from the
beginnings of Raku ceramics in the seventeenth century.

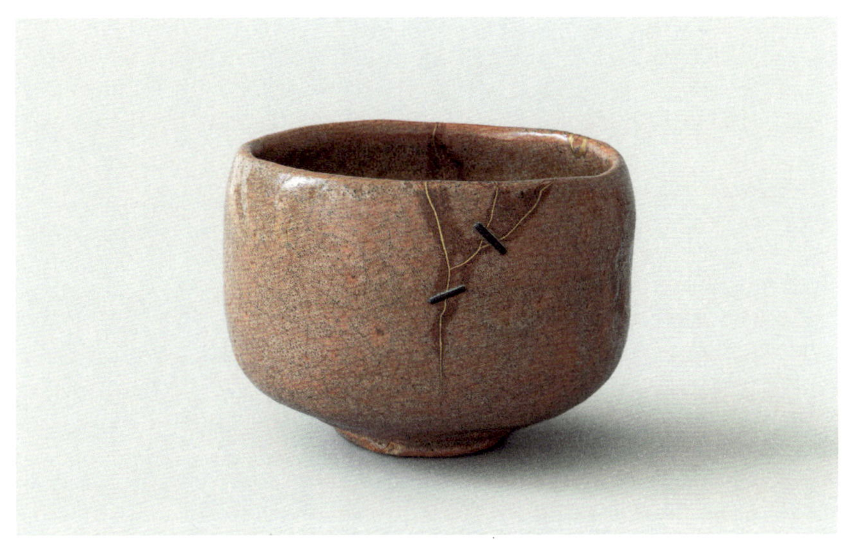

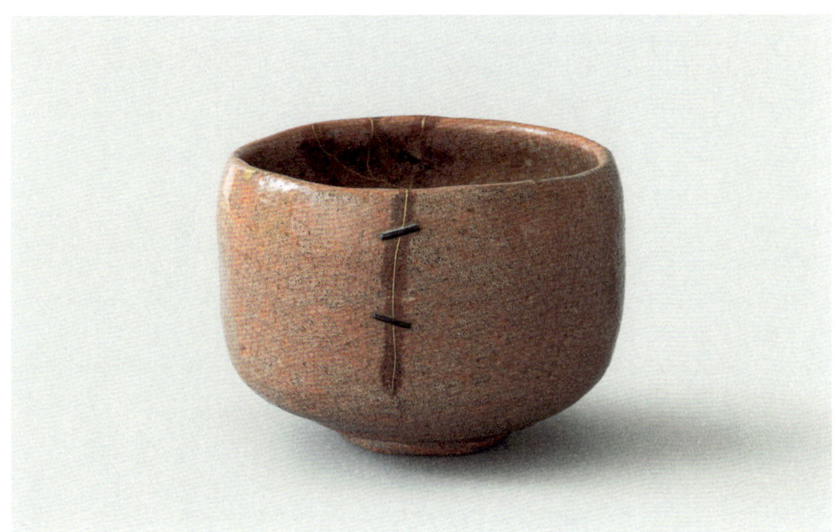

13

Aka-Raku chawan
Earthenware, glaze mostly brick-red
H 7.9, Dia 10.8 cm
Japan, Kyōto, Raku workshop, 18th/19th c.

W.M.P. 15, Wilhelm Peter Metzler collection (1818–1904), acquired 1904

The present bowl is characterised by a much freer design
than the seventeenth-century *Aka-Raku* bowl (cat. no. 13).
Hand-moulded without a potter's wheel, the piece's surface is
dynamic throughout, reminiscent of the loosely unfurling folds
of robes. Its shape nonetheless follows the contours typical of
raku – first projecting more or less horizontally above a narrow
foot with a wide foot rim and bending vertically upwards, the
lip moulded into waves. The glaze covering the entirety of the
body alternates between a brick-red base colour and, particularly at the lower portion of the wall, areas fired in black. The
milky grey of another transparent layer of glaze is also visible
in certain areas.

Born to an influential Frankfurt banking family, Wilhelm
Peter Metzler was one of the city's foremost art collectors.[1]
Influenced by *Japonisme*, he developed a particular passion for
Japanese art later in life. The Kunstgewerbeverein succeeded
in acquiring large portions of his collection for the museum
immediately after his death in 1904.

Lit.: Gabbert Avitabile 1983, no. 67

1   Metzler Bank is also one of the supporters of this exhibition.

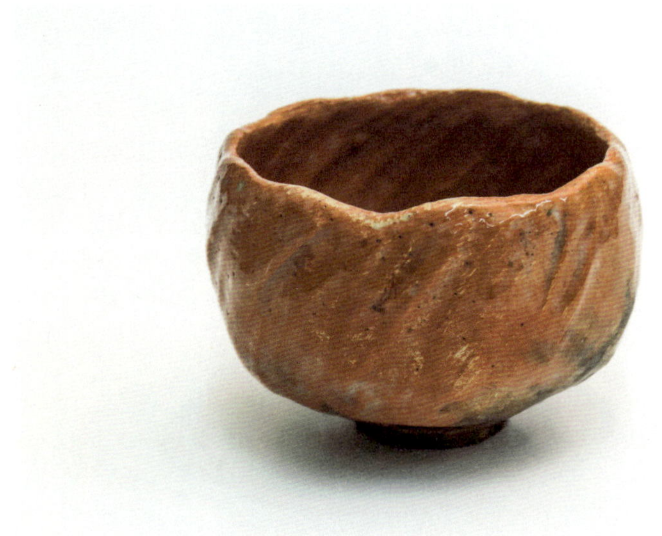

14

Kuro-Raku chawan
Earthenware, thickly applied glaze with drips, gold lacquer repair (*kintsugi*)
H 8.5, Dia 11.5 cm
Japan, Kyōto, Raku workshop, Edo period, 18th/19th c.

W.M.P. 16, Wilhelm Peter Metzler collection (1818–1904)[2], acquired 1904

The swirl-shaped marks at the base, within the short, wide
foot rim, could indicate that this bowl's basic shape was
turned on the wheel, in contrast to the usual method of raku
production. The bowl's irregular shape nonetheless reveals
that its final form was largely moulded by hand. This is a *Kuro
raku* ('black Raku') bowl which is, unlike the two red bowls (cat
nos. 13, 14), unglazed at the base and at the horizontal lower
section of the wall, revealing the bowl's brown body. There is
also an impressed raku mark (楽) in this unglazed area, but it
cannot be conclusively attributed to any of the eighteenth- or
nineteenth-century masters.

At the lower portion of the outer wall are sparse hints of loose
decorations of stylised grasses in red and beige, entering into
a delightful dialogue with the fine lines of the gold lacquer
repair, almost like lightning striking the moors.

2   On Wilhelm Peter Metzler, see the entry for cat. no. 14.

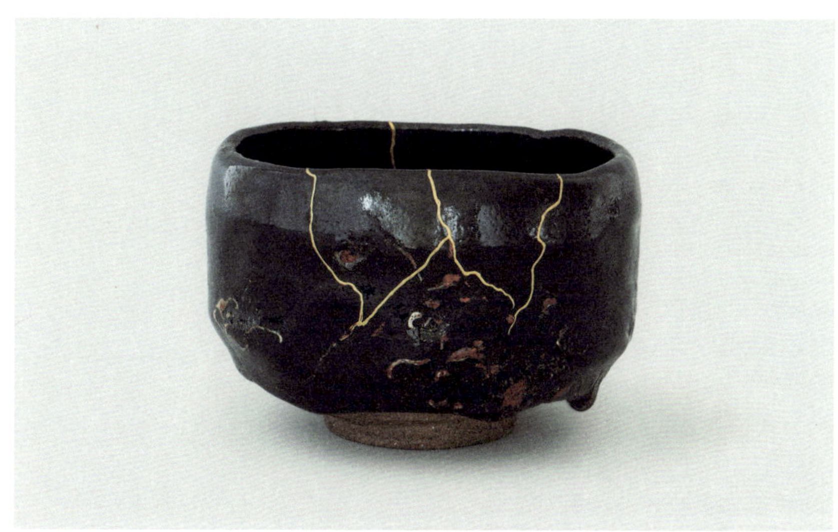

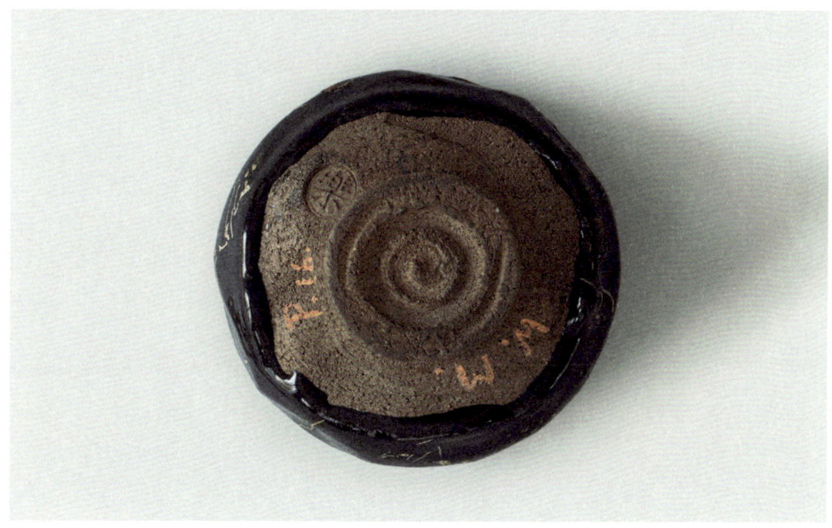

9. Raku-Meister Ryōnyū (1756–1834)
Kuro-Raku chawan
Earthenware, thick black glaze, gold lacquer repair (*kintsugi*)
H 7.5, Dia 12 cm
Japan, Kyōto, Raku workshop, Edo period, at latest 18th/early 19th c.

17298, donated by Eckhart Kremers 2012, acquired in Japan in the 1990s

The foot rim is somewhat imprecisely moulded compared to
the relatively wide and shallow bowl. Like cat. no. 15, a swirling
throwing mark can be seen within the foot rim, but the present
example was certainly not created on a potter's wheel. Raku
impressed mark (楽) to horizontal lower portion of the wall.
The black glaze, covering the entire surface of the body, has
been applied relatively evenly.

The inscription of the fourteenth raku master, Kakunyū
(1918–1980), on the wooden box attributes the piece to the
ninth master, Ryōnyū (1756–1834). He is considered the
greatest innovator of the raku workshop after it burnt down in
its entirety. Other blows dealt by fate, such as the deaths of
his brother, his wife, and finally his son, did not diminish his
creative vigour. His style is distinguished by striking sculptural
effects moulded with a spatula, as seen in the vertical section
of the wall of this bowl. Like no. 15, this bowl also bears elegant gold lacquer repairs.

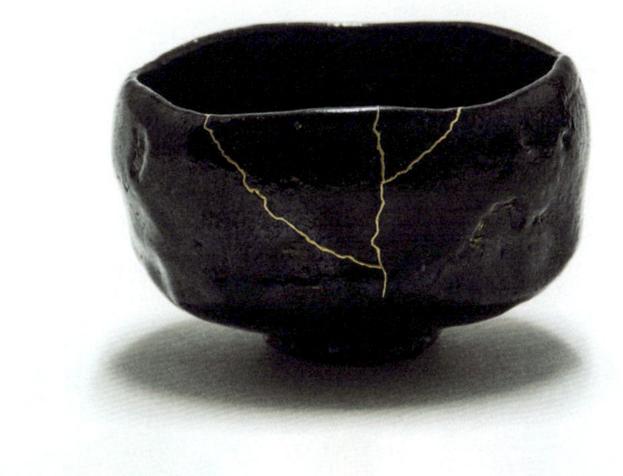

Oil plate (*aburazara*)
Stoneware, multicoloured decoration beneath transparent glaze
H 1.6, Dia 21.6 cm
Japan, Seto(?), Edo period, 18th/early 19th c.

17262, Gabriele Günther bequest, 2012, acquired from Japan Art/Frankfurt am Main

Round, shallow plate with a raised rim. Under a transparent glaze in bluish, brown, and beige is a stylised coastal
landscape featuring boats and amorphous hatching, perhaps
representing a highly stylised group of trees. The bluish-brown
portion of the plate's lower edge may represent the coastline.
The boats move in a boundless expanse of water. The motif
may also be interpreted as a view of a flat marshland studded
with grasses and plants. In either case, the figurative nature
of the work's decoration – and its ambiguity – offer a wide
variety of associations for the imagination.

Aburazara were placed under lanterns and used to collect
lamp oil. They are characterised by free, spontaneous decorations in the *mingei* (folk art) style. Typical features of *aburazara*
decoration include, as here, segments accentuated by bright
colours around the edge of the plate.

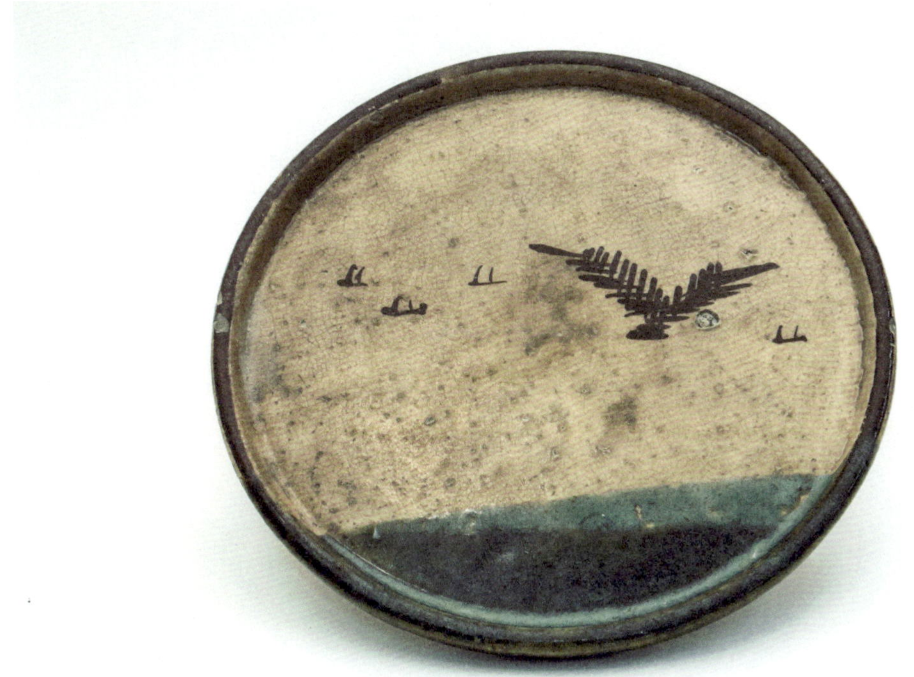

17

Oil plate (*aburazara*)
Stoneware, dark-brown decoration on a beige ground beneath transparent glaze
H 1.8, Dia 19.0 cm
Japan, Seto(?), Edo period, 18th/early 19th c.

17266, Gabriele Günther bequest, 2012, acquired from Japan Art/Frankfurt am Main

Aside from a wide foot rim, the entirety of this flat plate is
evenly covered with a transparent glaze, with craquelure on
the reverse. On the front is a dark brown underglaze drawing
of a nocturnal, moonlit landscape, within the plate's thick,
raised rim. A highly stylised scene spreads out along the water, rendered with loose, rapid brushstrokes. Behind the shore
is a scholar's hut with a fence, pictured beneath overhanging
trees. The beige-coloured ground under the transparent glaze
reveals brownish discolouration in several places.

The drawing's playful style is somewhat reminiscent of motifs
seen on Dutch tiles, though a mutual influence is unlikely.
Rather, saucers for oil lamps like this one were rapidly-pro-
duced commodities for which loose, swift decorations reminiscent of folk art were common.

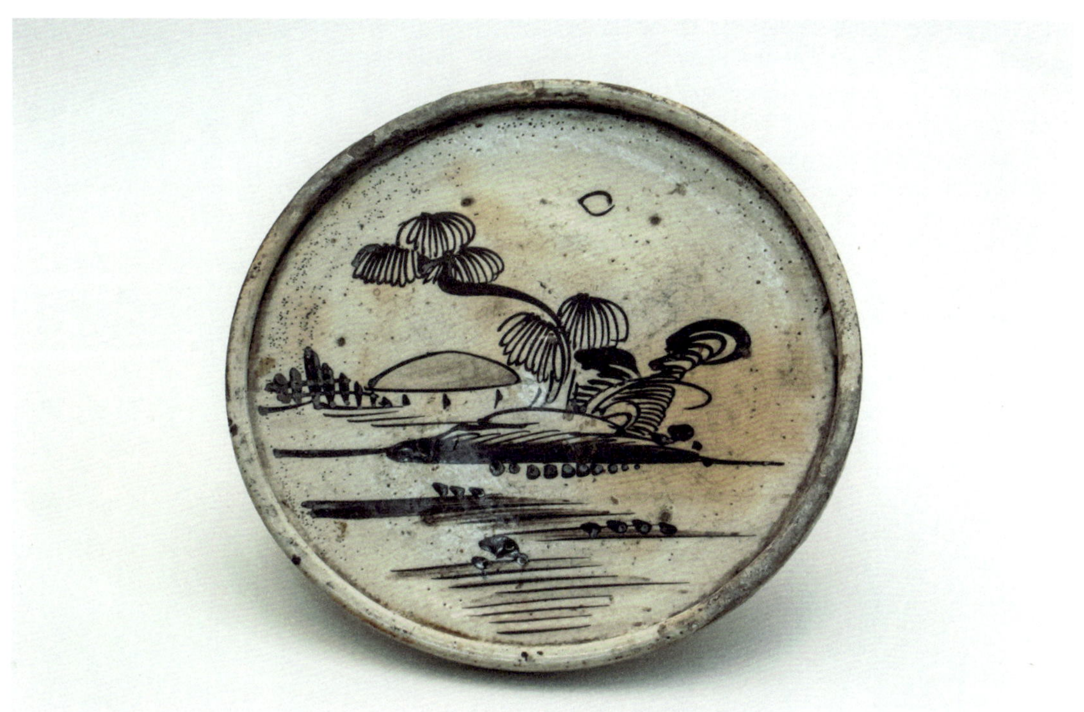

18

Plate
Porcelain, thick running glaze
H 5.3, Dia 27.1 cm
Japan, late Meiji/early Taishō era, probably around 1910

Stadt 253, acquired 1913

On the base within the unglazed foot rim are six brown dots
arranged in a circle around a central point, against a homoge-
neous light grey background. Both on the inside and outside
of the curved wall is a thick layer of running glaze with round
shapes ranging from violet to light blue and celadon-coloured
streaks against a crackled beige background. With some
imagination, one can associate the forms with an arrangement
of round fruits, but the motif can also be seen as entirely
abstract.

The unusual decoration is vaguely reminiscent of Chinese
Tang Dynasty *sancai* ware (Japanese *sansai*, "three colours"),
but is rather an expression of modernity, reflecting the joy of
experimentation of 1910s Japan.

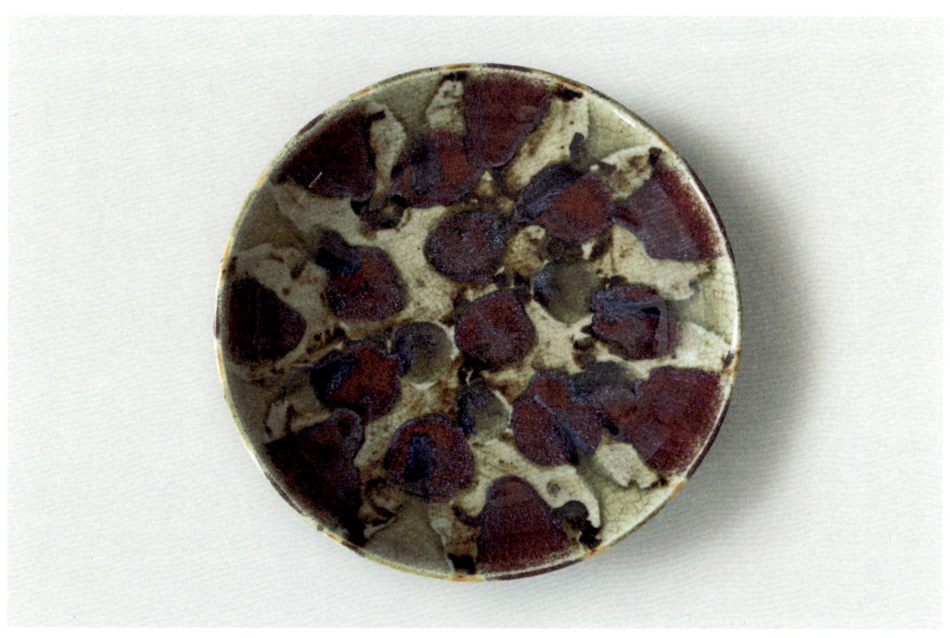

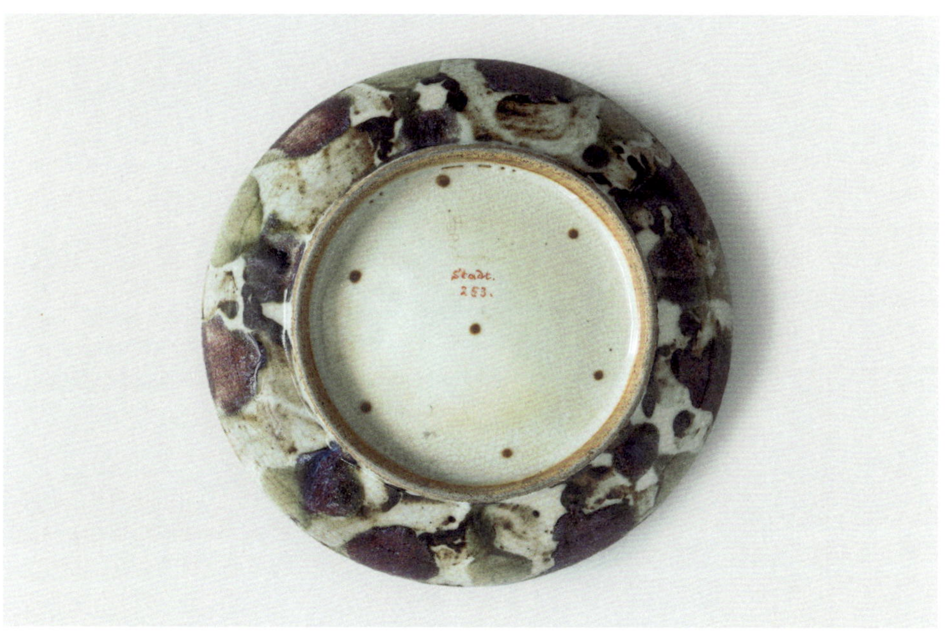

19

Mizuno Hanjirō (1926–2000)
Large dish
Fine-grained, white stoneware, *sansai* glaze
H 6, Dia 38 cm
Japan, Seto, circa 1985/86

17035, donated by Gisela Freudenberg, 2009

This large, impressive dish has been evenly thrown entirely on
the potter's wheel. The stoneware body, almost porcelain-like
with its fine graining and light colouring, is unglazed only on
and within the foot rim. The curving wall and the interior are
covered with a transparent glaze. Underneath, in green and
ochre stripes, are more or less parallel, almost calligraphic
striped brushstrokes with a few scattered spots against a
beige background. This type of glaze is freely borrowed from
Chinese Tang Dynasty three-colour glaze (*sancai*).

Born to a family of traditional ceramicists in the Seto pottery
centre in Aichi Prefecture, Mizuno Hanjirō worked as a lawyer
before becoming involved in the *mingei* (folk art) movement
after reading the work of Yanagi Sōetsu (1889–1961), and he
would take over his father's workshop in 1949. He was among
the most prominent masters of the second generation of
mingei ceramicists, who applied Yanagi's ideas to ceramics
following the Second World War. The movement's focus was
simple, everyday objects of the highest quality; it is therefore
fitting that tea ceramics play a minimal role in Mizuno's *oeuvre*.

Lit.: Schulenburg 2005, cat. no. 3-3

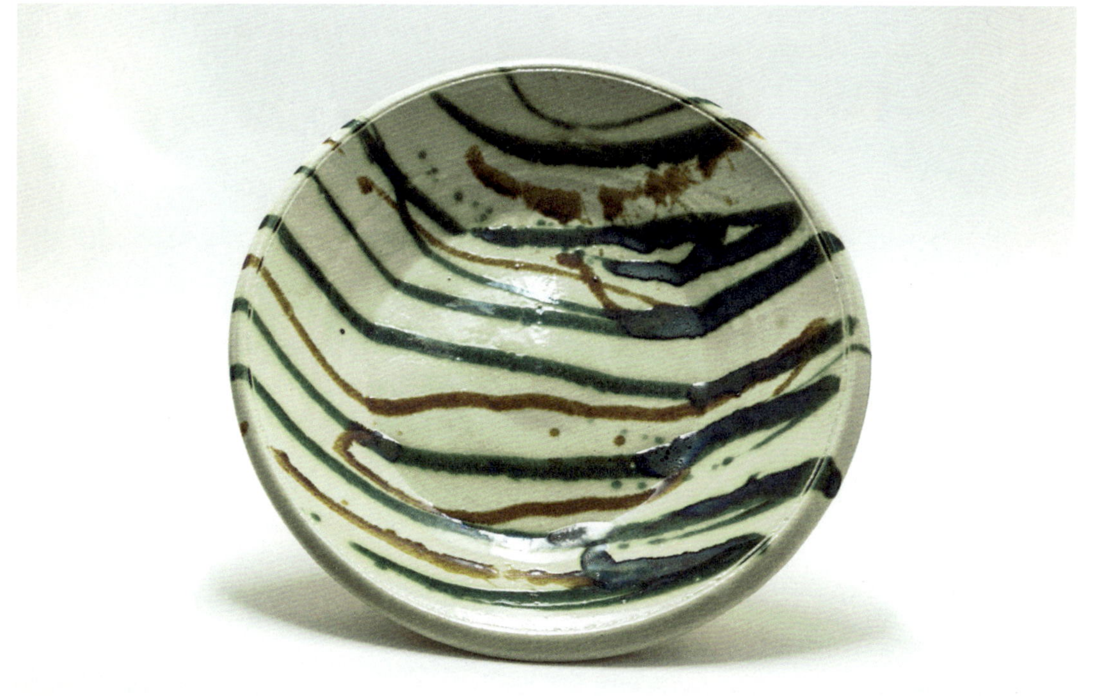

Mizuno Hanjirō (1926–2000)
Large dish
Fine-grained, white stoneware, *sansai* glaze
H 9, Dia 45 cm
Japan, Seto, circa 1985/86

17036, donated by Gisela Freudenberg, 2009

Though very similar in shape to cat. no. 20, this dish is even
larger and stands on a wider foot rim. The *sansai* decoration in
green and ochre, with a transparent glaze over a beige background, here appears even more expressive, as though Mizuno
had intended to create a Jackson Pollock in ceramic.

Large-scale dishes or plates like this one are typical of Mizuno
Hanjirō ceramics. Sometimes the forms are even deeper and
are perhaps better described as bowls; in such cases, the
artist would often let wide swaths of three-coloured – or
two-coloured glazes in green and white – run from the wall
into the centre of the vessel. Mizuno's inspiration for this element of his work is allegedly a Persian ceramic in the Chinese
Tang Dynasty *sancai* style which he discovered in 1968.

Ceramics such as these, which allow for chance effects and
dynamic movement, are tied to the theme of our exhibition.

Lit.: Schulenburg 2005, no. 3-5

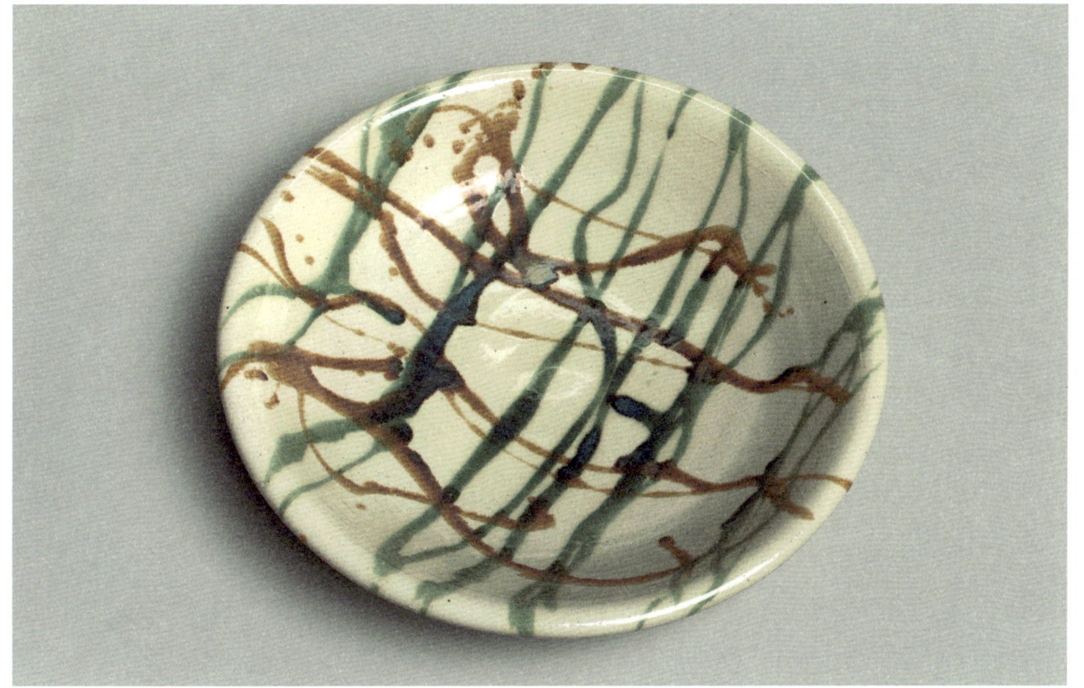

Takahara Shōji (1941–2000)
Chawan
Pale stoneware, ash glaze
H 7, Dia 12.5 cm
Japan, Bizen, Okayama Prefecture, late 20th c.

17241, Gabriele Günther bequest, 2012, acquired from Japan Art/Frankfurt am Main

The basic shape of this bowl has been thrown on the potter's
wheel, but the wall has then been reshaped by hand or with
a spatula. Not dissimilar to a raku bowl (c.f. cat. nos. 13–16),
the wall runs largely horizontally before rising more or less
vertically to form an irregular, wavy lip. Around the foot rim are
reddish fire markings (*hidasuki*, literally "cords of fire"), caused
by the burning of straw wrappings during the firing process.

At the base is a carved, cross-shaped workshop mark. The exterior of the wooden box is inscribed *Bizen chawan* (Bizen tea
bowl), signed *Shōji-zō* (made by Shōji) and with the workshop
mark.

Takahara Shōji was known primarily for his tea ceramics.
His style is characterised by a sense of modest restraint,
which can be seen in the rather unexpressive design of this
tea bowl, as well as the comparatively minimal traces of ash
glaze. Bizen, where Takahara grew up, is the second oldest of
the Six Ancient Kilns, many of which had been in existence
since the Heian period (794–1185) and were rediscovered in
the sixteenth century by the masters of the tea ceremony. The
bright red fire markings against the beige body are the result
of bands of straw (*hidasuki*) placed around the ceramics and
would become the hallmark of Bizen ceramics.

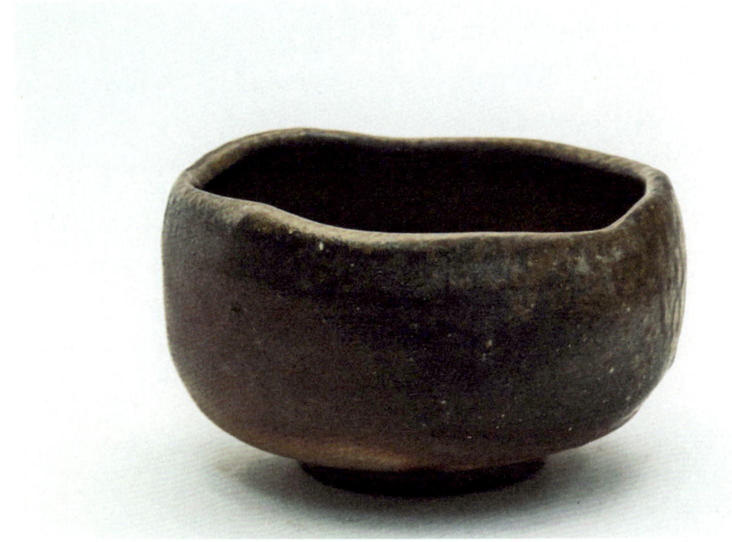

Takahara Shōji (1941–2000)
Kinuta hanaire
Stoneware, ash glaze
H 22, Dia 14 cm
Japan, Bizen, Okayama Prefecture, Shōwa era, circa 1982

14353, donated by the artist, 1982

The wall rises into an irregular, cylinder above a flat base
before narrowing into a cylindrical neck roughly halfway up.
The majority of the brownish body of fired stoneware has been
covered by a shiny grey-black, crusted ash glaze which lies
relatively flat against the ceramic surface and gives the base,
with its cruciform workshop mark, a silvery lustre.

The vase (*hanaire*) imitates the shape of a washing paddle
(*kinuta*), as is popular in Japanese tea ceramics. The wooden
box is labelled accordingly: *Bizen kinuta hanaire* ('Bizen. Washing paddle vase, made by Shōji').

Lit.: Schulenburg 2005, no. 7-5

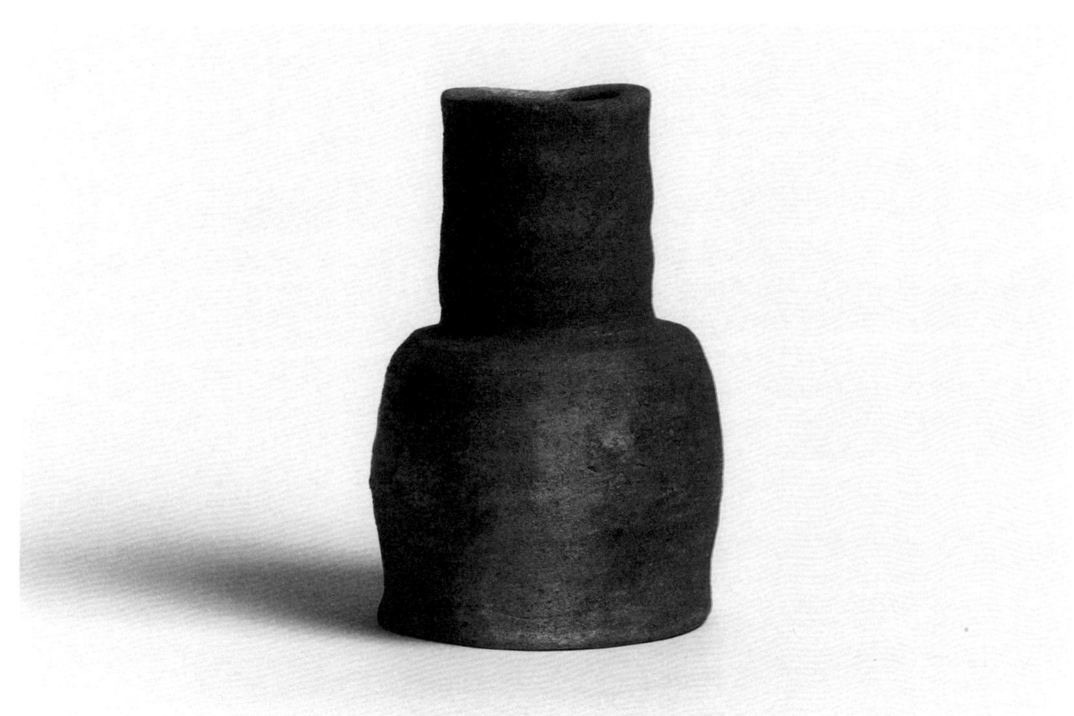

Takahara Shōji (1941–2000)
Mizusashi
Beige stoneware, ash glaze
H 20.8, Dia max. 21 cm
Japan, Bizen, Okayama Prefecture, circa 1980s

17271, Gabriele Günther bequest, 2012

The body of the vessel ascends more or less cylindrically
above a flat foot. The neck is indented below the upper edge,
below which a looped handle has been attached on either
side. The flat lid is likewise made of stoneware. The outer wall
and the lid partially show rough, slagged burn marks from
the ash in the kiln, as well as reddish firing marks from straw
bands (*hidasuki*) typical of Bizen ware.

Mizusashi were vessels filled with cold water which would
be ladled out with a wooden spoon to brew tea, and were
common accessories in the Japanese tea ceremony.

The wooden box bears the inscription *Bizen mimitsuki
mizusashi* ('*mizusashi* [from] Bizen, fitted with ear[handles]'),
signed *Shōji-zō* ('made by Shōji'), with a workshop mark.

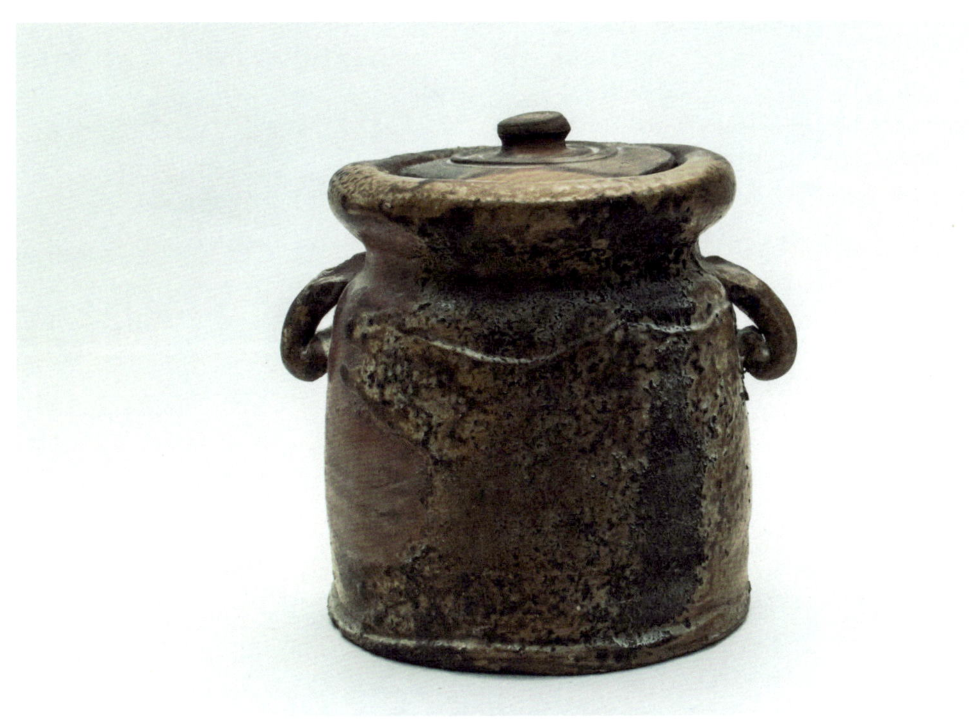

Takahara Shōji (1941–2000)
Square dish with rounded corners
Red-fired stoneware, partial ash glaze
H 9.8, L/W 33.4 cm
Japan, Bizen, Okayama Prefecture, Japan, Shōwa era, dated 1986

14677, donated by the artist

A fairly wide, terraced square base with a slightly sloping –
but overall rather flat – bowl, circular at the centre and with
rounded corners on the outside. The circular portion displays
vivid, bright red *hidasuki* fire marks against a dark red background, which look almost like fallen Mikado sticks. Outside
the curved segments are heavy, partly encrusted traces of ash.

At the base, inside the foot rim, is the inscription "on the third
day of the first month of the Year of the Tiger Shōwa 61 (1986)".
The lid is inscribed *Bizen daibachi* 備前台鉢 (Bizen bowl),
signed *Shōji-zō* (made by Shōji), with a workshop mark.

Lit.: Schulenburg 2005, cat. no. 7-6

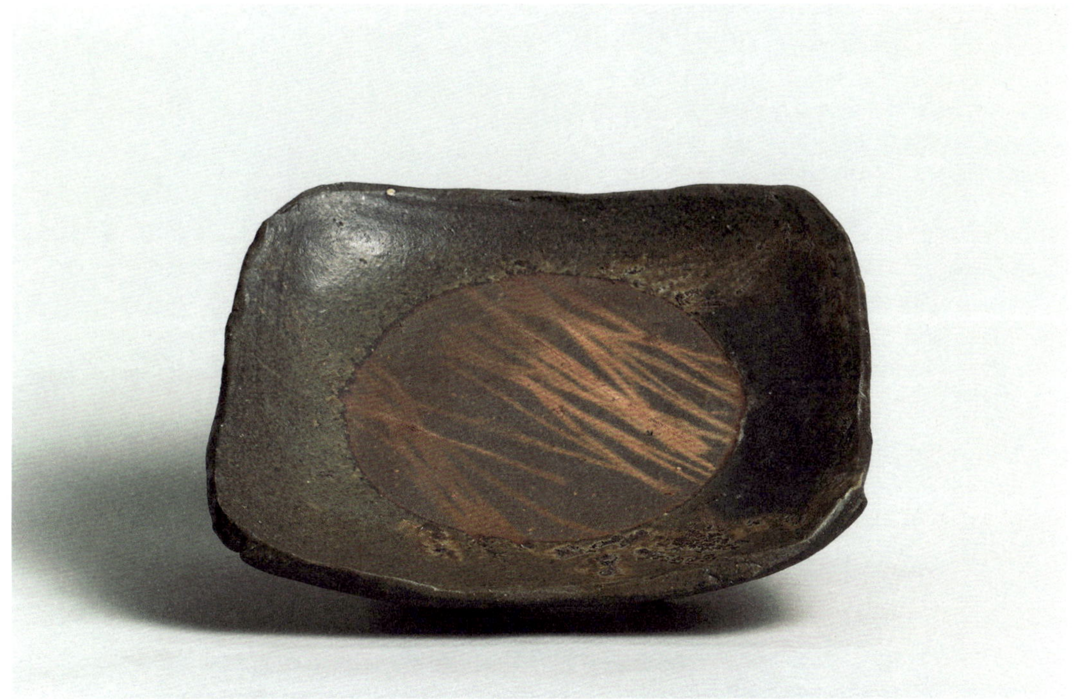

Chūroku IV (Furutani Hiromu, 1922–2012)
Kinuta hanaire
Pale stoneware, ash glaze
H 25.8, Dia 18 cm
Japan, Shigaraki, Shiga Prefecture, 1985

14612, acquired 1986

A cylindrical wall rises above a flat foot bearing the artist's
incised mark "Chūroku"; with an almost horizontal shoulder
beneath a slender neck with two small looped handles. The
body features light-coloured quartz typical of Shigaraki. The
surface is coated entirely in an ash glaze ranging in colour
from amber to blackish-grey, lending the piece both a particular patina effect and an extraordinary sense of dynamism.

Chūroku IV honed his craft in a traditional pottery family in
Shigaraki, a region classified as one of the Six Ancient Kilns.
He built by hand two *anagama* (tunnel kilns), already common
in Japan prior to the introduction of the *noborigama* (climbing
kilns) introduced from Korea in the sixteenth century. Chūroku
is best known for his tea ceramics.

On the *kinuta* (washing paddle) shape, c.f. cat. no. 23. The
accompanying wooden box is labelled *Shigaraki-yaki. kinuta.
Chūroku-zō* (Shigaraki pottery, kinuta, made by Chūroku), with
two seals (*Shigaraki-yaki* and personal seal).

Lit.: Schulenburg 2005, cat. no. 9-4

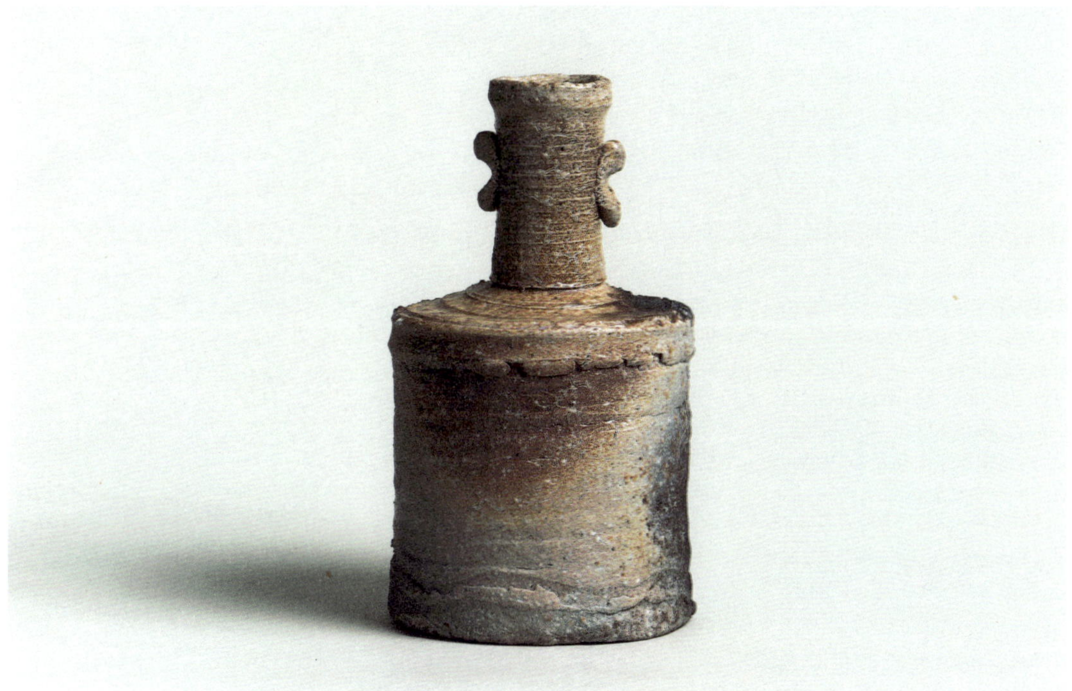

26

Ichino Shinsui (1932–1997)
Large square platter (*kaku-zara*)
Red-brown stoneware, partial ash glaze
H 6, L 47, B 21 cm
Japan, Tanba, Hyōgo Prefecture, circa 1986

17026, donated by Gisela Freudenberg, 1991

A bulky, rectangular slab, deformed during the firing process,
is mounted on two elongated, runner-like feet. The body, fired
in the manner typical of Tanba ware, ranges from purplish to a
deep brown, with a mustard-coloured ash glaze in the upper
right corner providing an extraordinarily varied spectrum of
colours.

Tanba, in Hyōgo Prefecture west of Kyōto, is another of the Six
Ancient Kilns, the high quality of its ceramics here represented
by Ichino Shinsui. Ichino came from an established family
of ceramicists in Tanba. His style can be characterised as
classical, and he produced both tea ceramics and everyday
objects. The large signature *Shinsui* has been etched into the
base; the lid of the wooden box (*kiri-bako*) is labelled *Tanba
manaita kaku-zara* ('Tanba. Rectangular plate in the shape of
a chopping board'), signed *Shinsui-zō* ('made by Shinsui') and
with the seal *Shinsui*.

Lit.: Schulenburg 2005, cat. no. 16-3

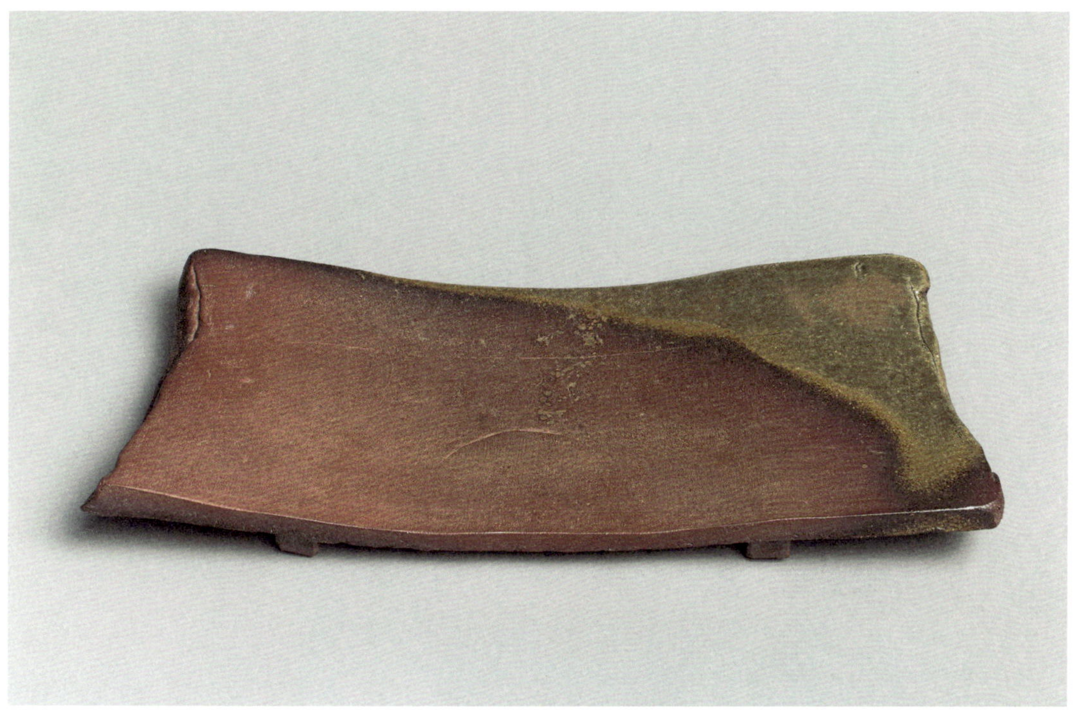

27

Ichino Shinsui (1932–1997)
Large dish (*ōzara*)
Red-brown stoneware, partial ash glaze
H 12, Dia 55 cm
Japan, Tanba, Hyōgo Prefecture, circa 1986

15615, donated by Gisela Freudenberg, 1992

This substantial, heavy bowl stands on a broad foot rim. Above
it, the wall curves gently as it rises toward the flattened rim.
The fired-body, aubergine in colour, is characteristic of Tanba
and is here covered with a thick layer of ash glaze, which
runs down in bands along the outside and slopes downward
toward a mustard-coloured pool on the inside. The imposing
work thus appears almost like a bird's-eye view of a water
landscape, a manifestation of flow in the form of ceramics, as
it were.

The master has incised his signature *Shinsui* within the foot
rim. The lid of the accompanying wooden box (*kiri-bako*) is
labelled *Tanba ōzara* ('Tanba. Large plate') and bears the
signature *Shinsui-zō* ('made by Shinsui') as well as the seal
Shinsui.

Lit.: Schulenburg 2005, cat. no. 16-2

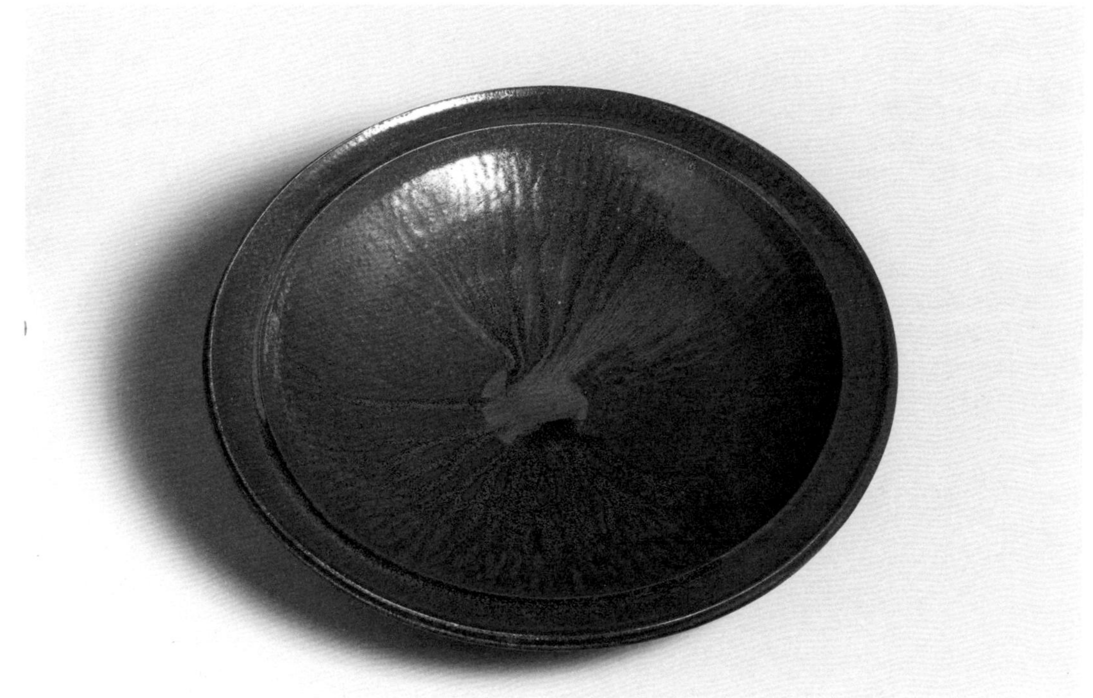

28

Ichino Motokazu (b. 1956)
Large sake bottle
Red-brown fired stoneware, ash glaze
H 32.3, Dia 21.8 cm
Japan, Tanba, Hyōgo Prefecture, circa 1980s/90s

V.956, on permanent loan from Kunstgewerbeverein in Frankfurt am Main e.V., donated by Herbert Meyer-Ellinger, 2015

Above a flat foot bearing five traces of firing supports and the artist's signature (*Moto* 元), the weighty vessel, thrown on the potter's wheel, curves into a bulbous form that flares out widely before slowly tapering as it approaches a very narrow neck. The lip is likewise slightly flared. The blackish to mustard-coloured traces of ash glaze against an aubergine-coloured base are typical of Tanba and lend the surface an extraordinary vibrancy.

Born in 1956, Ichino Motozaku belonged to the next generation of Tanba's traditional Ichino workshop following Shinsui (cat nos. 27, 28). The style visible here is characterised by a classical restraint and reveals a refined understanding of the firing process, in the tradition of the Ancient Kiln of Tanba.

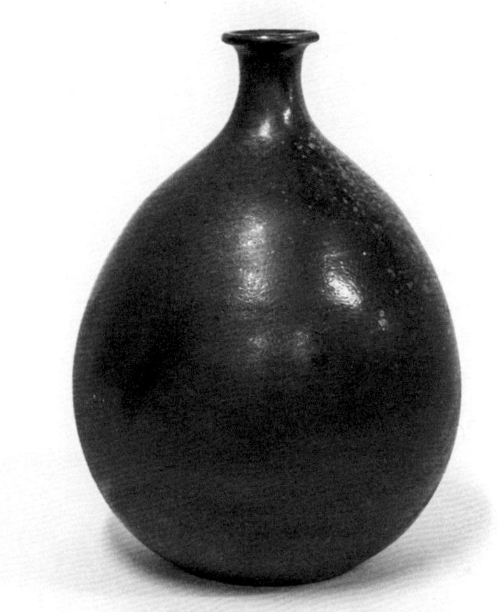

Tsujimura Shirō (b. 1947)
Chawan in the shape of a shoe
Red-fired Shigaraki stoneware, ash glaze
H 6.5, Dia 14.0 cm
Japan, Nara, circa 1990

16845, donated by Gisela Freudenberg, 1992

The wall first juts out widely above the rather narrow,
irregularly shaped foot before bending into a short vertical
line. Tsujimura here makes use of reddish Shigaraki clay, characterised by several inclusions of white quartz. The ash glaze,
along with the pockets of quartz (some of which protrude
from the surface), creates a rough surface and a lively range
of colours.

On the accompanying wooden box, the work is labelled _Shiga-
raki kutsu chawan_ 信楽沓茶碗 ('Shigaraki shoe tea-bowl') and
bears the signature _Shiro_ and the seal _Shi. Kutsu_, or _kutsugata_
('shoe-shaped') tea bowls have a rounded, compressed shape
vaguely reminiscent of a shoe, although this hardly pertains
to the comparatively rounded, even shape of this bowl. The
signature _Shi_ 史 is incised beside the base of the vessel.

Following art studies in Tōkyō, Tsujimura became a largely
self-taught ceramicist and built an hermitage in the mountains
near his hometown of Nara as well as a teahouse and several
kilns. Despite the variety of styles resulting from the use of
multiple kilns, particularly in his tea bowls, Tsujimura's works
are highly distinctive, and the hand of the master can immediately be recognised.

Lit.: Schulenburg 2005, cat. no. 24-10

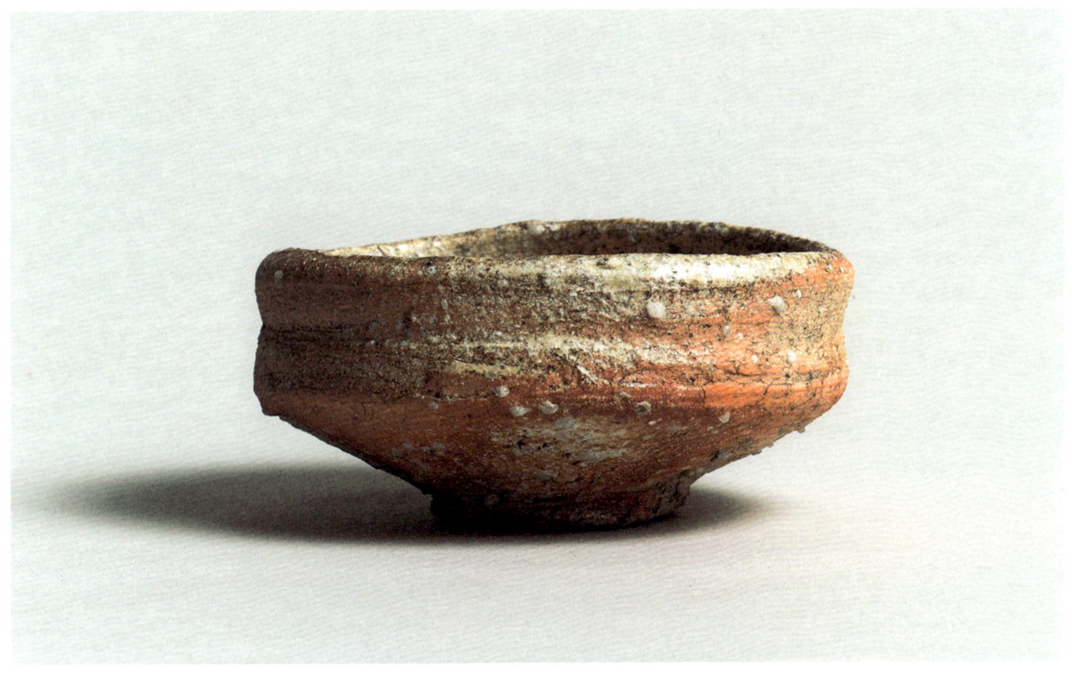

30

Tsujimura Shirō (b. 1947)
Winter tea bowl (*tsutsu chawan*)
Dark-brown fired stoneware, polychrome glaze
H 8.0, Dia 10.7 cm
Japan, Nara, early 1990s

17248, Gabriele Günther bequest, 2012, acquired from Japan Art/Frankfurt am Main

High-walled bowls such as these, used during the winter to
keep tea warm for longer, are known as *tsutsu-gata* 筒型
('tube-shaped') in Japanese ceramic. Above a short foot, the
wall projects horizontally before bending into a high vertical
section. The glaze is exceptionally vivid; in tea ceramics, the
term for such glaze effects is *keshiki* 景色 ("landscape" or
"scenery"). Here, a moss-green underglaze has been overlaid
with beige engobe, which in part drips down thickly and has a
reddish colour in places. The signature *Shi* 史 is incised by the
base of the vessel.

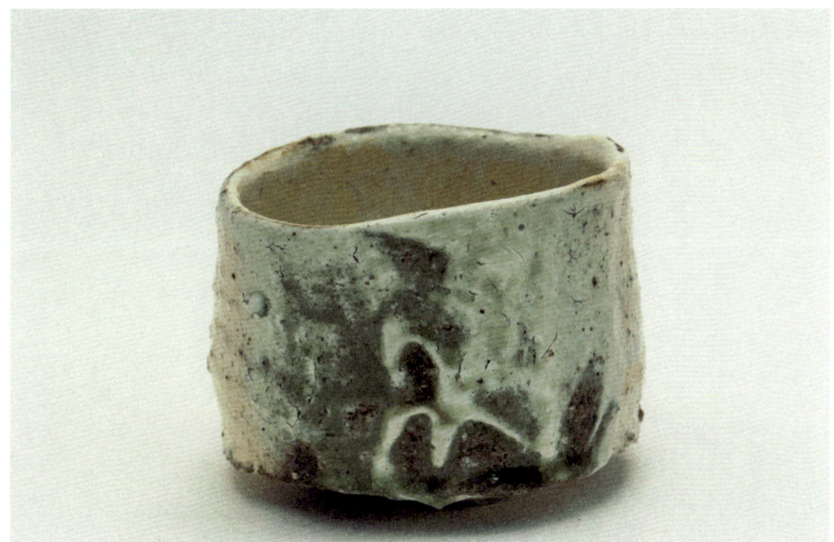

31

Tsujimura Shirō (b. 1947)
Winter tea bowl (*tsutsu chawan*)
Stoneware, black Raku glaze
H 9.5, Dia 10.5 cm
Japan, Nara, circa 1990s/early 2000s

17246, Gabriele Günther bequest, 2012, acquired from Japan Art/Frankfurt am Main

Above a short foot, the horizontal wall bends vertically into a
tall, more or less cylindrical shape. A rich, black raku glaze (c.f.
nos. 13–16) covers the entirety of the bowl, including the base
ring. Below the centre of the wall is a bubbled surface effect
which lends the piece an appearance of patina. The signature
Shi 史 is incised by the base.

Bowls of this type are commonly used in tea ceremonies
during the winter months, as their high walls keep tea warm
for longer.

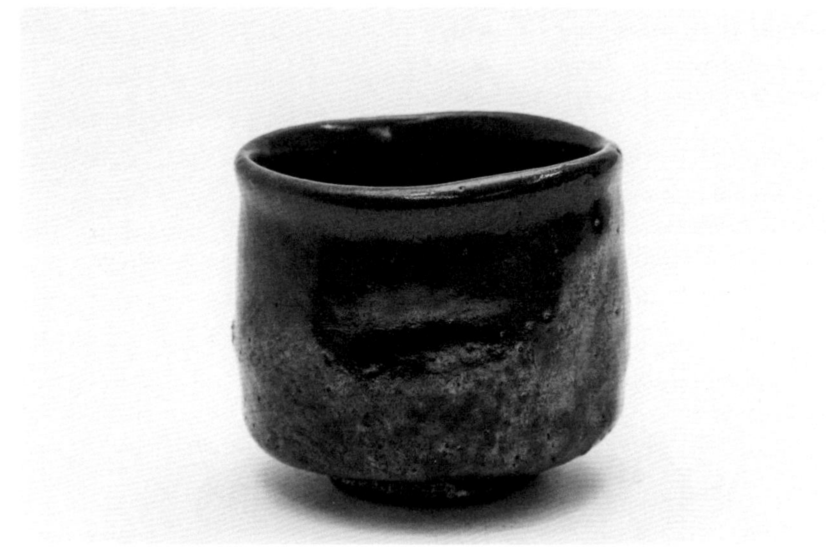

Kishimoto Kennin (b. 1934)
Incense burner (*kōrō*)
Beige stoneware, partial red ash glaze
L 18.5, B 13.8, H 20.2 cm
Japan, Mino, Gifu Prefecture, 1987

17032, donated by Gisela Freudenberg, 2009

A squat body on a flat base with an incised workshop mark.
Traces of five firing supports are visible at the base. The vessel's aubergine-shaped body, with its detachable, open-work
lid, has been freely moulded. The body of Iga clay contains
quartz inclusions similar to those found in Shigaraki (c.f. cat.
no. 26). Curiously, the shape can be interpreted as a rock or as
a cloth bag as a result of its diagonal, deeply incised bend.

The surprising formal ambivalence of the incense burner is
characteristic of the unconventional style of Kishimoto Kennin,
active in the ceramic centre of Mino, north of Nagoya. He is
particularly known for his stout vessels featuring superficial
fissures and cracks.

The wooden box is inscribed *Iga yakishime kōrō*伊賀焼締
香炉 ('high-fired [unglazed] incense burner from Iga'), with
signature and seal *Kennin* 謙仁.

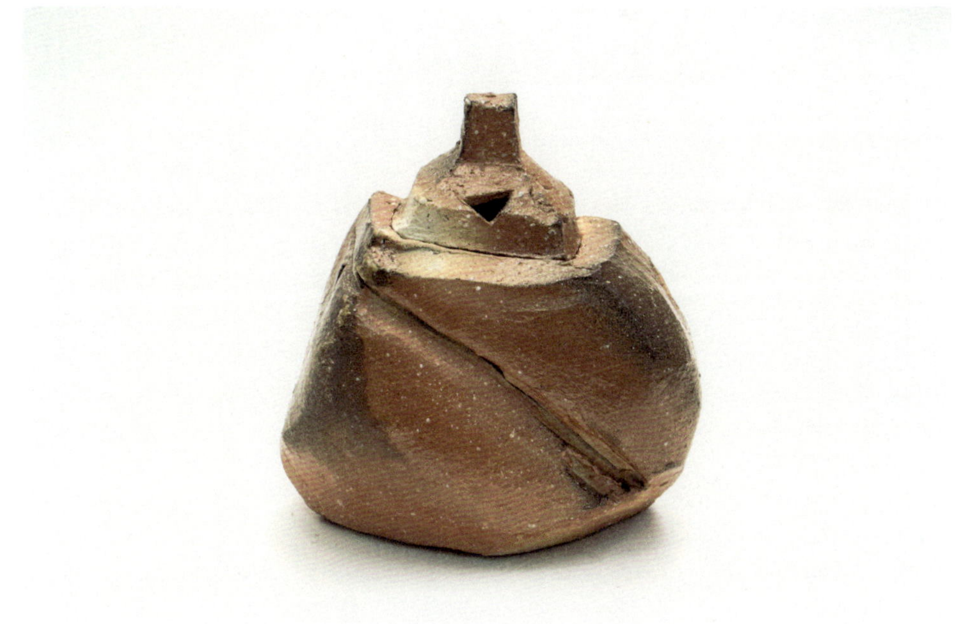

33

Sake bottle (*tokkuri*) in the shape of an aubergine
Stoneware, deep violet glaze
H 11.7, Dia 10.8 cm
Japan, Meiji era, circa 1900

4417, Johann August Parrot bequest, 1908

A beige-coloured stoneware body with dark speckles and a
dark, largely aubergine-coloured glaze. The star-shaped leaves
above the aubergine-shaped body are attractively sculpted.
Just beyond the leaves, the dark tone of the glaze changes in
part into a light grey-bluish colour and shows fine craquelure.

Small sake bottles in a variety of shapes were commonly used
as everyday objects in Japan. Playful, popular pieces like this
one would often take on surprising shapes – in this case, an
aubergine.

This small bottle belongs to the extensive collection of
Japonica bequeathed by Johann August Parrot in 1908 to
the Mitteldeutscher Kunstgewerbeverein, the basis of the
Kunstgewerbemuseum (now the Museum Angewandte Kunst).
Parrot, formerly Swiss consul to Sydney, later lived as a man of
independent means in Frankfurt.

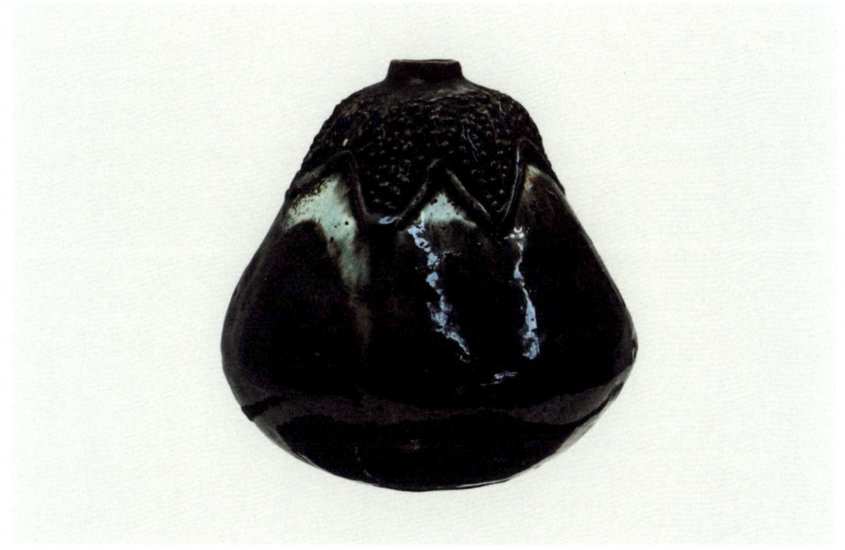

34

Sake bottle (*tokkuri*) in the shape of a bag
Dark-brown fired stoneware, brown and mustard-coloured glaze
H 10.4, Dia 8.0 cm
Japan, Meiji era, circa 1900

4441, Johann August Parrot bequest, 1908[3]

Traces at the vessel's flat base indicate that it was thrown
on the potter's wheel. The wall, tapered at the top to form a
narrow mouth, features several indents at the side, creating
the illusion of a cloth bag. Mustard-coloured spatters break up
the superficial dark brown glaze.

3   For the history of the Parrot Collection, see the entry
for cat. no. 34.

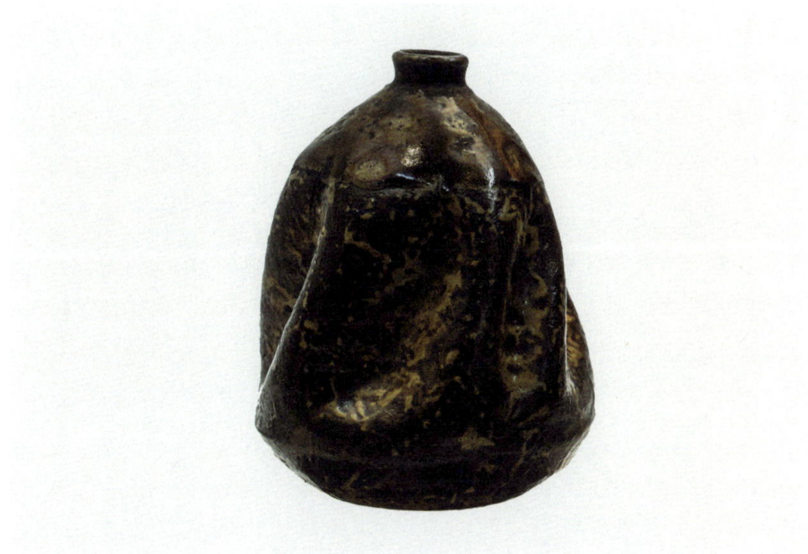

35

Low bowl

Cloisonné, *plique-à-jour (shōtai shippō)*
H. 8.3, Dia 18.4 cm
Probably late Meiji/Taishō or early Shōwa era, ca. 1910–30

17932, donated by H., 2016

Cloisonné, i.e. enamel or liquid glass placed between metal supports, was a technique introduced to China from the Mediterranean centuries ago, although it only began to flourish in Japan from the Bakumatsu and Meiji period (second half nineteenth century onward). In 2016, the Museum Angewandte Kunst received one of the most internationally significant collections of its kind as a donation from the H Collection (the name of the benefactor and collector remains undisclosed in keeping with his widow's wishes).

The piece shown here is an undisputed masterpiece from this encyclopaedic collection of over four hundred objects. The *plique-à-jour* technique, which flourished only briefly in Japan between in 1910 and 1930, takes cloisonné to a new extreme: after the vessel has been completed, it is stripped entirely of its basic metal core using acid, resulting in transparent, ephemeral glass fluxes. The magnificent chrysanthemums symbolise the Japanese imperial family, representing splendour, dignity, and beauty; the ephemerality of their blooms, however, also renders them metaphors for transience. Furthermore, the flat vessel is shaped like a beggar's bowl, which – countering the splendour and the masterful execution of this piece – is perhaps an ironic reference to the Buddhist monastic condition, *i.e.* a life of poverty dedicated to the spiritual quest for perfection and liberation from earthly *samsara*.

Lit.: Schulenburg 2019, no. 8–1.

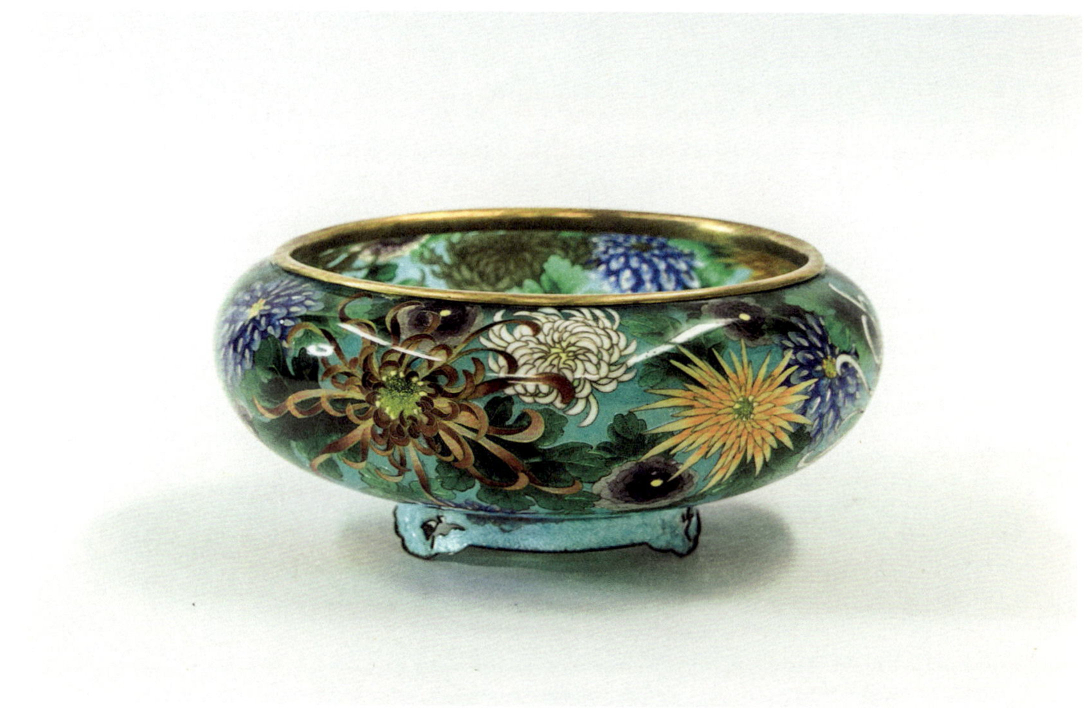

The Butterfly Dance (*Genji monogatari*, "Kochō" chapter)
Fan, paint on paper, gilt, h of fan segments
H. of fan segments 17.9, W 47.0 cm
Tosa Mitsuyoshi (1539–1613) or associates, Japan, Momoyama period, at latest 16th c.

V.320, on permanent loan from Kunstgewerbeverein in Frankfurt am Main e.V., acquired from R. Gaus, 1976[4]

Three courtiers, among them an imperial prince, regard eight children performing the Bugaku dances Karyōbin und Kochō beneath blossoming trees. Karyōbin represents the dance of celestial birds from Buddhist mythology. Its complement, Kochō, the dance of the butterflies, was devised during the Heian era. One chapter of the *Genji monogatari* depicts the young Prince Genji attending such children's dances with peerless beauty and grace.

This work is part of a group of twelve fine fan leaves previously mounted on a screen, and in this exhibition forms a complement to the poetry of Mari Kashiwagi.[5]

The charming leaf portrays an episode titled *Kochō* ('Butterfly') from the twenty-fourth chapter of the *Genji monogatari*, composed by the gentlewoman Murasaki Shikibu in the early eleventh century. The corresponding passage of the novel reads:

'The Empress began her Sutra reading that day. Many were yet to return home from the festival; they had spent the night here and were now putting on their everyday clothes. Only those who were not able to do so departed.

At noon, those who had remained at the Rokujō-in went to the Empress and sat in their assigned places, with Genji at the head. Not a single Denjōbito was missing. The ceremony was unusually dignified, its splendour largely the result of Genji's reputation.

Flowers were offered to the Buddha at Murasaki's request. The eight page girls who would make the offering looked lovely, dressed half as birds, half as butterflies. Those dressed as birds carried cherry blossom branches in silver vases, and those dressed as butterflies carried golden dead-nettles in golden vases. The bouquets were simple, but the most beautiful ones had been chosen. [...]

The girls dressed as birds danced to music which resounded beautifully, mixed with the cheerful twittering of the nightingale, and the birds on the pond called on all sides; the dance slowly came to an end in this way, so beautifully that one never grew tired of listening. The girls dressed as butterflies, even more light-footed than the birds, finally danced into the flowering shadows of the hedge, in which the golden dead-nettles shimmered.'[6]

4   A detailed description of this work is available in Schulenburg/Jesse 2000, pp. 312–14.

5   C.f. Motto, p. 10.

6   Murasaki 1966, vol. 1, pp. 700–01.

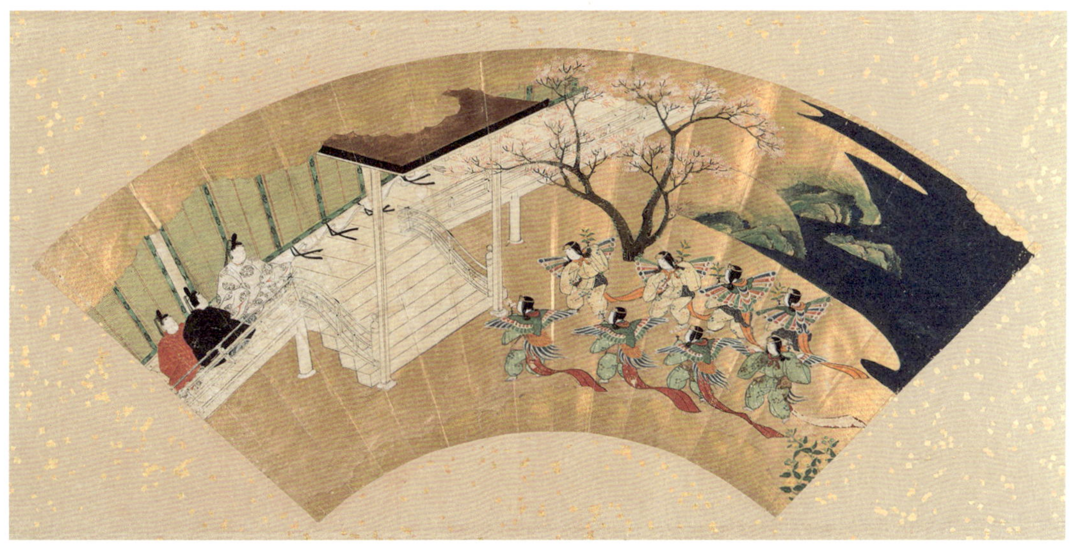

37

Spring landscape with cherry blossom festival
Folding screen, ink and paint on paper, leaf gold and gold paint
H 161, W 366 cm
Japan, early Edo period, 17th c.

12883, Ernst Arthur Voretzsch collection, acquired 1959

This radiant, cheerful spring picture takes cherry blossoms
as its focus, a subject long enthusiastically celebrated in
Japan. The place depicted might be Arashiyama near Kyōto or
perhaps Yoshino, south of Nara: both are popular excursion
destinations during cherry blossom season. The foreground-
ed tableau with the raftsmen evokes Hiroshige's woodblock
print cat. no. 64, depicting a similar raft beneath the cherry
blossoms of Arashiyama.

The blossoming trees are arranged across the large-scale
pictorial image, like the flow of water and the golden clouds.
The focus is on the cherry blossom festival in a village centre
on a platform near a bridge over the river shown in the bottom
left, where people have already gathered to celebrate. The
expansive scene also shows a group of swimmers in the top
left and raftsmen, fishermen, and rice farmers at work in the
foreground. There are also hikers observing a waterfall in the
top right. Both delight in the moment and the consciousness
of the transience of all human activity are impressively conveyed in this imposing work.

This unsigned folding screen is probably the work of a city
painter (*machi-eshi*). The style of painting suggests they were
perhaps from Kyōto, as the influence of the Kanō school and
other painting traditions of early modern Japan are evident.

Lit.: Schulenburg 2000, no. II-20

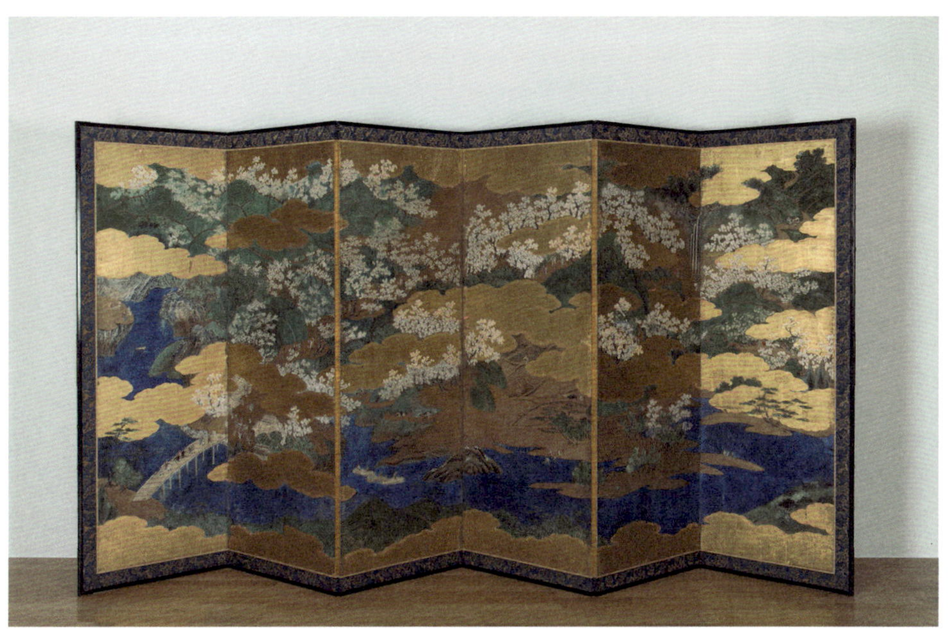

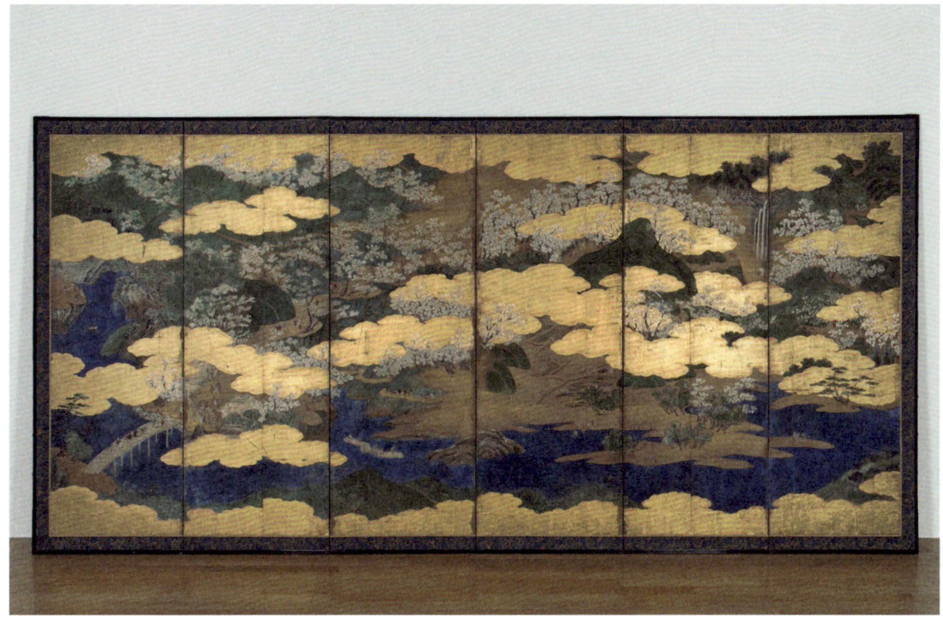

38

The Trade Route from Edo to Nagasaki

Scroll, ink and paint
H 52.5, L 1741 cm
Japan, Edo period, 18th/19th c.

Ernst Arthur Voretzsch collection, private loan

This very long scroll also serves as a map with written place
names and a narrative depiction of the cities and landscapes
which line this major trade route. Beginning at the capital city
of Edo, the cities along the route are depicted from a fore-
shortened perspective. The act of journeying across country
roads is also integrated into the image, as in the scene directly
before Edo's city gates: there we see palanquins and standard
bearers in front of them evidently waiting for the travelling
party of a daimyō returning to his home prefecture. Striking
information about mountains (including Fuji) are depicted with
a certain naturalism.

The scroll's wooden storage box displays the following text:
Tōkaidō gojūsan eki emakimono 東海道五十三駅絵巻物
(handscroll of the fifty-three stations of Tōkaidō). Since the
ancient trade route between Edo and Kyōto is simply given as
Tōkaidō, the title ignores the sea route shown running further
west to Nagasaki. This city was Japan's sole international harbour during the Edo period, mostly engaging in sea trade with
Korea and China as well as acting as the sole base for Western
countries thanks to the Dutch mission, enabling exchange with
other regions in Asia and with Europe.

Paintings with such panoramas seem to have been in wide
circulation, which speaks to the heavy traffic on this important
long-distance trading route of Japan.

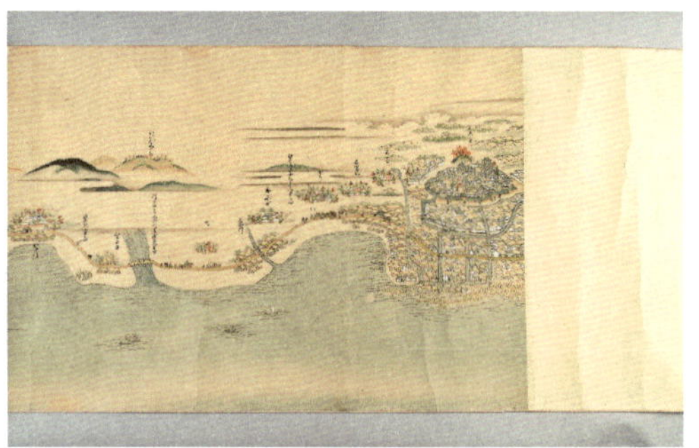

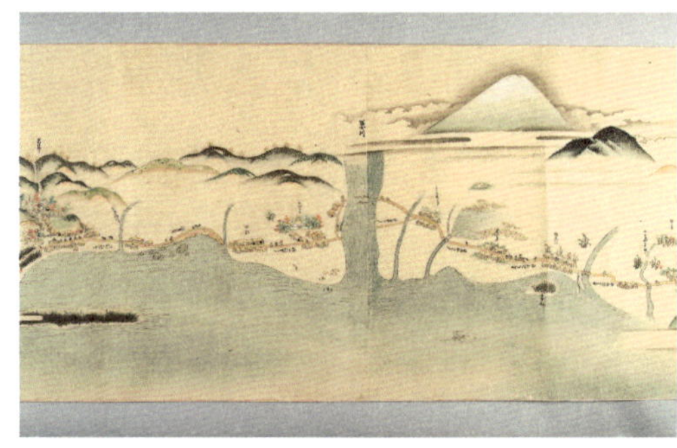

Image on right page:
Nagasaki and surrounding areas

Images on this page:
The start of the trade route near Edo (top) and
the trade route near Mount Fuji (bottom)

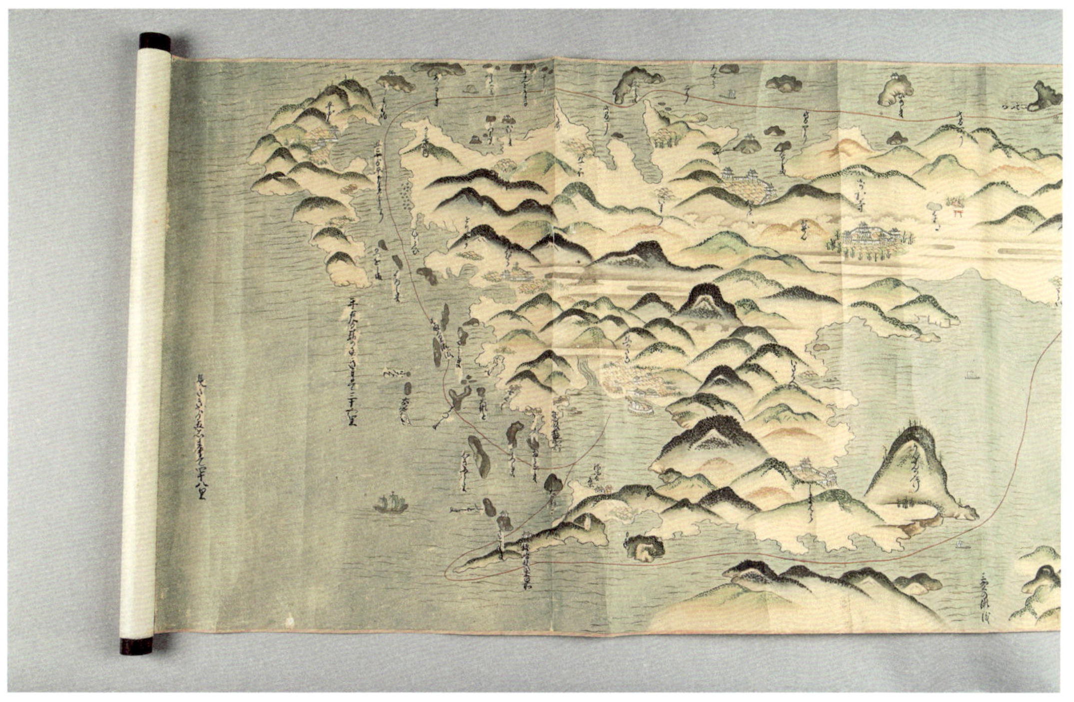

39

Attributed to Watanabe Kazan (1793–1841)
Goldfish in Basin
Hanging scroll, ink and paint on silk, signed: Kazan 崋山, unidentified seal
H 31/131.5 cm, W 36/50.3 cm
Japan, Edo period, first half of 19th c.

19539, donated by Hisako Kashiwagi, 2024

This meticulously detailed and naturalistic painting shows
a small globe containing a goldfish against a blank background. Two lengths of string slumping downwards have been
secured to the top of the globe. The hopeless nature of the
fish, confined to a miniscule space, evokes the inner feelings
of those living in the last days of the late Edo period following
a devastating war. At this time, the Shōgun rulers' strict edicts
and the enforced isolation of the country increasingly began
to be perceived as a burden.

Watanabe Kazan was one of the first trained painters as well
as working for a provincial gentryman and acquainted with
Western science, administration, and defense strategies.
His critical views on the inner structures of the Shōgunat
repeatedly brought him into conflict with the rigid laws of the
land. He was imprisoned before essentially being forced to die
by suicide.

As an artist, Kazan was influenced both by literati painting and
the Western-tinged *ranga* (painting in the Dutch style). As of
now, we do not know if this is one of his early works or a later
copy.[7]

7   We are grateful to Dr. Alexander Hofmann of Museum
für Asiatische Kunst Berlin for his kind assistance with appraising
this work.

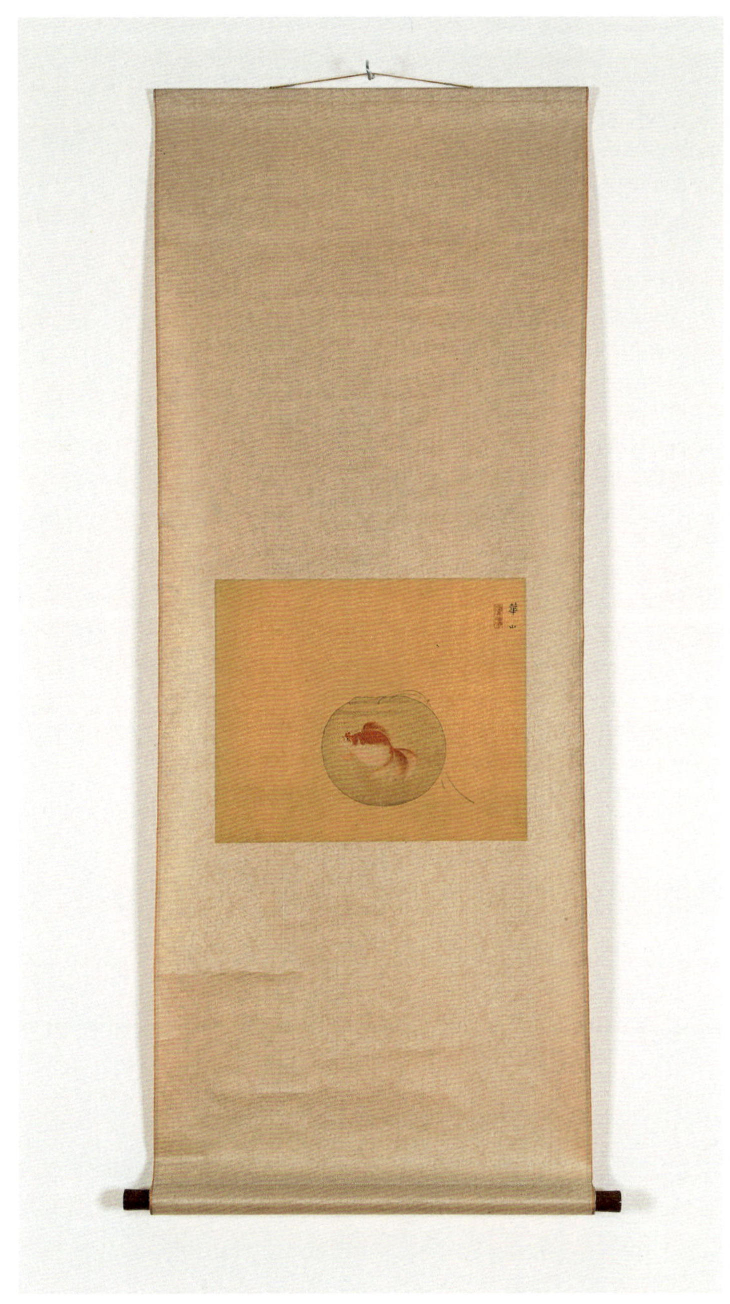

40

Yokoyama Seiki (1793–1865)
The Yōrō Waterfall
Hanging scroll, ink on paper
H 137.2/206.5 cm, W 31.0/33.4 cm
Japan, late Edo period, dated 1862

V.516, on permanent loan from Kunstgewerbeverein in Frankfurt am Main, acquired from Japan Art/Frankfurt am Main, 1992

This extraordinary scroll bears the inscription "Facing the Yōrō
Waterfall, by the seventy-year-old man Seiki". The waterfall
is depicted with only a few brushstrokes at the upper right
edge of the work. The picture is otherwise empty, save for
the small inscription at the lower left. The subject is the Yōrō
Waterfall ("solace for old age") in the Gifu Prefecture; in the
eighth century it was visited by the Empress Genshō (in power
715–724) and has since been venerated as a fountain of youth.
Its waters are said to smooth the skin, darken the hair, and
sharpen eyesight. The waterfall, pushed into the corner of the
work, becomes a final trace of life, a *memento mori* of sorts
made a few years before the death of the elderly Seiki.

The scroll preserves its original nineteenth-century mounting,
lending a sense of harmony to the work's portrait format; its
composition, on the other hand, is decidedly unusual for its
time and, curiously, already appears to anticipate the minimal-
ism of twentieth-century art.

Lit.: Bauer 1998, p.256f.; Soltek 1999, no. 30, p.156f.

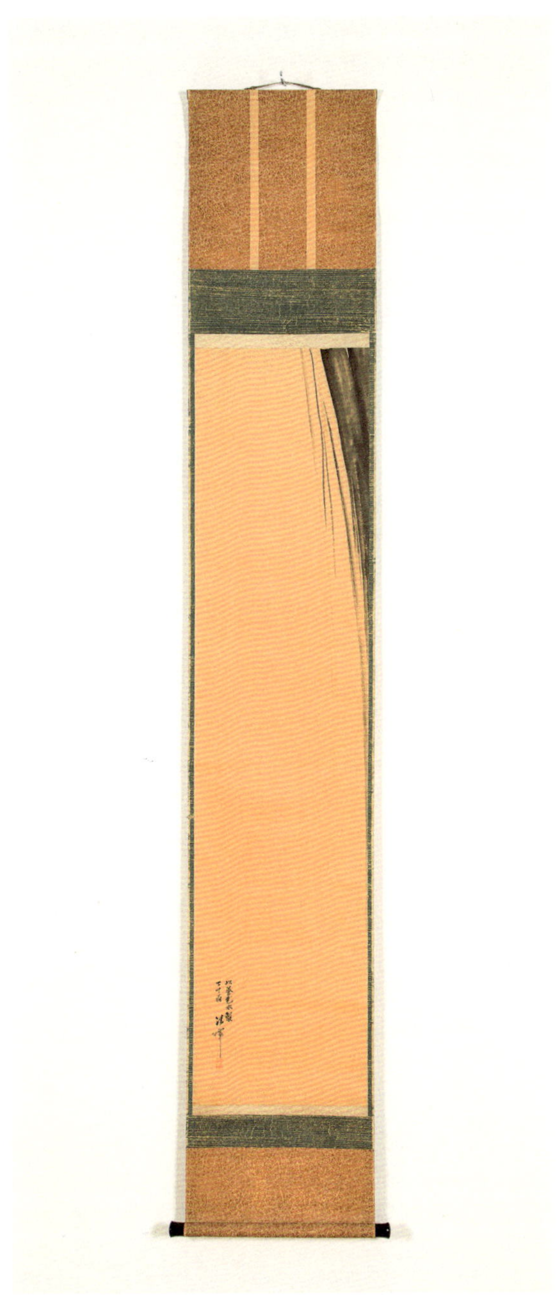

41

The Prehistory of the Gods of Kumano (*Kumano no honji*)
Nara ehon, two volumes bound together, ink and paint on paper
Signature: Tosa no kami Mitsumoto (active 1530–1569), seal: Eiroku(?)
7.5 x 26 cm
Japan, Momoyama period, late 16th c.

12782, Ernst Arthur Voretzsch collection, acquired 1959

This story of an Indian prince and his murdered mother is
based on a Buddhist teaching which was translated into
Chinese in the fifth century, transformed in Japan in the fourteenth century into the founding myth of the three shrines at
Kumano: disgusted by the atrocities committed by his jealous
wives, the Maharaja travels to Japan with his son and his son's
spiritual teacher, where they reveal themselves to be the three
deities of Kumano. Pictured here is the prince mourning the
treacherous murder of his mother, and below the Maharaja's
celestial chariot on its way to the Kumano shrine.

Nara ehon are illustrated manuscripts depicting folk stories
(*otogi-zōshi*), widespread in Japan from the sixteenth to the
eighteenth century. The texts are largely written in syllabary
(*hiragana*) so that they could also be read by women, who
were less likely to be literate. They were frequently given
as dowry gifts and later inherited as family heirlooms. A
particularity of this copy of this popular history of the gods
(*honjimono*), now held in Frankfurt, is the signature of Tosa
Mitsumoto, although its authenticity cannot be verified. The
style of the illustrations identifies this as a very early *nara
ehon*, from the late sixteenth century.

Lit.: Schulenburg/Jesse 2000, no. I-1

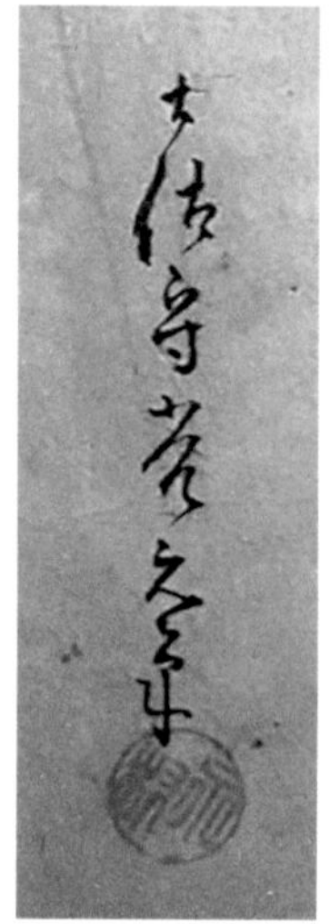

Images on right page:

top:
The prince mourning the treacherous murder of his mother

bottom:
The horrified Maharaja, the prince, and the holy man leave
India in a chariot to settle in Japan as the three deities at
the Kumano Shrine.

Image on this page:
Signature
Tosa no kami Mitsumoto

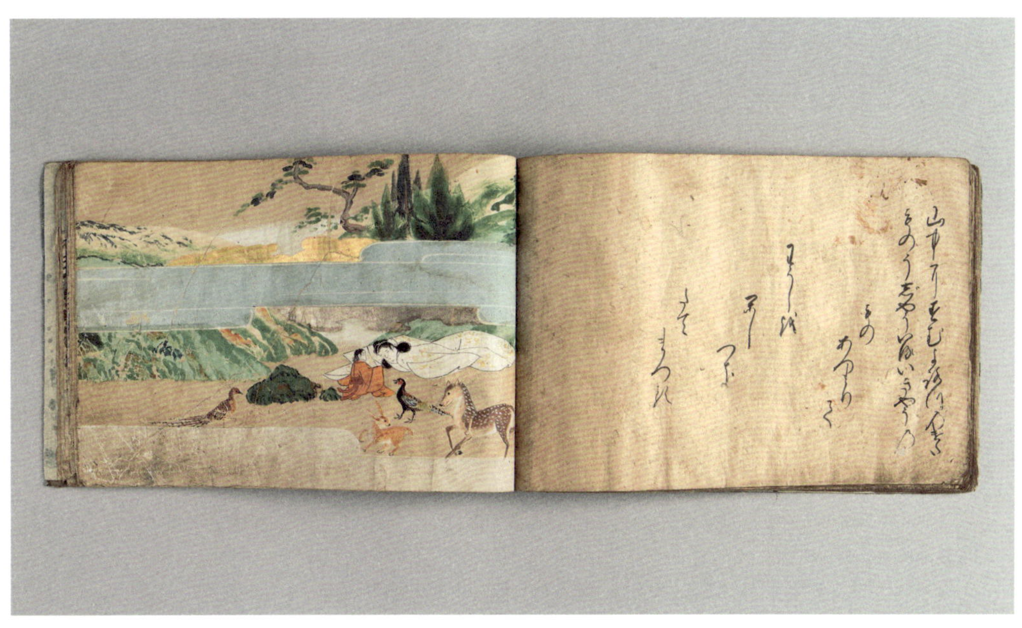

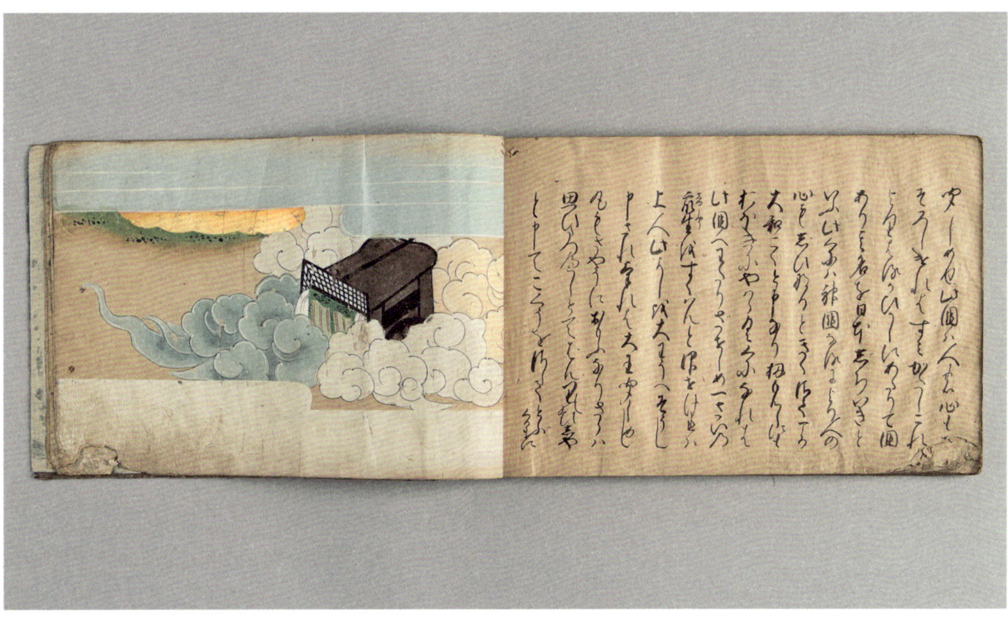

42

The Buddha Legend (*Shaka no honji*)
Nara ehon, one of three volumes, ink and paint on paper
17.6 x 24.5 cm
Japan, Momoyama period or early Edo period, at latest 16th/early 17th c.

12795, Ernst Arthur Voretzsch collection, acquired 1959

The surviving books of the *Lives of the Buddha* are either
one-volume illustrated manuscripts or three-volume printed
works. As the Frankfurt text begins with the marriage of Prince
Siddhartha, this edition presumably first appeared in several
parts, and the accounts of earlier incarnations of the Buddha
which usually precede it have been lost. The story was likely
compiled by preachers based on Chinese canonical writings
and the Buddhist stories (*setsuwa*) then widespread in Japan.
The spread pictured here depicts the prince Siddhartha on a
celestial horse, rising into the air.

Lit.: Schulenburg/Jesse 2000, no. I-2

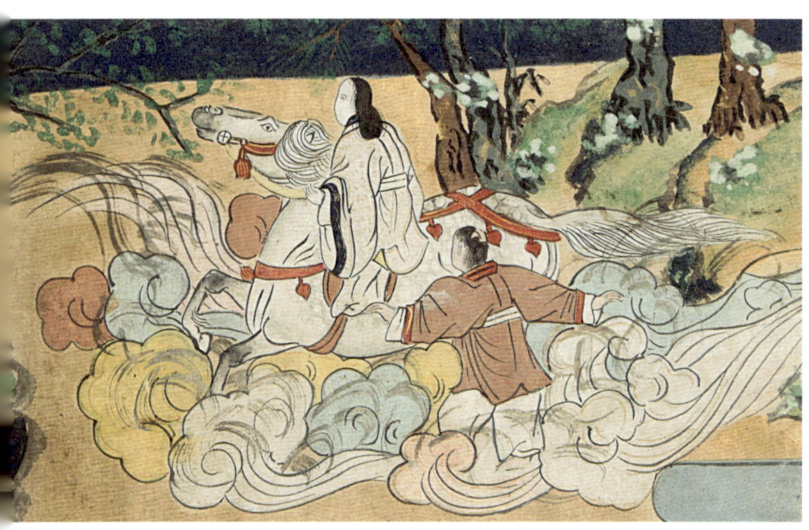

Detail: Prince Siddhartha rising into the air on a celestial horse.

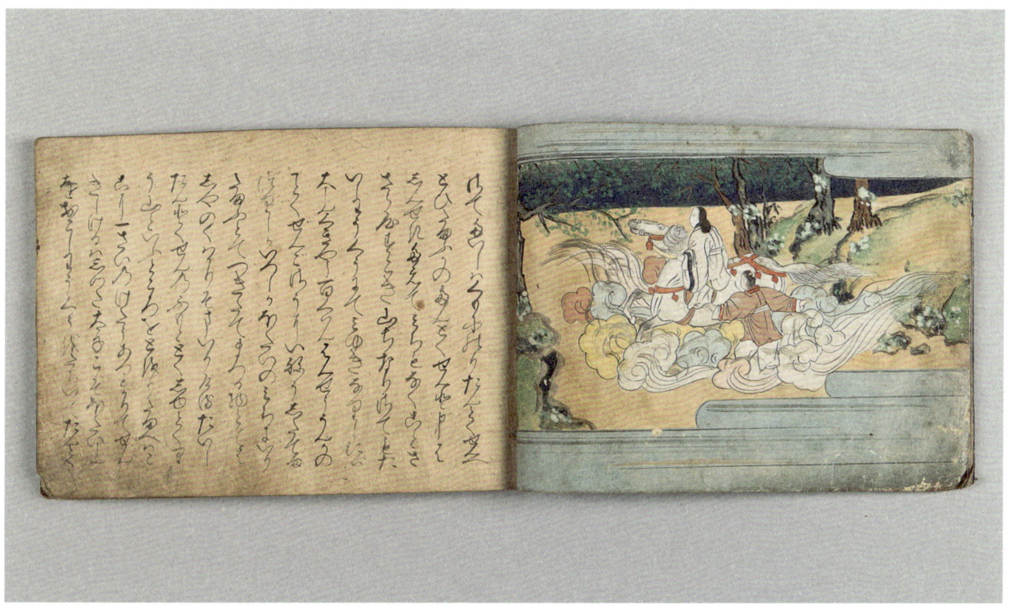

43

The Salt Merchant Bunshō (*Bunshō no sōshi*)
Nara ehon, 2 volumes, ink and paint on paper
18.0 x 24.5 cm
Japan, Edo period, prob. Genroku era to Hōei era (1688–1711)

12804 a, b, Ernst Arthur Voretzsch collection, acquired 1959

The success story of the salt merchant Bunshō was one of
the most widely-read "social books" (*otogi-zōshi*).[8] Scrolls and
manuscripts depicting the legend were popular bridal gifts
for daughters of wealthy merchants. The auspicious story
was traditionally read at New Year's in the hope of bringing
prosperity and blessings for the new year. Though naive in
style, the illustrations are extraordinarily original, and the
manuscript is among the most fascinating manuscripts in the
Frankfurt collection. Pictured above is the courtier on his way
to Bunshō; below is his return to the capital with his bride, the
salt merchant's daughter.

Lit.: Schulenburg/Jesse 2000, no. I-16

Images on right page:

top:
The courtier on his way to Bunshō

bottom:
Return to the capital with his bride

8   A summary of the Bunshō legend can be found in the
introduction, p. 26.

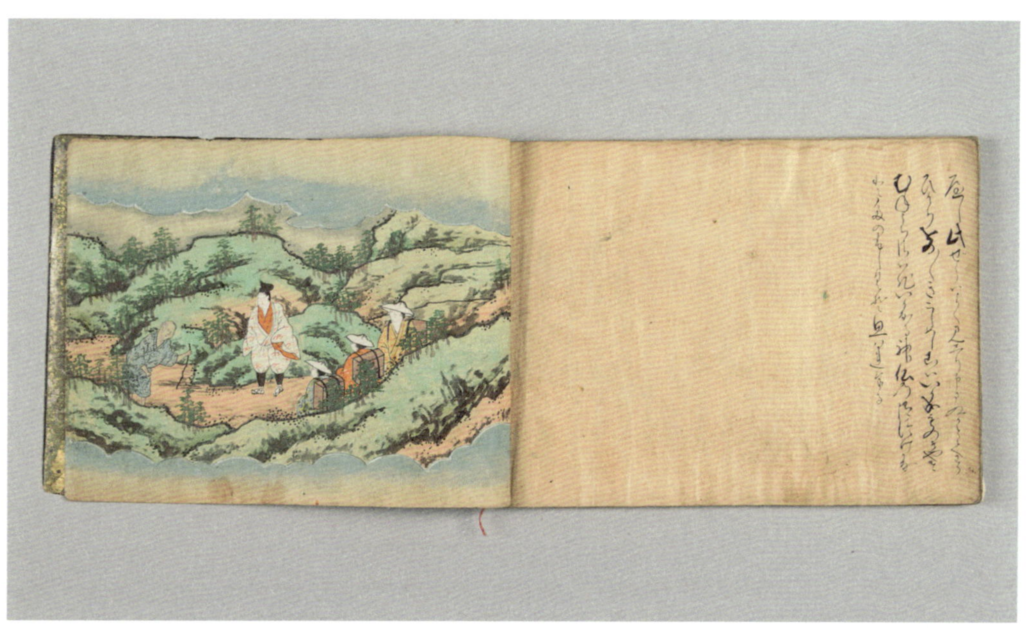

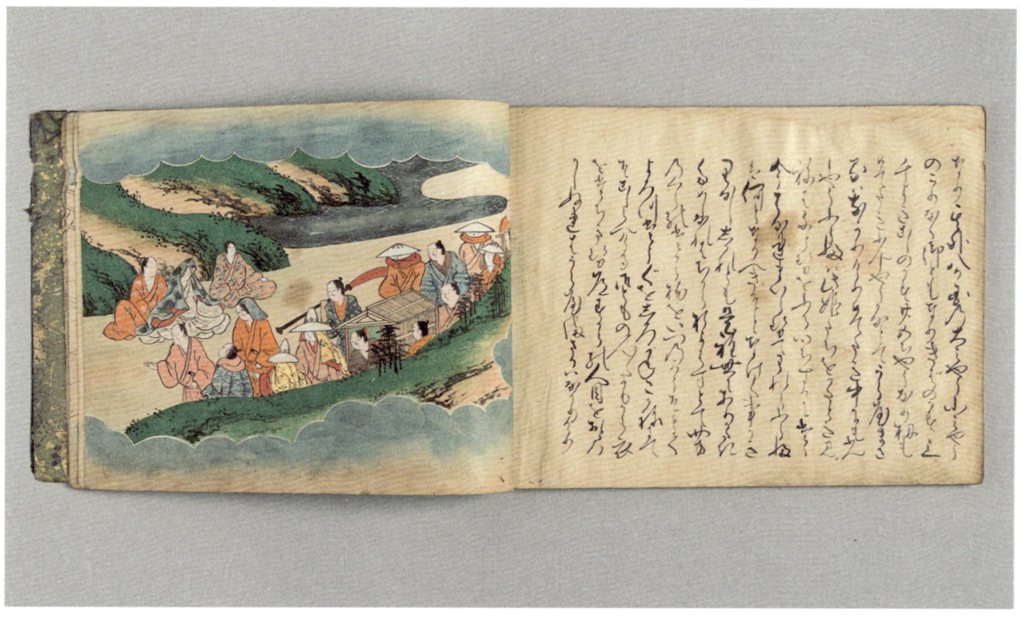

44

The Salt Merchant Bunshō (*Bunshō no sōshi*)
Nara ehon, 3 volumes, ink and paint on paper
15.9 x 23.0 cm
Japan, Edo period, prob. Jōkyō or Genroku era (1684–1704)

12793 a-c, Ernst Arthur Voretzsch collection, acquired 1959

Despite its plain covers of plain blue wax paper, the manuscript's interior reveals vibrant illustrations, carefully executed
and accompanied by personalised inscriptions. They again
depict the courtier's journey to his bride-to-be and his return
with her to Kyōto (*cf.* no. 44).

Lit.: Schulenburg/Jesse 2000, no. I-17

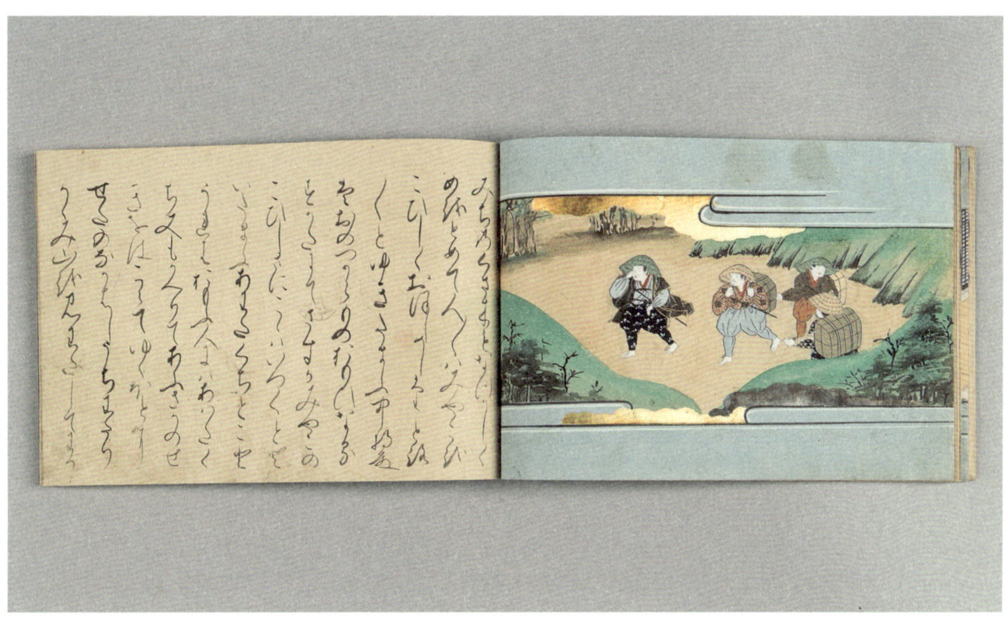

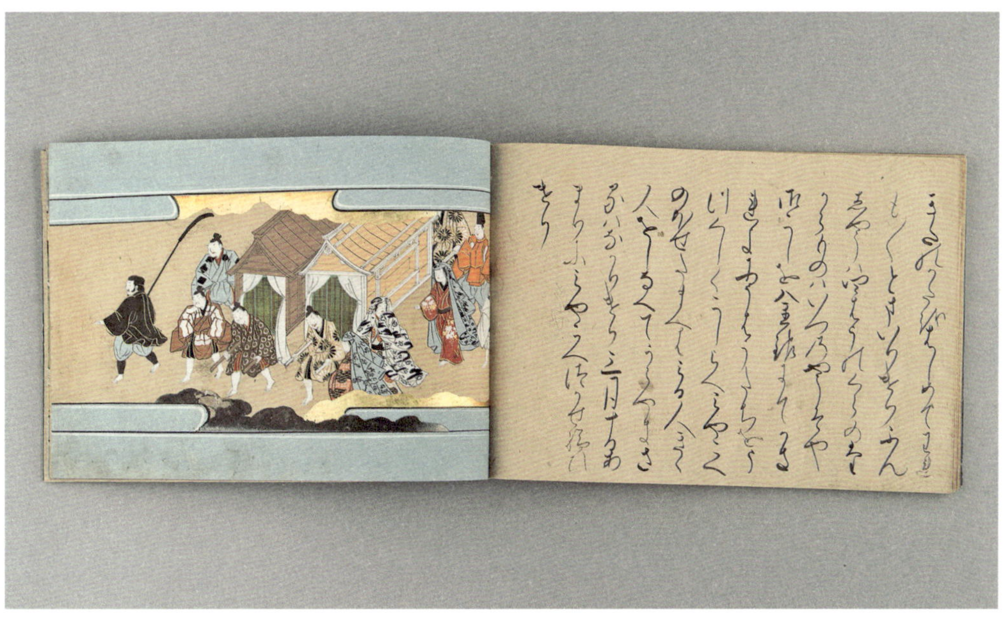

45

Fujiwara no Kamatari (*Taishokan*)
Nara ehon, fragments from 3 volumes, ink and paint on paper
17.0 x 23.5 cm
Japan, Edo period, prob. Kanbun or Enpō era (1661–1681)

12799 a–c, Ernst Arthur Voretzsch collection, acquired 1959

The daughter of the powerful statesman Fujiwara no Kamatari
(614–669), wife of the Chinese emperor Taizong, sends precious treasures to her homeland, among them a magical jewel.
The transport ship is, however, attacked by the coast of Shikoku by the Dragon Kings, and the jewel is stolen. Fujiwara no
Kamatari travels to Shikoku, where he befriends a pearl diver,
who sacrifices her life to recapture the jewel. The Confucian
virtues the legend exemplifies, as well as its dramatic content,
make it likely one of the most popular subjects among the
Nara ehon.

The two-page spread pictured here depicts the sea mon-
sters attacking the Chinese ship and the pearl diver about to
retrieve the stolen jewel from the underwater palace.

Lit.: Schulenburg/Jesse 2000, no. I-10

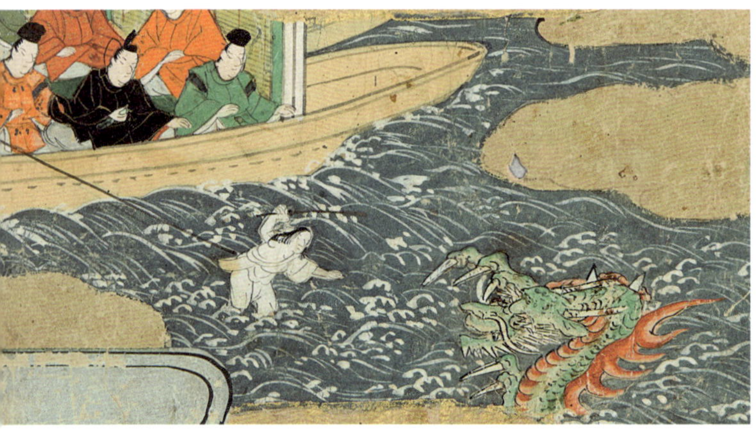

The pearl diver on her way to the dragon's palace on the ocean floor, where she
retrieves the jewel and returns it to the ship, sacrificing herself in the process.

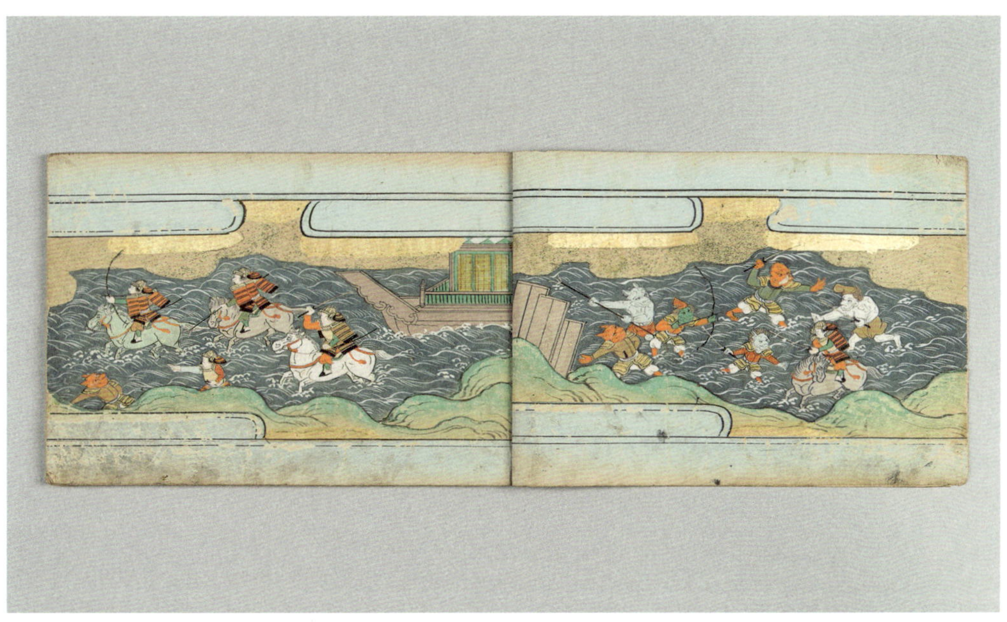

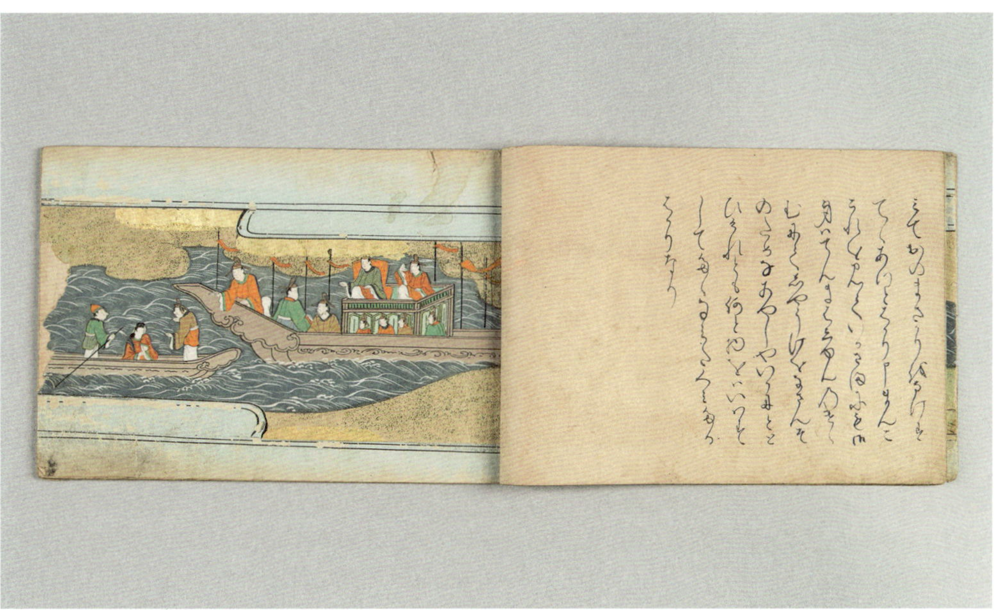

そのめさるりもけるを
てあり、ほそりやうに
うちくやんくいっるふをに
見へてんこ、ちそんのきて
しめくへうりともましんそ
のうらもあるしやうみをて
いられも何ところといつて
しておくもくろへつもあろ

Drinking with the Man-eater (*Shuten-dōji*)
Nara ehon, 3 volumes, ink and paint on paper
23.5 x 17.5 cm
Japan, Edo period, late 17th c.

12785 a-c, Ernst Arthur Voretzsch collection, acquired 1959

The tale of the man-eater *Shuten-dōji*, conquered by Minamoto
no Yorimitsu (Raikō, 948–1021) with the aid of the gods, was
so popular that it was included in a bestselling printed edition
of twenty-three short stories (*otogi-zōshi*) by the Shibukawa
press in Ōsaka at the start of the eighteenth century.

The unusually high number of double-page illustrations,
five in total, may be a result of the subject's popularity in
emaki painting, with its large, landscape-format scenes. The
illustrations depict the ascent of Yorimitsu and his warriors
to Shuten-dōji's palace, and the dramatic moment of the
man-eater's beheading.

Lit.: Schulenburg/Jesse 2000, no. I-3

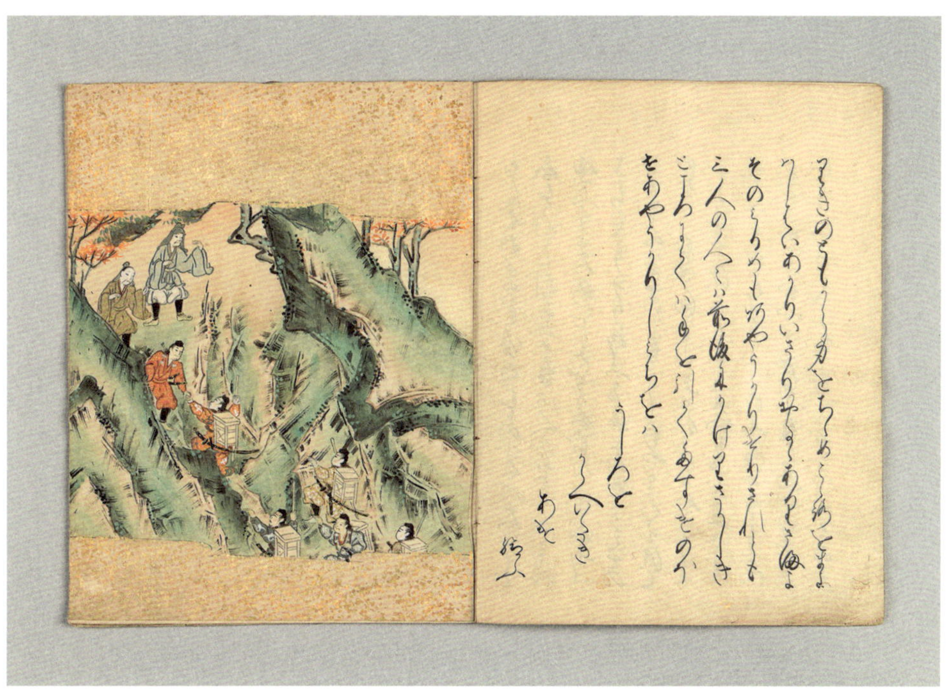

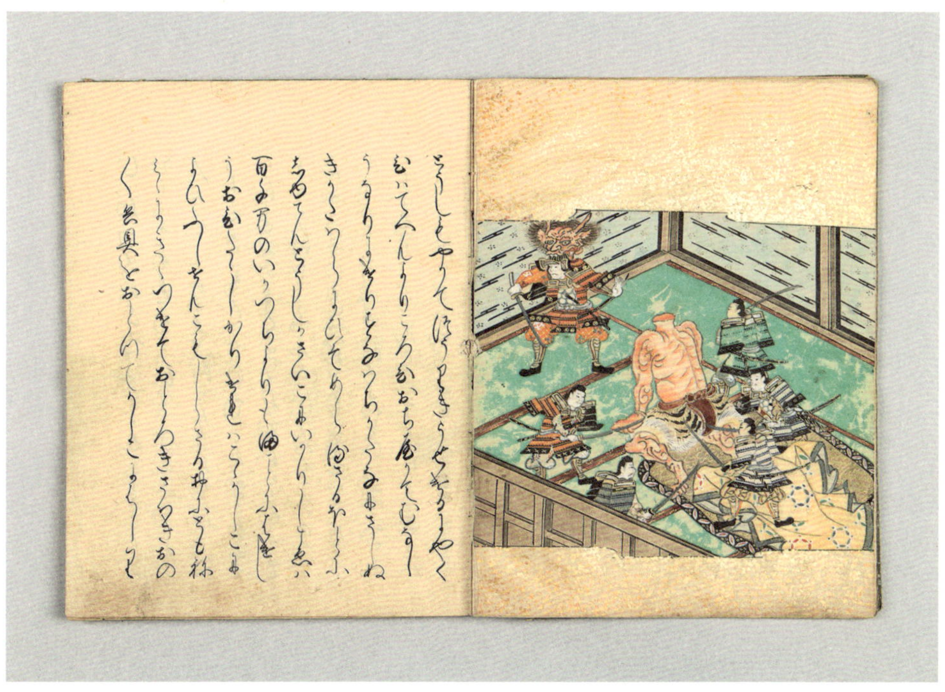

47

The boy Hōmyō (*Hōmyō-dōji*)
Nara ehon, 2 volumes, woodblock print
25.8 x 18.6 cm
Japan, Edo period, dated "Kanbun 8" (1668)

12786 a, b, Ernst Arthur Voretzsch collection, acquired 1959

The boy Hōmyō forfeits his potential to become a rich son
and makes himself a human sacrifice to a dragon to help his
impoverished mother. The boy's fervent prayer, however, frees
the dragon and transforms him into a youth. Hōmyō is named
Mahārāja, goes looking for his mother and cures her blindness
through prayer. The only block-printed work among the books
of the Voretzsch collection, *Hōmyō-dōji* is characterised by its
varied and lively illustrations. Pictured here is Hōmyō on his
way to the sacrificial altar and the moment in which a host
of Buddhas hear his prayers, descending from the heavens to
save him.

Lit.: Schulenburg/Jesse 2000, no. I-21

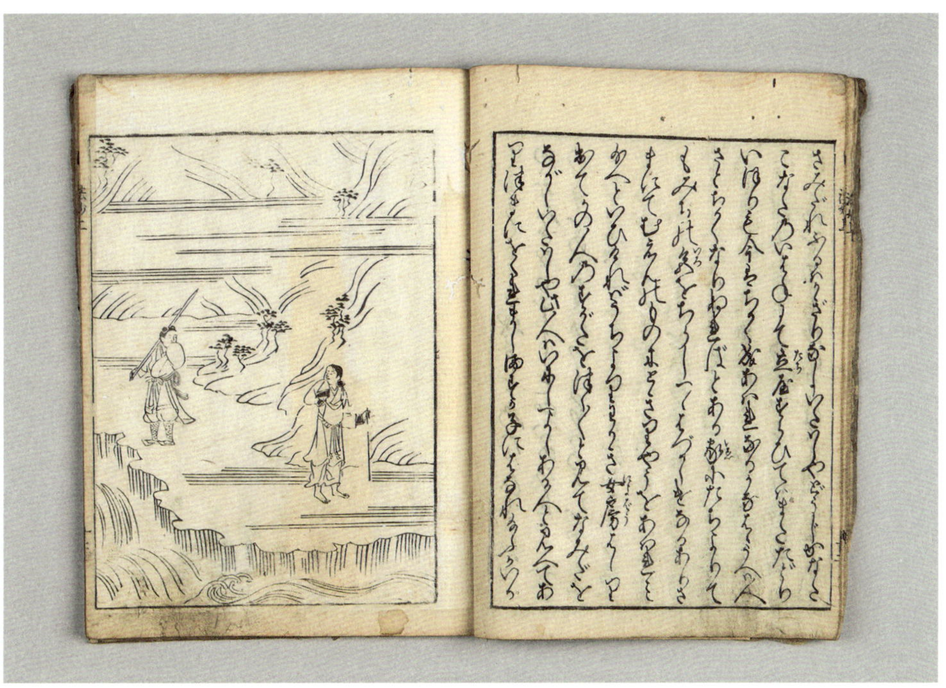

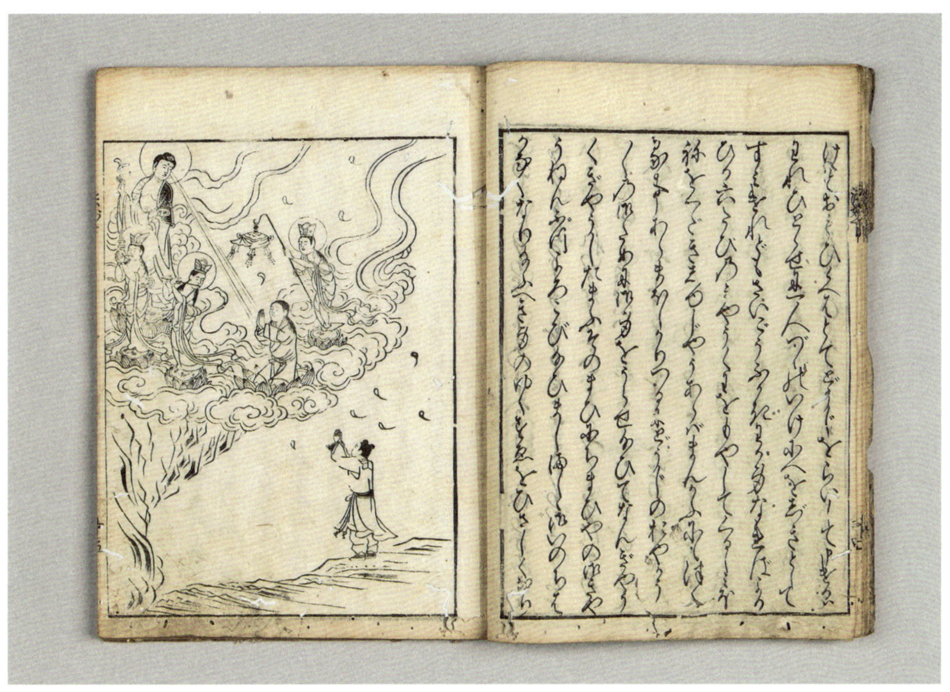

48

The girl Sayohime (*Sayohime*)
Nara ehon, 3 volumes, ink and paint on paper
23.5 x 17.5 cm
Japan, Edo period, prob. Kanbun era (1661–1673)

12784 a-c, Ernst Arthur Voretzsch collection, acquired 1959

In order to pay for her deceased father's funeral, the girl
Sayohime offers herself to the great serpent of Adachi as a
sacrifice. When the snake appears, Sayohime sings from the
Lotus Sūtra, transforming the snake back into a young girl,
who gives her a magical pearl in thanks.

Commercial storytellers perhaps used motifs from the book
of *Hōmyō-dōji* in this story about a child's love (*cf.* no. 48).
Sayohime is a typical dowry book, providing a lesson for the
bride in promoting the female virtue of self-sacrifice, which is
here rewarded with a happy ending. The spreads pictured here
show Sayohime passing Mount Fuji on her way to Mutsu, and
the girl on the sacrificial altar, before her the snake of Adachi.

Lit.: Schulenburg/Jesse 2000, no. I-6

Images on right page:

top:
The girl Sayohime passes salt works on the coast beneath
Mount Fuji on her way to the sacrificial site

bottom:
The singing girl on the sacrificial altar and the man-eating
snake of Adachi

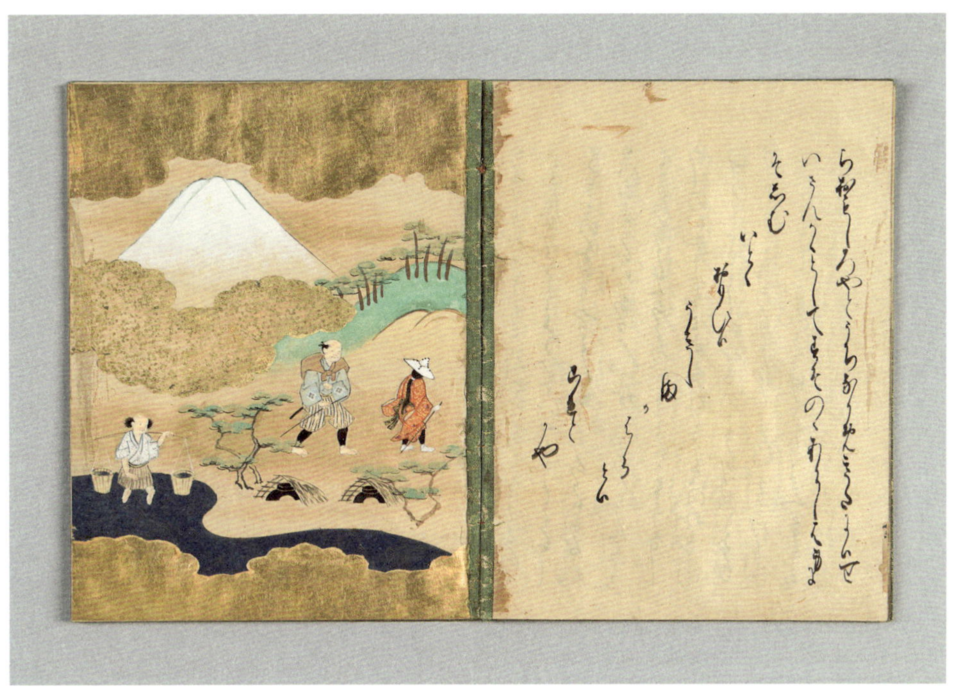

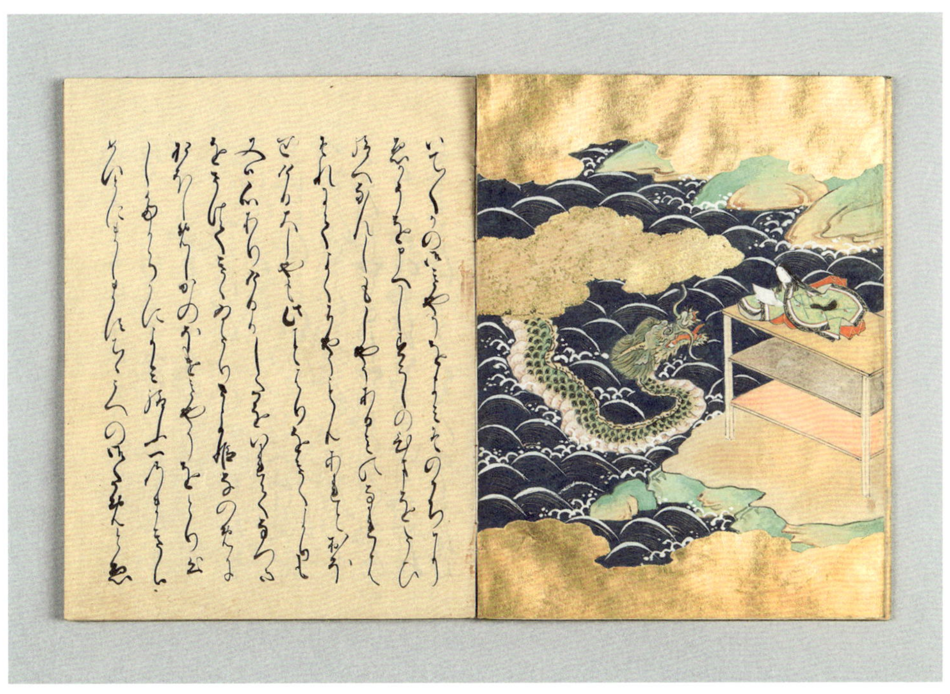

49

The Battle of the Dead Souls (*Sagamigawa*)
Nara ehon, 2 volumes, ink and paint on paper
23.5 x 17.5 cm
Japan, Edo period, prob. Kanbun era (1661–1673)

12783 a, b, Ernst Arthur Voretzsch collection, acquired 1959

This story recounts the legend of the feud between the
generals Kagetoki and Shigetada, augmented by stories of the
vengeful spirit of Yoshitsune from the *Hōryaku-kanki* chronicle
(1156–1338) and the wrathful souls of the Taira, here repro-
duced in a distinctly modified manner. The Frankfurt volumes
represent the only known illustrated copy of this book. The
work's high artistic quality and meticulous illustrations
suggest that such books were purely decorative objects
and would have rarely been read, explaining this copy's fine
condition. The open illustrations show the lifeless Shōgun
falling from his horse in the wake of uncanny events; below is
a boat journey.

Lit.: Schulenburg/Jesse 2000, no. I-4

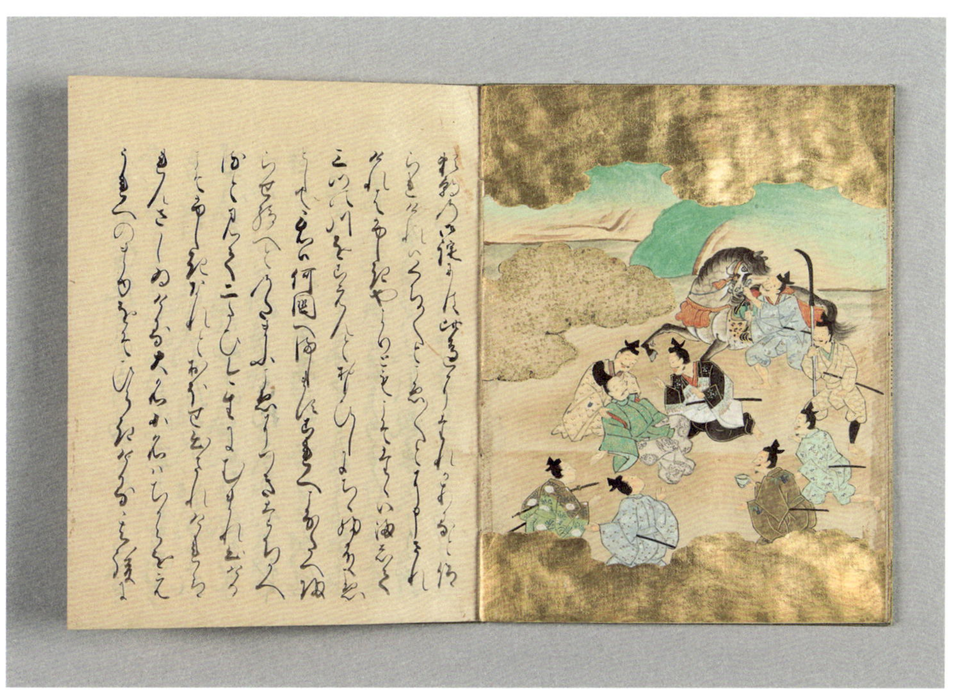

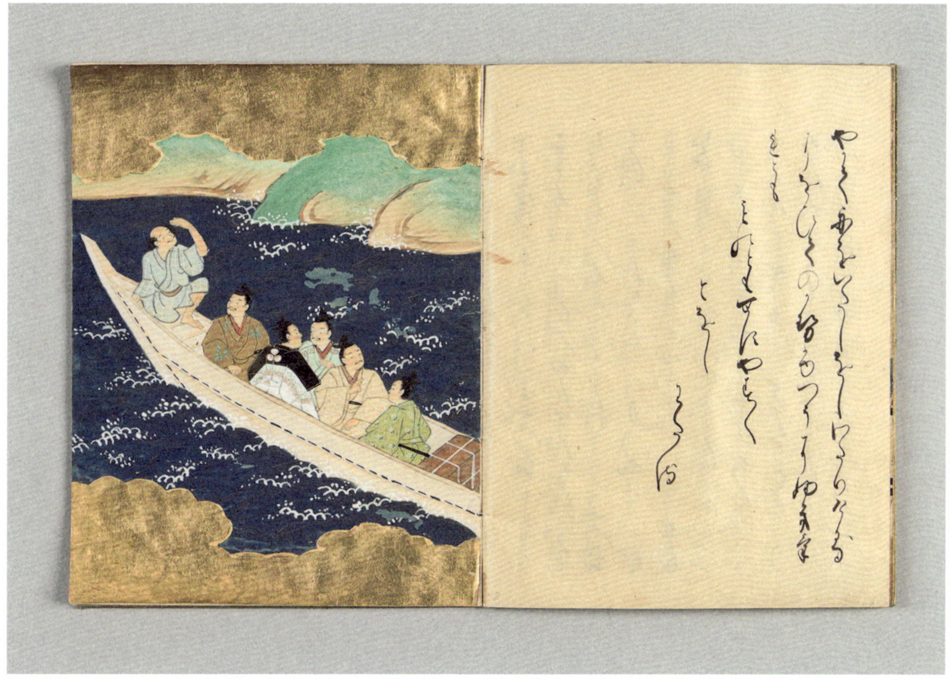

50

New Piece (*Shinkyoku*)
Nara ehon, ink and paint on paper
23.7 x 17.5 cm
Japan, Edo period, prob. Kanbun or Enpō era (1661–1681)

12806 b, Ernst Arthur Voretzsch collection, acquired 1959

This love story is likely the prose rendition of a ballad-like
stage play (*kōwakamai*) of the same name, first performed
in 1554. Hata no Takebun, Prince Ichinomiya's loyal vassal,
takes his own life in order to free his liege's abducted wife
in the form of a ghost. The illustrations have been executed
using relatively modest materials, though the figures seem
expressive and animated. Here, we see Hata taking his life in
the hope of serving his lady as a ghost.

Lit.: Schulenburg/Jesse 2000, no. I-9

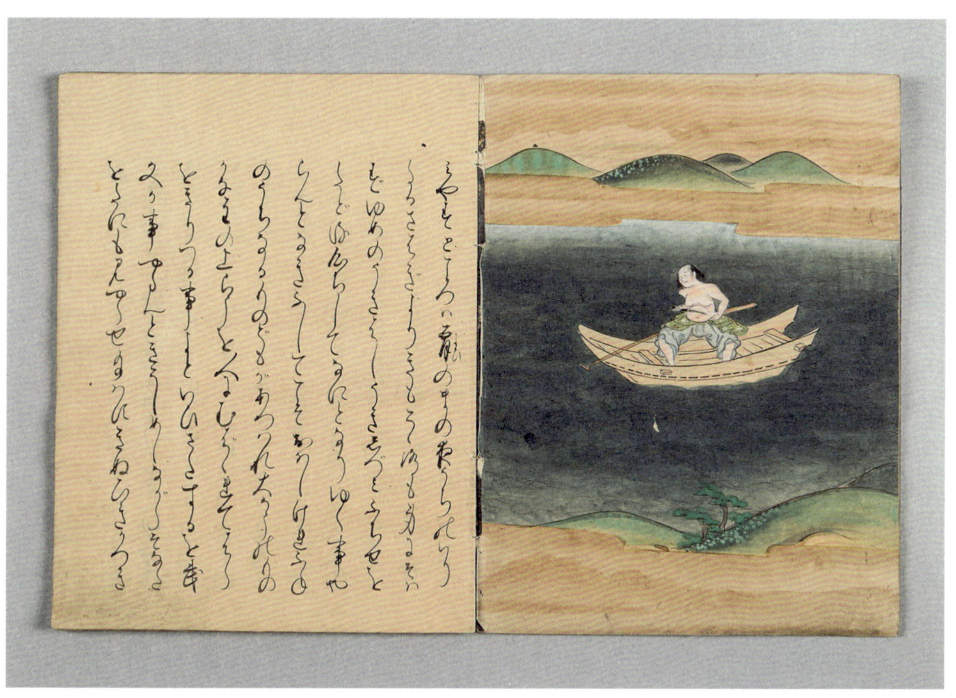

51

Sugimura Jihei (active 1681–1704)
Couple with Voyeur
Hand-coloured woodblock print, *ōban*
25.8 x 37.8 cm
Japan, Edo period, ca. 1685

16399, Johann Georg Geyger collection, acquired 2001

A single leaf from an unidentified erotic series (*shunga*). A
couple locked in a passionate embrace are observed by a
youth, whose head sticks out of the heavy blanket. The woodblock print exemplifies Jihei's typical mode of composition,
in which the visual space is rhythmically arranged around a
central scene. It is governed entirely by an artistic strategy
which eliminates the superfluous and creates a richly struc-
tured, self-contained image. The flatness of the dramatically
billowing fabric verges on the abstract, hinting at an erotic
plot of fiery tension. The tip of a sword emerging from the
fabric may also symbolise a phallus – a world in flux, of a sort.
This magnificent print is the only known copy worldwide.

Lit.: Schulenburg/Höhn 2009, no. 11

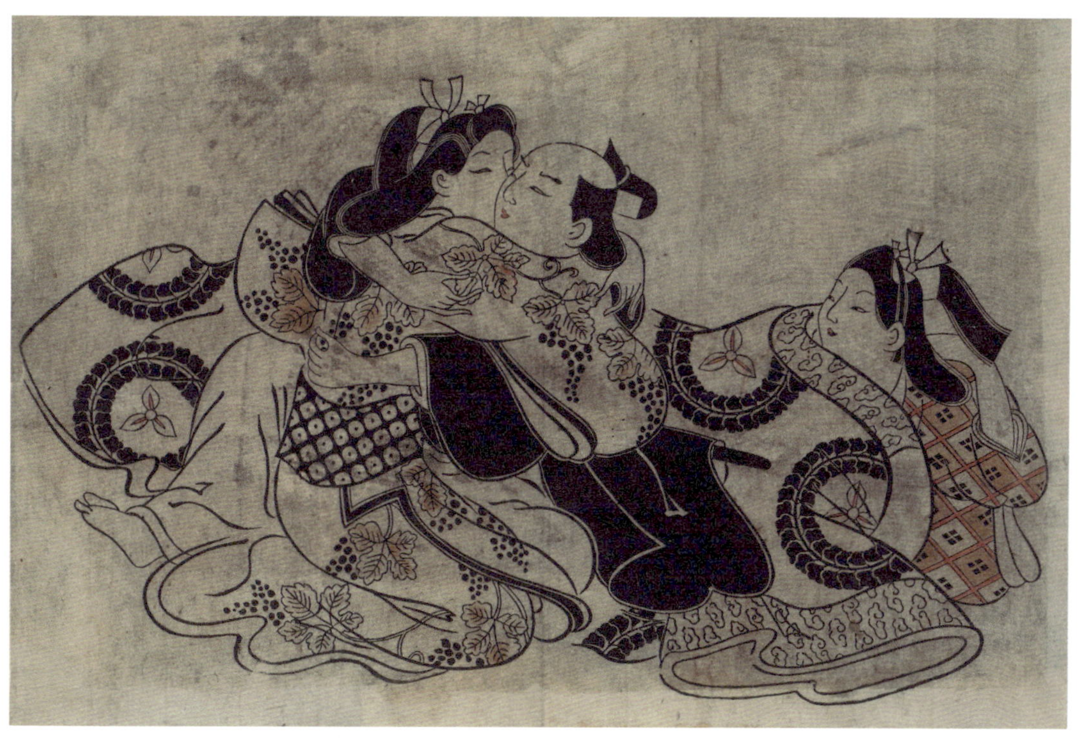

52

Sugimura Jihei (active 1681–1704)
Yoshida kaidō – "Street in Yoshida, the 34th Station of the Tōkaidō"
Woodblock print, *kakemono-e, ō-ōban*
57.0 x 29.5 cm
Japan, Edo period, 1684–1687

16358, Johann Georg Geyger collection, acquired 2001

This masterfully composed large-format print is one of the
earliest examples of *ukiyo-e* as an independent art form
(*ichimai-e*, or single-page images). This *mitate-e* parodies
contemporary *kabuki* theatre figures in a manner typical of
ukiyo-e. This form of dramatic entertainment was common
since the Edo period. Especially in its early days, it pushed the
boundaries of what was permitted. particularly when it came
to erotic elements. Portraits of *kabuki* actors later became one
of the most important genres of *ukiyo-e* woodblock prints.

The diagonal lines in the centre of the image suggest a raised
first floor on the opposite side of the street while also displaying a leap in time of eighty years. Above, seated with her
servant is Miyako no Ōkuni (ca. 1572–1613), founder of *kabuki*
theatre, while below, the men shown on the street are the
retreating novel hero Ukiyonosuke and the poet Ihara Saikaku
(1642–1693) holding an umbrella over *jōruri* singer Kantō
Koroku. Headings displayed beside the protagonists reveal
their identities.

Lit.: Schulenburg/Höhn 2009, no. 13

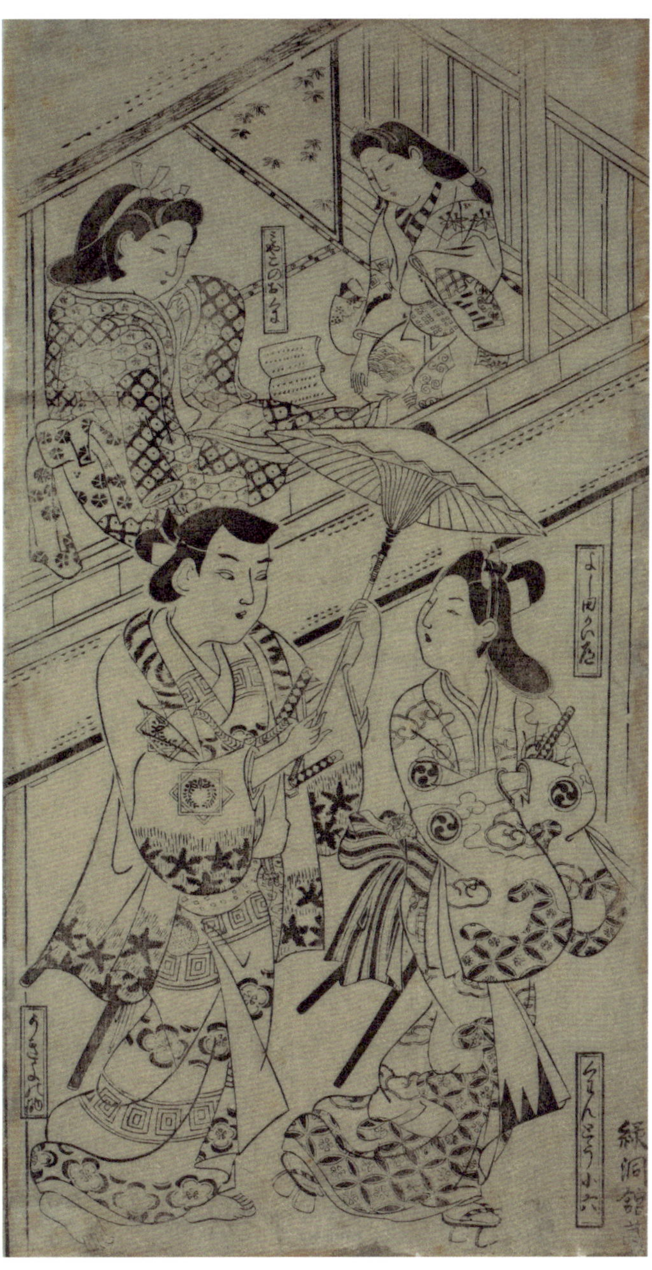

53

Early Torii master
Two Women on a Raft
Hand-coloured woodblock print, *ōban*
21.4 x 29.9 cm
Japan, Edo period, ca. 1718–1720

17300, Otto Riese collection, acquired 2012

This single leaf, bearing only the publisher's seal "Komatsuya",
is attributed to the early Torii school and shows two elegantly
dressed ladies on a raft, clad in travelling hats and observing
the cherry blossoms which descend upon them and float
into the water – perhaps a literary motif. The scene may also
refer to the cherry blossom festival (*cf.* no. 38). The seated
figure holds in her right hand a *shaku*, a symbol of dignity. The
woodblock print has been hand-coloured in orange and yellow
(*tan-e*), the riverbank and the raft accentuated with sprinkled
metal powder.

The shoreless scenery and the raft, drifting slowly amidst
waves and cherry blossoms, create a dreamy, flowing effect.

Lit.: Schulenburg/Höhn 2009, no. 28

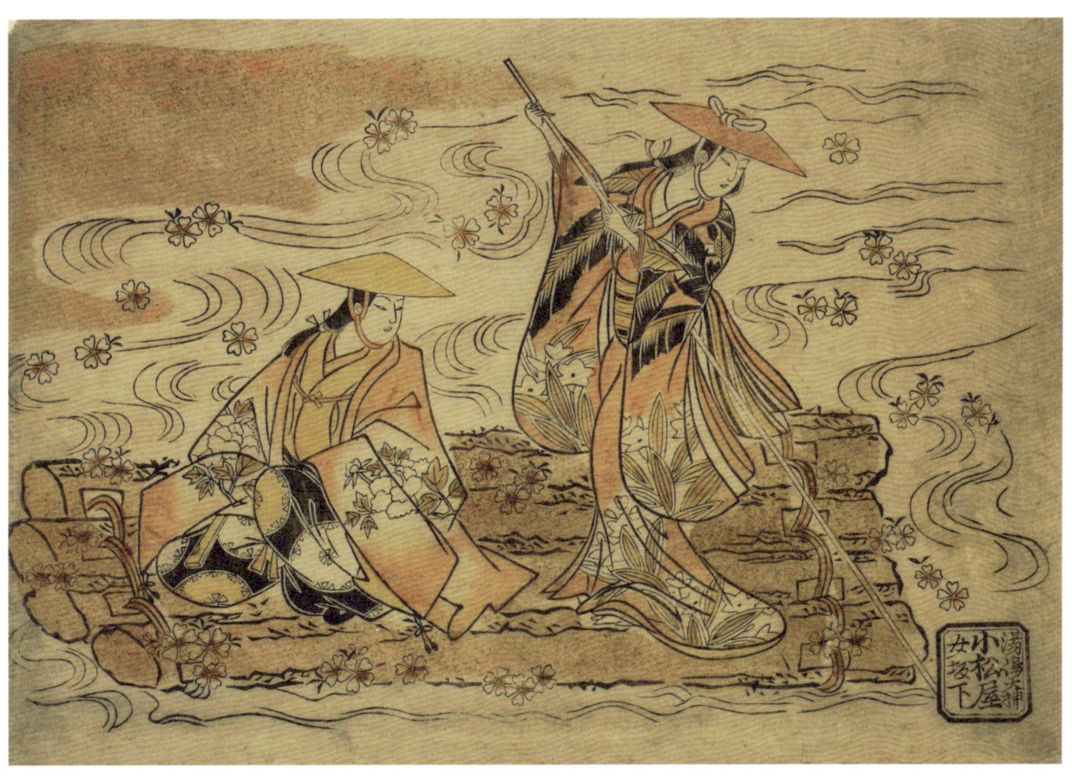

Utagawa Kuniyoshi (1798–1861)
Miyamoto Musashi Slays the Whale
Colour woodblock print triptych, three *ōban*
36.9 x 74.7 cm
Japan, late Edo period, 1847-50

17402, Otto Riese collection, acquired 2012

With both hands, Miyamoto Musashi thrusts his sword into the
back of the enormous sperm whale. A title label describes the
legend. Kuniyoshi frequently depicted the popular swordsman,
artist, and folk hero Miyamoto Musashi (1584–1645). In this
triptych, the general composition and the decorative representation of the whale, with its white belly and spotted dorsal
epidermis, are particularly striking.

In this highly dramatic composition, surrounded by waves,
Kuniyoshi impressively visualises the wild forces of nature.
The immense marine mammal appears at once formidable and
vulnerable, a symbol of the fragility of life.

Lit.: Schulenburg/Höhn 2009, no. 169

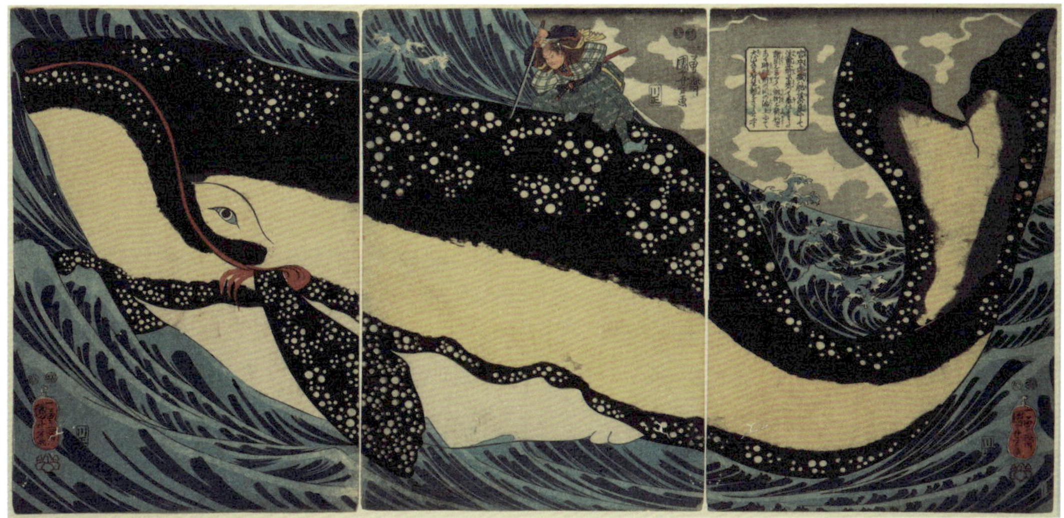

55

Katsushika Hokusai (1760–1849)
"The Great Wave off (the Coast of) Kanagawa", from *Thirty-Six Views of Fuji*
Colour woodblock print, *ōban*
25.5 x 37.5 cm
Japan, late Edo period, 1830

17409, Otto Riese collection, acquired 2012

The first of the *Thirty-Six Views of Fuji*. Hokusai was nearly
seventy years old when he produced this world-famous work.
Although Hokusai was well aware of the significance of his
work, the success of his Fuji series was a surprise; the thirty-six prints he originally planned then grew to one hundred.

The work shown here impressively depicts the fragility of
human existence. The flat fishermen's rowboats used to supply
fish to the large market in Edo are here unexpectedly caught
in rough waters. The beauty of the surging waves is breath-
taking; at the same time, however, the scene depicts a moment of great danger, one which could lead to disaster for the
fishermen in an instant.

When it was created, this fine work was among the cheapest
Japanese woodblock prints on the art market; on the internet,
it is now thought to be the single most popular artwork worldwide, surpassing even Leonardo's *Mona Lisa* or Van Gogh's
Sunflowers. There is likely no other work of art with such an
iconic impact, nor so many copies, adaptations, or parodies.[9]

Lit.: Schulenburg/Höhn 2009, no. 177

9   See also Guth 2015.

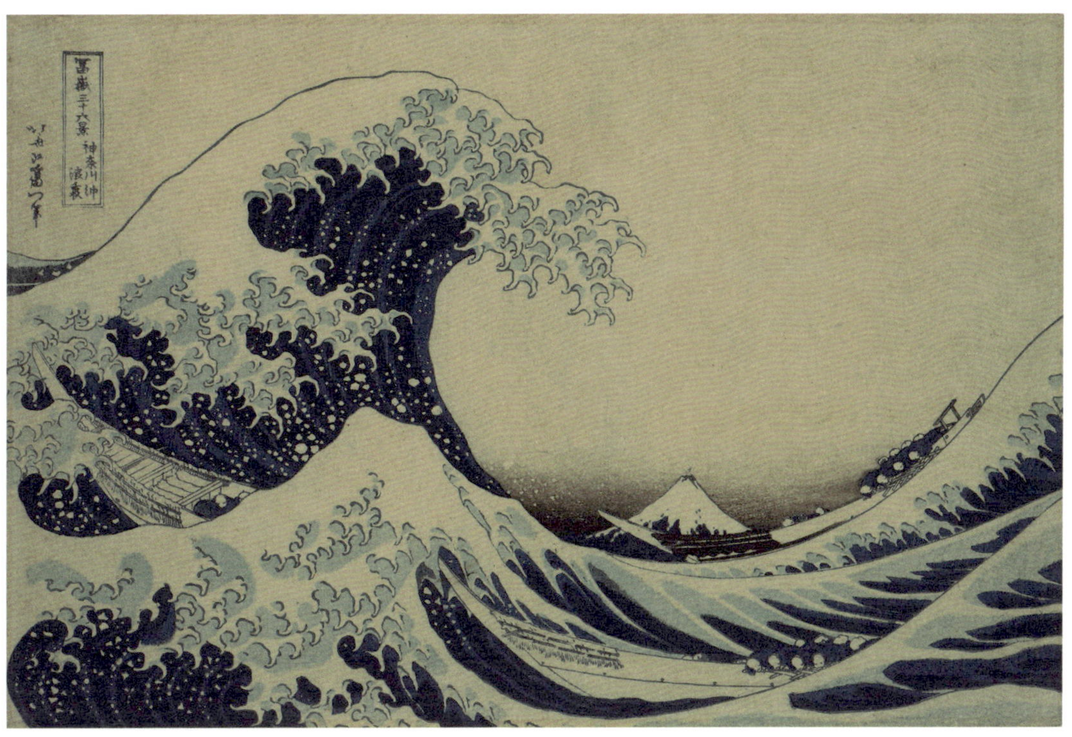

56

Katsushika Hokusai (1760–1849)

"Kajikazawa in Kōshū (Kai Province)", from *Thirty-Six Views of Fuji*

Colour woodblock print, *ōban*

25.8 x 37.9 cm

Japan, late Edo period, 1830

17410, Otto Riese collection, acquired 2012

A lone fisherman stands at the edge of a cliff, battered by
surging waves, holding the lines of his net against the storm.
Behind him crouches his companion, holding a fish basket.
The outline of Mount Fuji emerges from beyond the wide band
of mist that runs horizontally across the image, against white
streaks of clouds amidst the shadowy blue sky. Both fishermen
are almost exactly in the centre, the standing fisherman in
particular highlighting the instability of the ground on which
they stand, between the looming volcano and the roaring
waves. He may be seen as a metaphor for the collective fragility of human existence.

With its masterful composition, this high-quality print is
among the most exceptional of the series of *Thirty-Six Views of
Fuji*. Aside from the rather faded red stamps of the publisher
and the censor in the lower right corner, it is also an excellent
example of a true *aizuri-e*, an attractive blue print in various
shades of Berlin blue (*bero-ai*), the synthetic Prussian blue
which had then only recently begun to be imported from
Europe.

Lit.: Schulenburg/Höhn 2009, no. 181

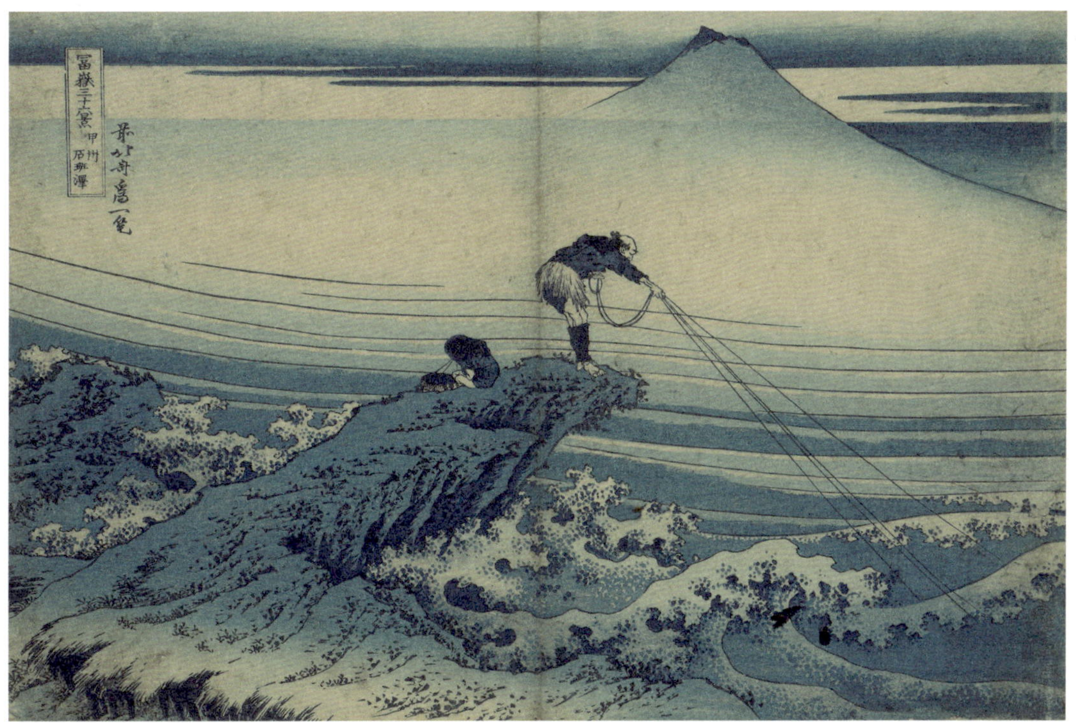

57

Katsushika Hokusai (1760–1849)
"Ejiri in Sunshū (Suruga Province)", from *Thirty-Six Views of Fuji*
Colour woodblock print, *ōban*
25.0 x 37.0 cm
Japan, late Edo period, 1830

17413, Otto Riese collection, acquired 2012

Farmers and travellers fight against a violent storm on a path
winding through the marshland on a barren plain beneath
Mount Fuji. Withered trees bend to one side, some of their
leaves blowing away. A woman in the foreground loses her
papers – perhaps sheets of poetry, or handkerchiefs. They
sail across the picture into the distance, as does the porter's
straw hat. Curiously, he is the only figure who does not appear
"headless" in the composition. As in *The Great Wave* (cat.
no. 56) and *Kajikazawa* (cat. no. 57), the true theme is man's
struggle with the superior forces of nature.[10]

The first edition of this print, scarcely found today, was printed
entirely in blue (*aizuri-e*). In the present edition, only the
contours of the line block are printed in blue. The other three
colours, typical of the 1830s and early 1840s, testify to the
enormous popularity of the Fuji cycle during Hokusai's lifetime.

In this exhibition, the present work is accompanied by a parody by Shiriagari Kotobuki (p. 209).

Lit.: Schulenburg/Höhn 2009, no. 178

10   Jason Farago published a clever animation of this
print for the New York Times online (7 August 2020), under the title
"A Picture of Change for a World in Constant Motion": https://www.
nytimes.com/interactive/2020/08/07/arts/design/hokusai-fuji.
html?referringSource=articleShare (accessed 25 June 2024).

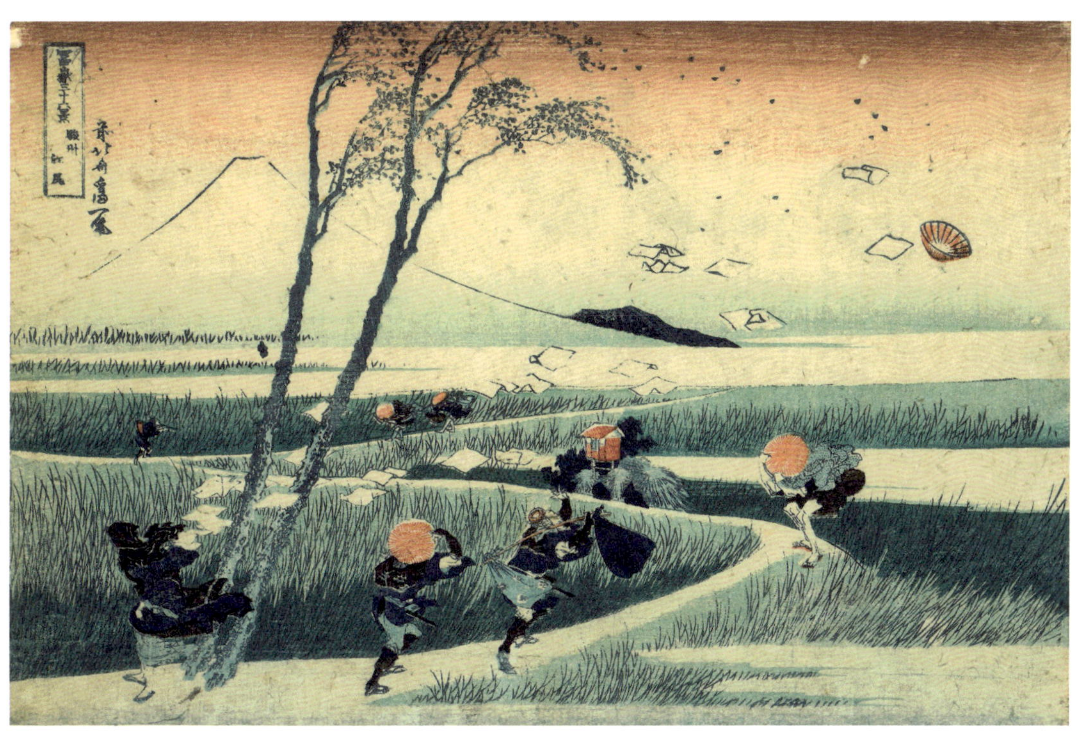

Katsushika Hokusai (1760–1849)

"The Rōben Waterfall in Ōyama in Sōshū (Sagami Province)", from *A Tour of the Waterfalls of the Provinces*
Colour woodblock print, *ōban*
38.5 x 26.3 cm
Japan, late Edo era, 1834/35

17418, Otto Riese collection, acquired 2012

The waterfall streams smoothly over a rocky slope, overgrown
with bushes, into a pool. A group of pilgrims with wooden
prayer boards perform their ablutions in the pool and, drying
themselves off, return to the bank. The seal and individual
characters of the publishing house Eijudō can be seen on the
pilgrim's cloak on the left, and on the pilgrims' hats on the
right, at the Fuji-no-bō roadhouse.

Ōyama, situated near Edo in the present-day Kanagawa
Prefecture, was the site of the Afuri shrine, devoted to a
rain-bringing deity. Pilgrimages to Ōyama from Edo had been
popular since the early eighteenth century, and a festival
was held there at the height of summer each year. Before the
pilgrims could ascend to the shrine with their wooden planks,
they first ritually cleansed themselves in the waterfall's pool
one last time. If they neglected to do so, the impure pilgrims
would expose themselves to *tengu*, long-nosed demons living
in the mountains, who would tear them to shreds as they
continued their ascent.

Lit.: Schulenburg/Höhn 2009, no. 184

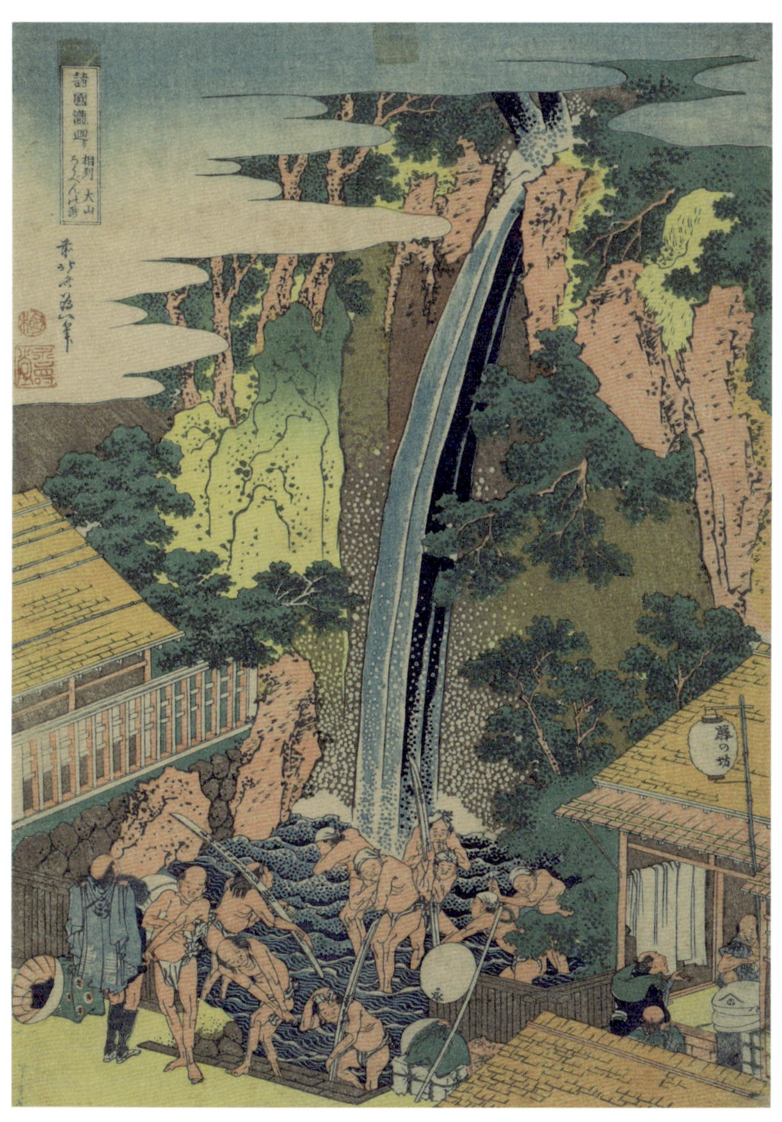

Katsushika Hokusai (1760–1849)
"The Waterfall near Ono at Kisokaidō", from *A Tour of the Waterfalls of the Provinces*
Colour woodblock print, *ōban*
38.0 x 27.5 cm
Japan, late Edo era, 1834/35

17419, Otto Riese collection, acquired 2012

A waterfall, almost like an enormous crystalline structure in
appearance, cascades vertically from the high mountain face
into the depths pictured at the left. We see the waterfall's
spray – indicated by small dots – only at the lower edge,
where the torrent of water pours into a natural basin. From a
footbridge over the stream, five travellers watch the impressive
natural spectacle as it flows on. In the foreground on the left,
we can make out a wooden roof weighed down with stones,
and on the right bank, a small shrine on a rocky cliff juts out
by the waterfall. Further to the right, an overhanging cliff,
almost level with the waterfall, emerges from a zone of bluish
mist.

This waterfall may have been a product of Hokusai's imagination; unlike most of the other waterfalls in the series, it cannot
be located in the real world.

Lit.: Schulenburg/Höhn 2009, no. 185

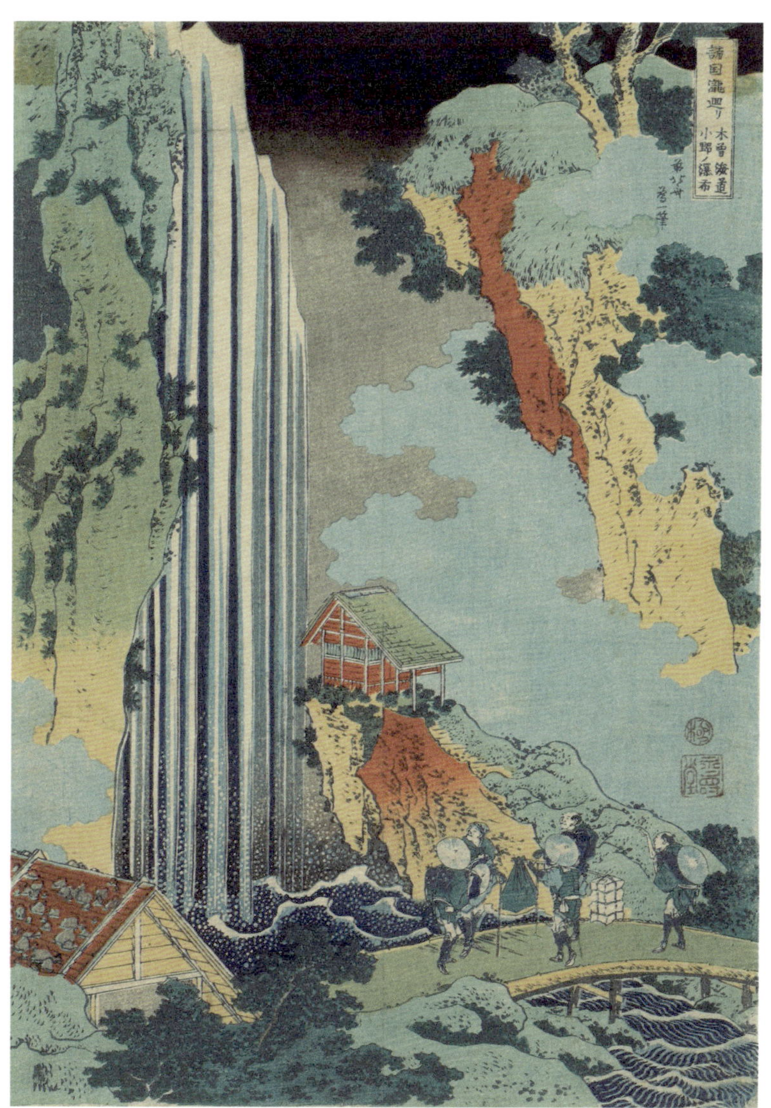

Katsushika Hokusai (1760–1849)
"The Waterfall near Aoigaoka in the Eastern Capital (Edo)", from *A Tour of the Waterfalls of the Provinces*
Colour woodblock print, *ōban*
38.5 x 26.0 cm
Japan, late Edo era, 1834/35

17420, Otto Riese collection, acquired 2012

A small waterfall cascades, foaming, from a lotus-covered
pond into a basin surrounded by walls, at the edge of which
two porters rest on the road in the foreground. At the lower
edge, a building emerges from the clouds. On the left is a road
populated by porters and pedestrians, leading uphill along
the green embankment to Aoigaoka ('Mallow Hill'), located
in the Minato-ku district of present-day Tōkyō. The two small
buildings at the base of the pool and at the top of the hill are
seemingly lookout posts, as the area was home to noblemen
and samurai who valued peace and order in their neighbour-
hood.

Compared to Hokusai's previous waterfall motifs from the
series, the present scene appears far less dramatic; its urban,
civilised appearance can also be seen in the neat stone wall
surrounding the lower water basin.

Lit.: Schulenburg/Höhn 2009, no. 186

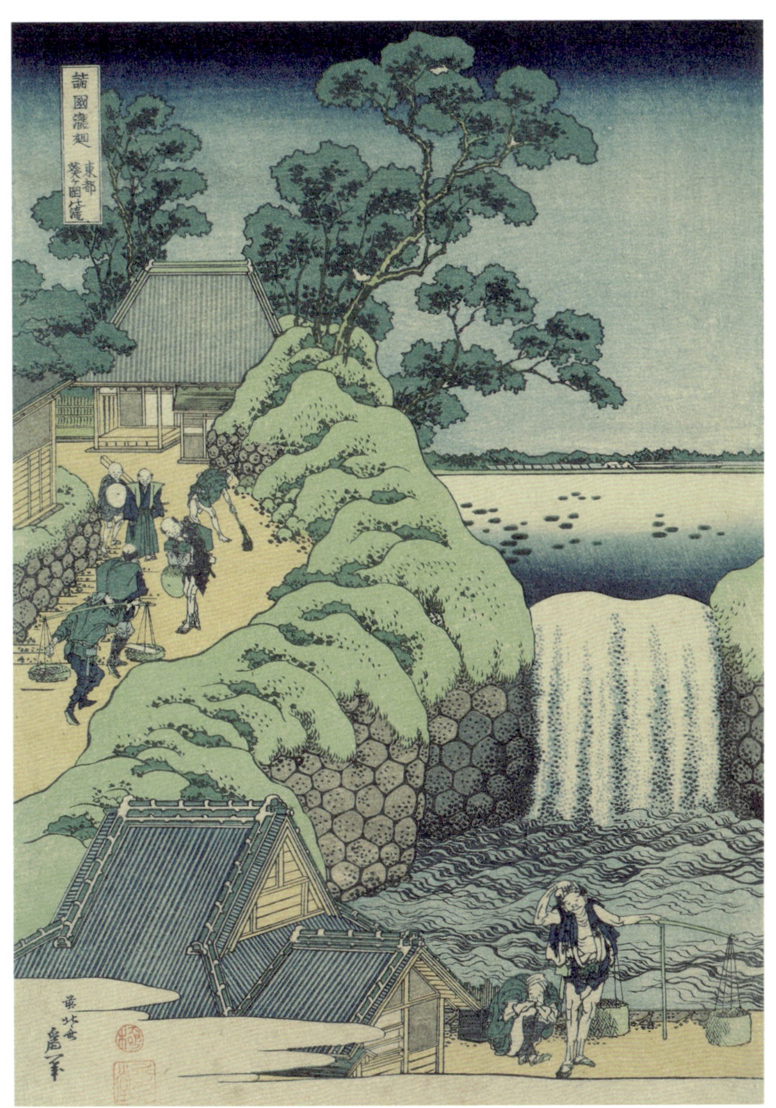

Katsushika Hokusai (1760–1849)
"The Amida Waterfall at Kisokaidō", from *A Tour of the Waterfalls of the Provinces*
Colour woodblock print, *ōban*
36.9 x 25.2 cm
Japan, late Edo era, 1834/35

17421, Otto Riese collection, acquired 2012

The Amida waterfall cascades through an almost circular
hole in the rocks into the darkness of the depths. Plunging
downward in several jets, the waterfall is framed by steep,
rocky slopes covered in greenery. Two hikers, observing the
spectacular view, are seated on picnic mats on an overhanging plateau on the left, while a servant prepares tea.

The circular opening, whose shape is likely associated with
the third eye on the forehead of the Amida Buddha, may have
given the waterfall its name. Like the Ono Waterfall, however
(cat. no. 60), the present waterfall cannot be precisely located,
and it is also possible that the composition, inspired by the
name of the waterfall, is the product of Hokusai's imagination.

Unlike the other three waterfalls from the series in the Riese
collection, this print lacks the publisher's and censor's seals,
perhaps indicating a later edition.

Lit.: Schulenburg/Höhn 2009, no. 187

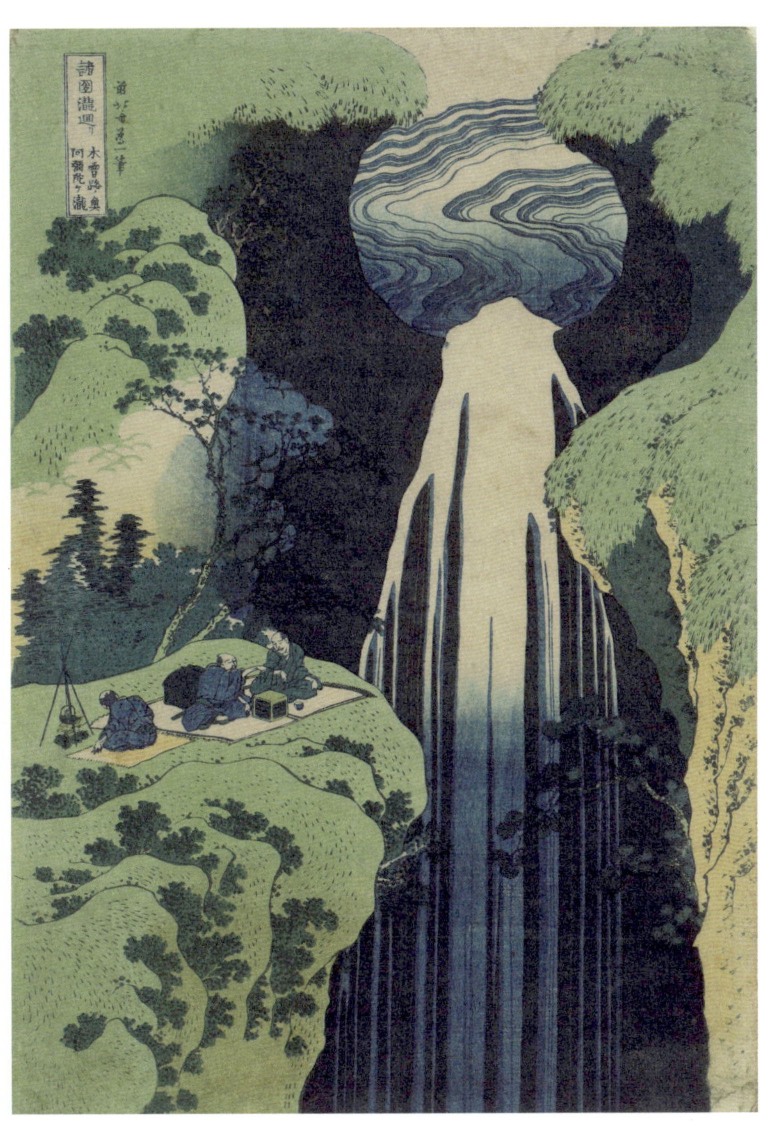

Utagawa Hiroshige (1797–1858)

"The Wakanoura Coast in the Kii Prefecture", leaf 53 from *Famous Views of the Sixty-odd Provinces*

Colour woodblock print, *ōban*

31.0 x 24.0 cm

Japan, late Edo era, 1855

17471, Otto Riese collection, acquired 2012

A group of five cranes flies through the morning sky across the Wakanoura coast of the (former) Kii Province, which lies south of the present-day city of Wakayama in central Honshū, in the southern part of the Kii peninsula. A small island with a temple can be seen in the middle ground, connected to the shore by a bridge with three arches.

In East Asia, cranes are seen as the creatures ridden by the immortals, which lends a metaphysical air to the picturesque, panoramic landscape depicted here. This dual meaning is emphasised by the viewer's elevated point of view; we find ourselves at the same height of the birds, almost floating.

The image, with the strongly contrasting colours of the morning sky – and the pinkish band of sky along the horizon – verges on the kitschy, but it is nonetheless a fine, early print, certainly created during Hiroshige's lifetime. The embossing on the upper crane and the blue of the centre crane's feathers seen here are indicative of the best state of printing.

Lit.: Schulenburg/Höhn 2009, no. 227

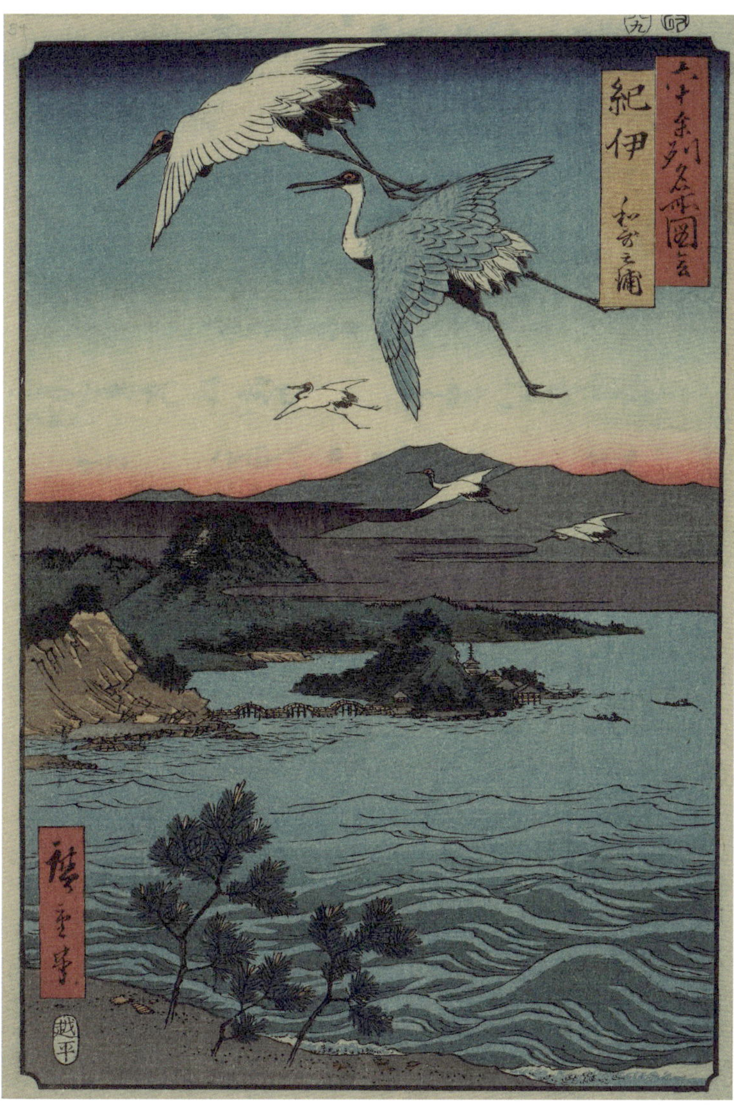

63

Utagawa Hiroshige (1797–1858)
"Arashiyama Cherry Blossoms in Full Bloom", from *Famous Views of Kyōto*
Colour woodblock print, *ōban*
23.6 x 35.9 cm
Japan, late Edo era, 1834

17452, Otto Riese collection, acquired 2012

The image is divided diagonally by the blue waters of the
Hōzu River. Upon it floats a brown raft, with two peasants
punting leisurely – one smoking, and the other looking at
the riverbank. A fire burns in the centre of the raft, a wisp of
smoke drifting upwards to the right. The water is a dark blue
by the shore, but is somewhat lightened by green lines in the
lower right-hand corner. Lone hikers and peasants walk along
the path by the bank, flanked by blossoming cherry trees. The
hillside is covered with pines and cherry trees in bloom; petals
fall down and float on the water.

Following the great success of his Tōkaidō cycle, Hiroshige
created further series of landscapes, among them this 1834
series of ten prints, *Kyōto meisho no uchi* (*Famous Views of
Kyōto*). In his designs, the artist drew from illustrated travel
guides (*meisho zu-e*), namely the 1799 *Miyako rinsen meisho
zu-e* (*Guide to Famous Places in Kyōto*), illustrated by Akasato
Ritō; here, Hiroshige transforms his inspiration, printed in
black, into evocative, colourful scenes. Arashima, in western
Kyōto, was renowned for its cherry blossoms; the season is at
its height in this magnificent springtime scene (see also cat.
no. 38).

Lit: Schulenburg/Höhn 2009, no. 214

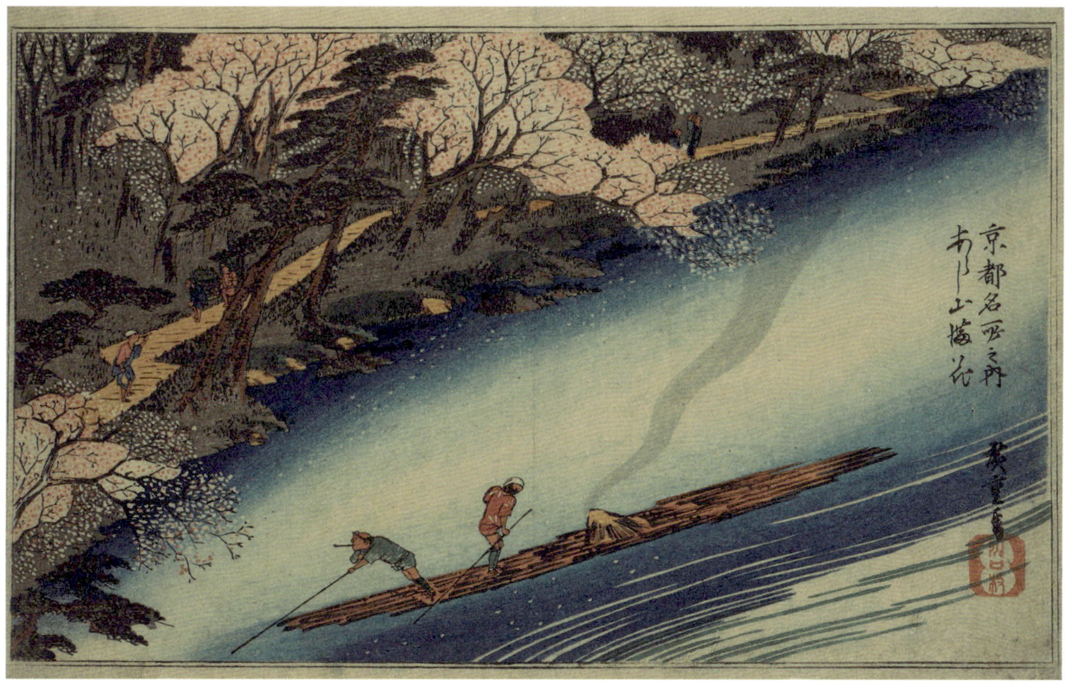
京都名所之内
あらし山満花
廣重画

64

Utagawa Hiroshige (1797–1858)
"The Ferry at Kawaguchi and the Zenkōji Temple", leaf 20 from *One Hundred Famous Views of Edo*
Colour woodblock print, *ōban*
36.3 x 24.5 cm
Japan, late Edo era, 1857

17462, Otto Riese collection, acquired 2012

As in the previous work, much of the visual space is taken up
by a river running diagonally through the image. The Arakawa
('Wild River') depicted here is the middle course of the Sumidagawa, at the northern end of old Edo. The S-shaped bend of
the river is here rendered as a site of lively movement, with six
men each arduously pushing a raft upstream. Nonetheless, the
waterway – in parts deep blue and almost white – is suffused
with a sense of meditative stillness.

In the foreground is a roadhouse, with travellers awaiting the
return of the boat disappearing at the right-hand edge of the
picture. Although he has several passengers, the ferryman
appears decidedly more relaxed than the rafters. Between the
trees at the upper right is the destination of the journey, the
temple of Zenkōji. Its main building is partially covered by the
work's title; perhaps the temple housed the figure of a "secret"
Amida Buddha (*hibutsu*), which was only publicly displayed
once every seventeen years.

The print is part of one of the master's most popular series,
Edo meisho hyakkei (*One Hundred Famous Views of Edo*), in
which Hiroshige, approaching the end of his life, once more
celebrates his native city in all its beauty.

Lit. Schulenburg/Höhn 2009, no. 228

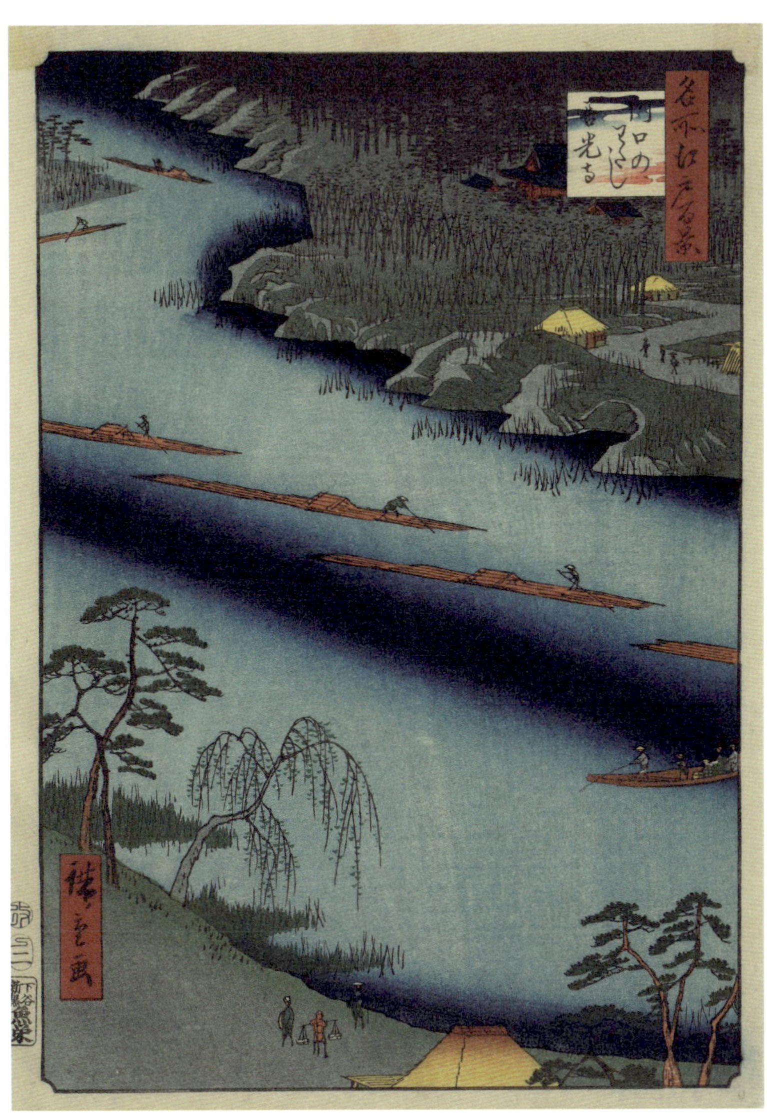

65

Utagawa Hiroshige (1797–1858)

"Evening Rain Shower on Ōhashi Bridge, near Atake", print 58 from *One Hundred Views of Famous Places in Edo*
Colour woodblock print, *ōban*
36.2 x 25.2 cm
Japan, late Edo period, 1857

17464, Otto Riese collection, acquired 2012

The print shown here is Hiroshige's most famous woodblock
print, undoubtedly the masterpiece of his *One Hundred Views*
of the capital. The hair-thin bands of rain cutting diagonally
through the work were created using grey and black printing
plates. This, as well as the gradual changes in colour (*fukibo-
kashi*) at the upper and lower edges of the image, presented
great technical challenges to the printer of this work. In fact,
early, clearly contoured prints with this motif differ clearly from
later ones, in which the linework is less precise. Likewise, the
black rain cloud at the upper edge of the image, initially wavy
in shape, is rendered in this work – and in a second edition –
as a straight, shaded line.

Depicted here is the imposing wooden Ōhashi Bridge, which
spans the wide Sumidagawa in northern Edo. Hiroshige
masterfully captures the moment in which the passersby on
the bridge, covering themselves with hats, umbrellas, or straw
mats, hurry to shelter from the storm. The raftsman, more or
less unfazed, continues his journey down the river alone.

As is frequently the case in *ukiyo-e* woodblock prints, the centre of attention is man, surprised by the overpowering forces
of nature, his miniature size deliberately contrasted with the
grand scale of nature (see for example, cat. no. 56).

The print, highly sought-after by Western collectors, also drew
considerable international attention thanks to Vincent Van
Gogh's 1887 oil painting copying this master print.

Lit.: Schulenburg/Höhn 2009, no. 229

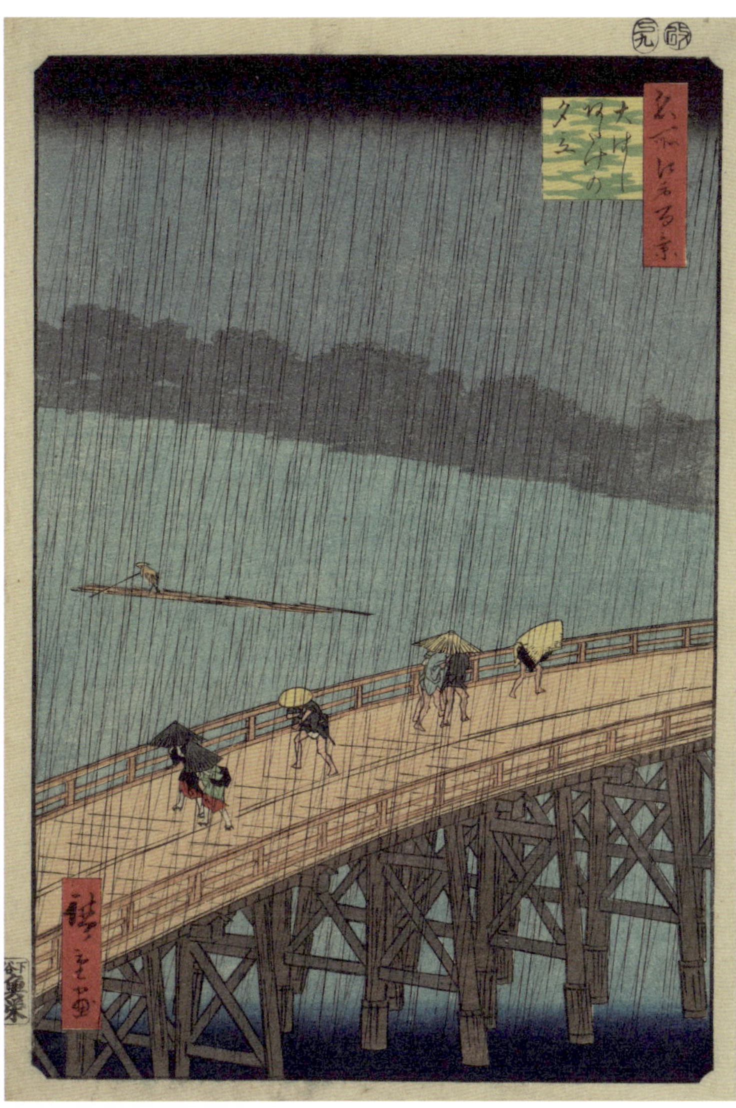

66

Kubota Beisen (1852–1906)

"Illustriertes Journal der verrückten Reise des (Herrn) Beisen" (*Beisen manyū gajō* 米仙漫遊画乗)

Book of woodblock prints in German protective cover ("Japanische Landschaften"), first of two volumes

ex libris: E. Schwabach-Maerzdorf, with "Christa Scholz" added by hand below

H 16.5 (16.9 cm with protective cover), B 23.2 (23.7) cm

Japan, dated Meiji 22 (1889)

18794, donated by Charlotte Orth, 2020

Raised in Kyōto, the painter, illustrator, and woodblock print
artist Kubota Beisen was regarded highly in his time and took
on commissions from the Japanese imperial family, amongst
others. In 1899 he travelled to the World's Fair in Paris as a
member of an official delegation, and later, in 1893, to the
World's Columbian Exposition in Chicago. He worked as a
newspaper illustrator in Tōkyō and in 1893–4 was commissioned to create war propaganda woodblock prints for the
Sino-Chinese war, widely distributed at the time.

The present woodblock print book contains twenty-four
double-page views of his journey to the World's Fair in Paris
in 1889. The woodblock prints depict various stages of his
journey, opening with a coastal panorama of Mount Fuji; there
follow scenes from Shanghai, Guangzhou ('Guangdong'), Hong
Kong, and Vietnam ('Annam'). It is the first volume, published
in 1899, and depicts only the first part of the sea voyage (a
second volume was published separately in 1890). In a humour
typical of its time, the covers of both volumes, each bound
with thread stitching, bear a small steamship with a Japanese
flag in the middle of a porcelain bowl filled with water.

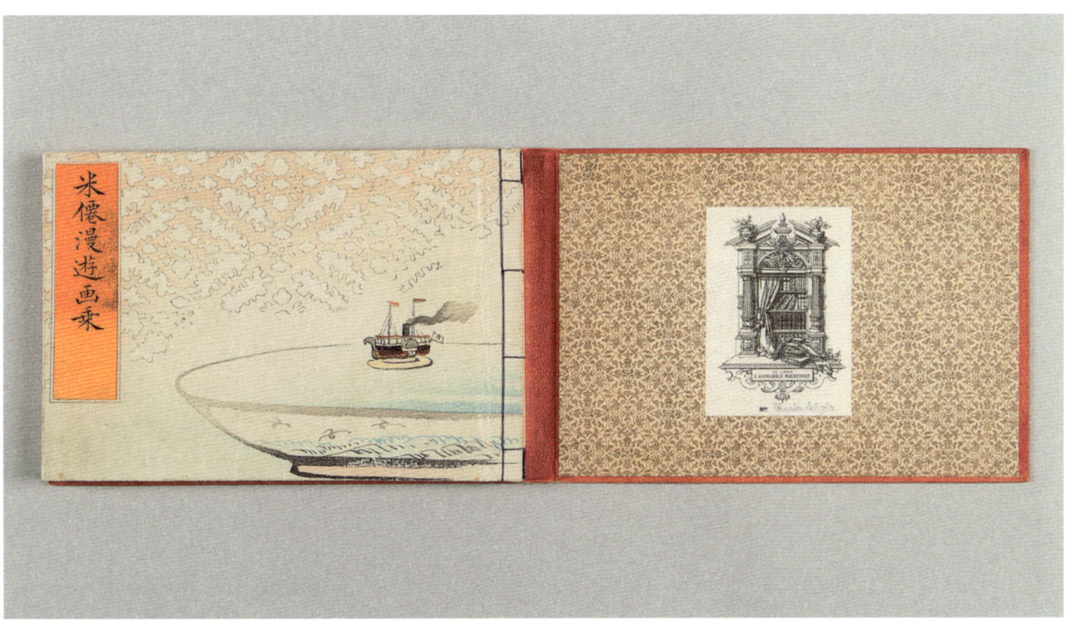

67

Inoue Yūichi (1916–1985)
Economic Growth (経済成長 *keizaiseichō*)
Hanging scroll, ink on paper
91.3 x 105.5 cm
Japan, Shōwa era, 1978

15938, acquired by Japan Art/Frankfurt am Main, 1995

Today, Inoue Yūichi is thought to be one of the most significant
calligraphers of the twentieth century. The artist, who grew
up in Tōkyō and made his living as a primary school teacher,
lived his life in the shadows of Japan's calligraphic circles,
however, which considered themselves part of an intellectual
and artistic elite. He was nonetheless invited to the São Paulo
Biennial in 1957 and to Dokumenta II in Kassel in 1957 on an
insider tip of sorts.

The great trauma of his life was the destruction of Tōkyō by a
massive US air raid in March 1945, in which he, then teaching
at a school in the Japanese capital, nearly lost his life. His
entire calligraphic oeuvre may be interpreted as an attempt
to contend with this existential shock. In contrast, the work
shown here is a striking representation of his critical detach-
ment from Japan's post-war economic growth. His characters,
jumbled together and sometimes crossed, lend the work a
powerful disorder and can be interpreted as a visual representation of the text's message.

This expressive visualisation of inner chaos, which repeatedly
occurs in the artist's work, is likely a conscious reference
to a famous work, the Chinese calligrapher Yan Zhenqing's
(709–785) *Requiem* for his murdered nephew.[11] Inoue Yūichi's
condemnation of the destructive "madness" of modern industrial society highlights the dramatic processes of change to
which our world in flux, is subject, now more than ever.

Lit.: Unagami 2000, vol. 3, no. 78220, p.252

Transcript and translation:

経済成長
浪費拡
大巨大高速路
望無限然
破壊環境汚
染狂気
暴込如斯国亡

keizaiseichō
rōhi kaku-
dai, kyodai kōsokuro
nozomi mugen, shizen
hakai, kankyō-o-
sen, kyōki
abarekomu, sono gotoku
kuni horobu

Economic Growth
Waste
increases, huge highways,
greed unbounded, natural
destruction, Environmental
pollution, madness rages,
thus the country expires

11   C.f. http://www.chinaonlinemuseum.com/calligraphy-
yan-zhenqing-requiem.php (accessed 27 August 2024).

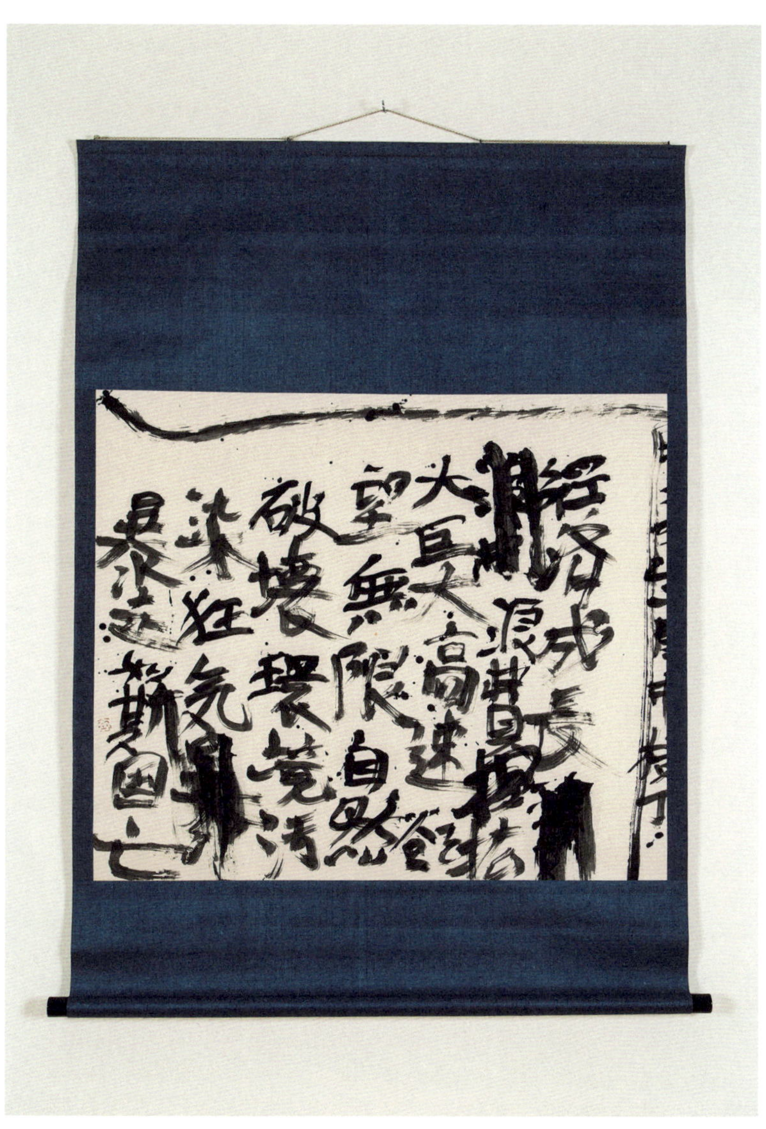

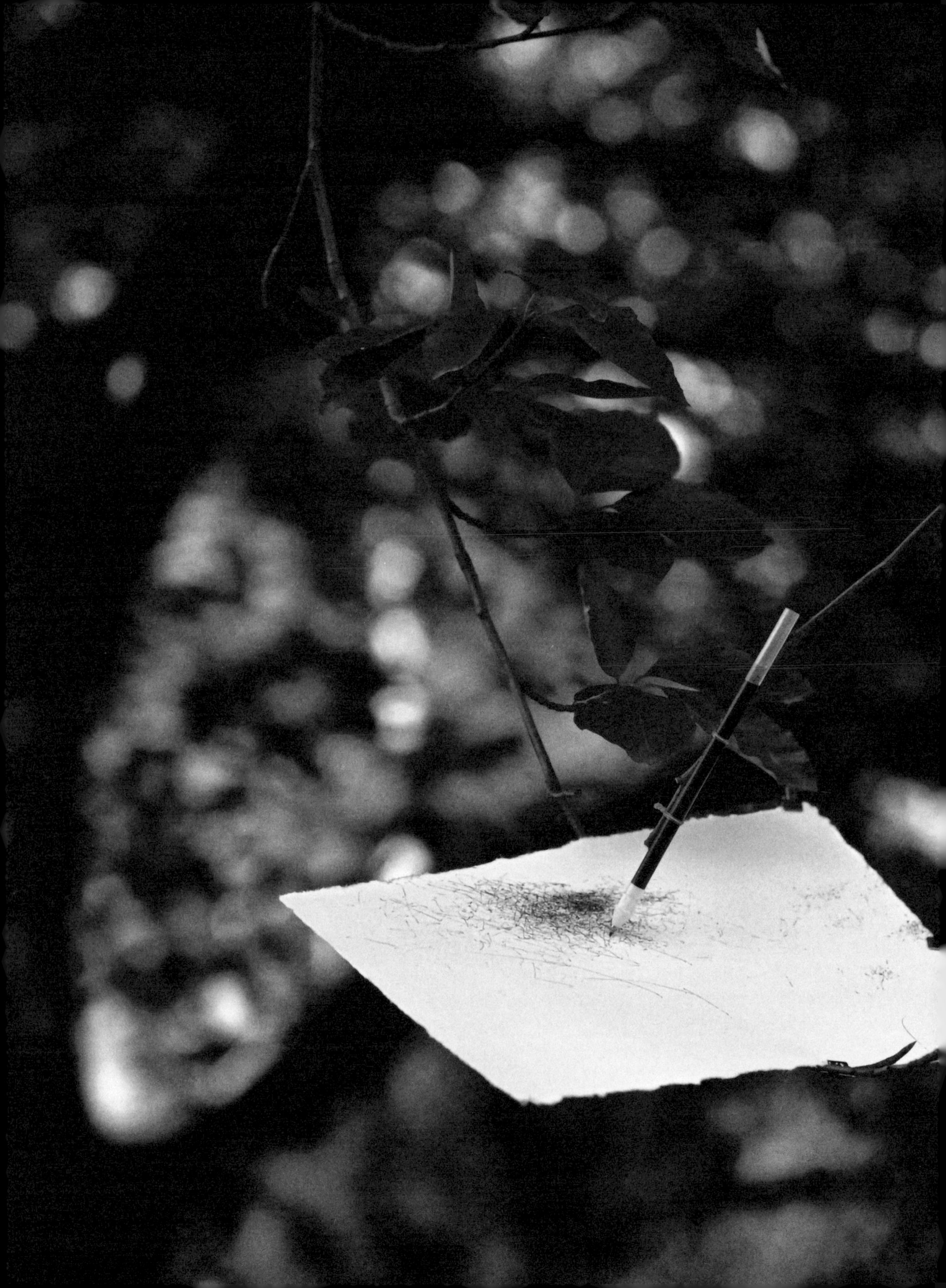

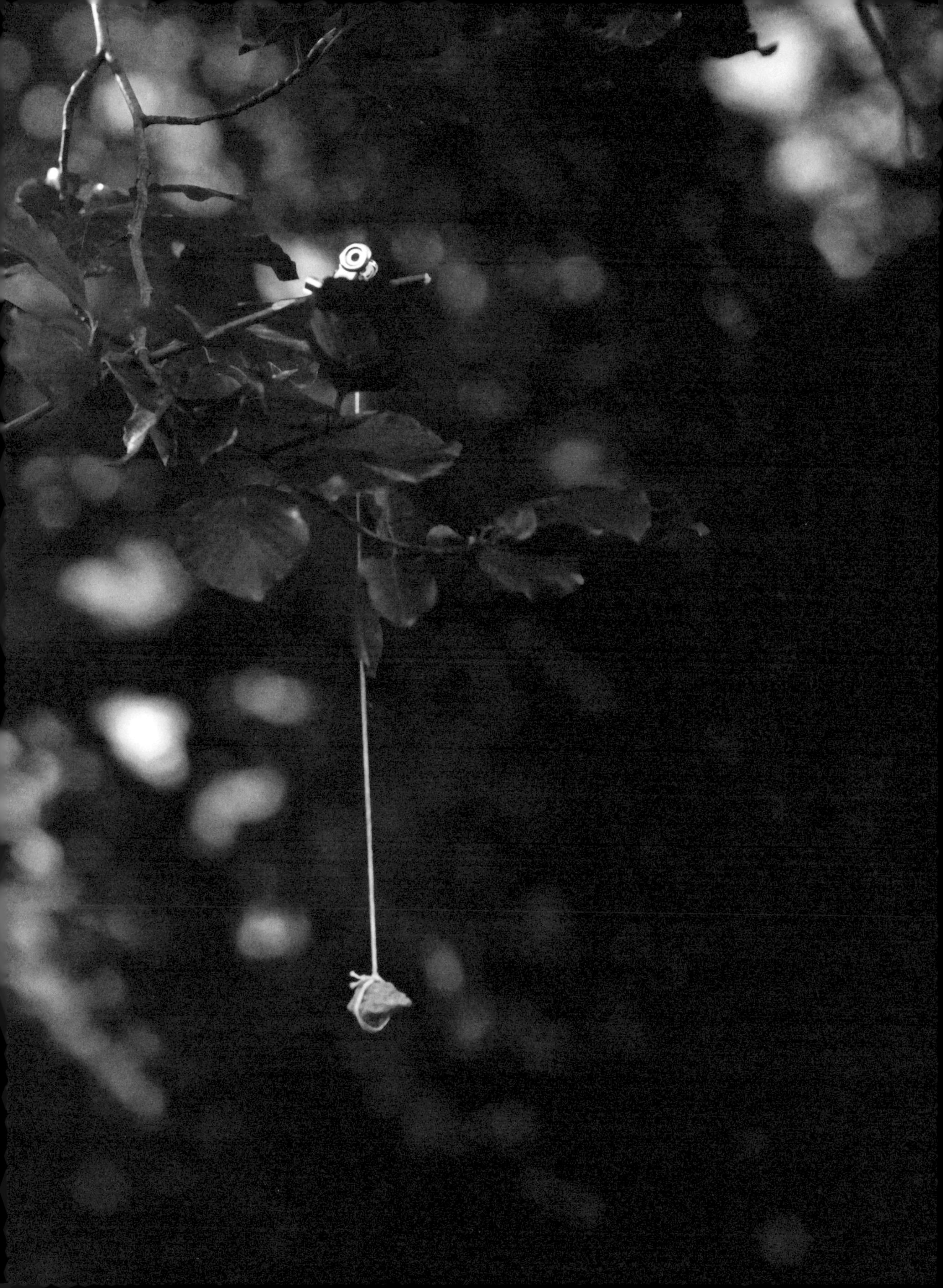

Rikuo Ueda was born in Ōsaka Prefecture in 1950. He embarked on a journey around the world in 1973, spending three years visiting first London, then Norway, Morocco, Turkey, Iran, Pakistan, and India. Following what was evidently a highly conventional study of art in Ōsaka, which he found uninspiring, he supported himself for an extended period through a series of odd jobs. He discovered his topic of the wind as a master of artistic expression in Denmark in 1997. Since then, the wind has "assisted" Ueda in different ways in his abstract drawings on paper. Moreover, he has captured the wind across the world in small film canisters on which he has noted precisely where and when the gust of wind has originated. When capturing the first spring storm (haru ichiban), he consciously or unconsciously follows the Japanese tendency to artistically arrange life according to the passing seasons. Thus his actual "preserved winds" and his open wind drawings made with ballpoint pen, wax crayon, or brush and ink become a kind of memory reserve, a mysterious trace of our existence in the world.

Rikuo Ueda lives and works in the ancient harbour city of Sakai near Ōsaka – when he isn't working in the United States, Denmark, Germany, the Netherlands, Israel, Taiwan, People's Republic of China, or other places in Japan.

On the artist and his work, see:
https://de.wikipedia.org/wiki/Rikuo__Ueda
https://www.mikikosatogallery.com/de/kuenstler/rikuo-ueda/
https://www.youtube.com/watch?v=Gv2TovQdvLM
https://vimeo.com/113597835
https://www.facebook.com/earways/videos/typhoon-no11-rikuo-ue-da/693640454151142/ (accessed 27.6.2024)

We thank Mikiko Sato Gallery in Hamburg, which has represented the artist for over twenty years, for their kind support.

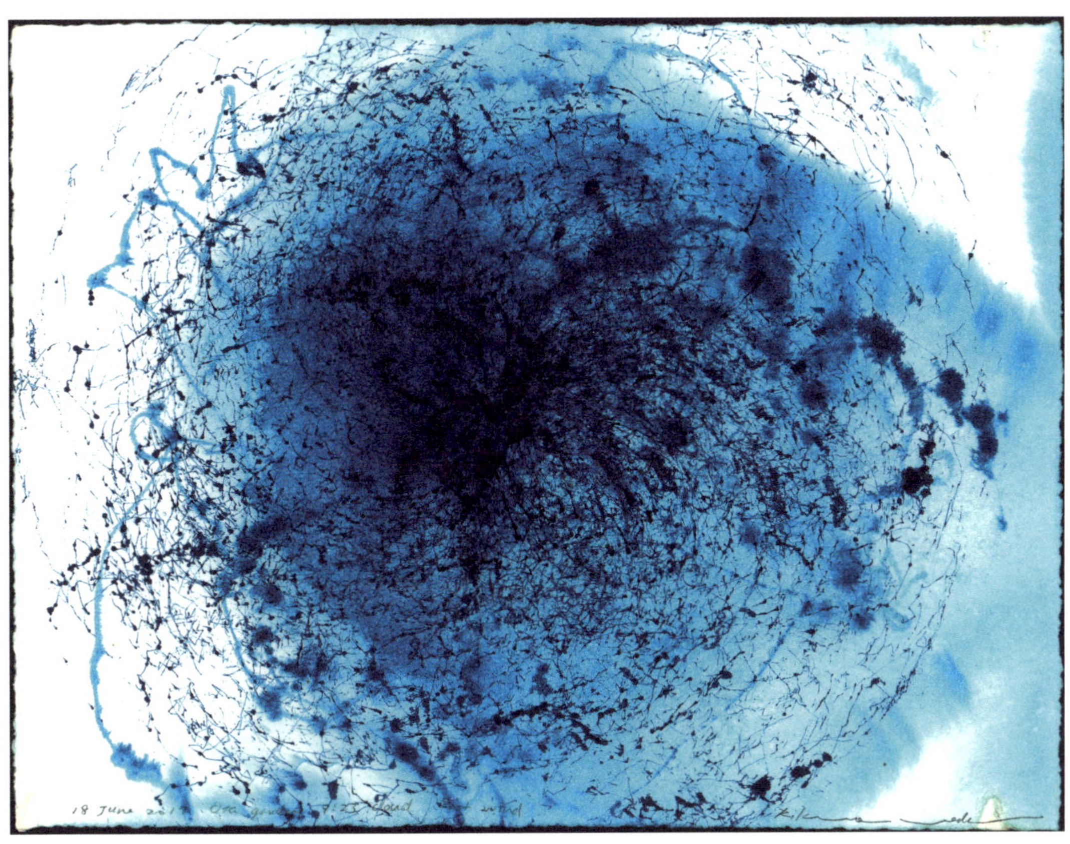

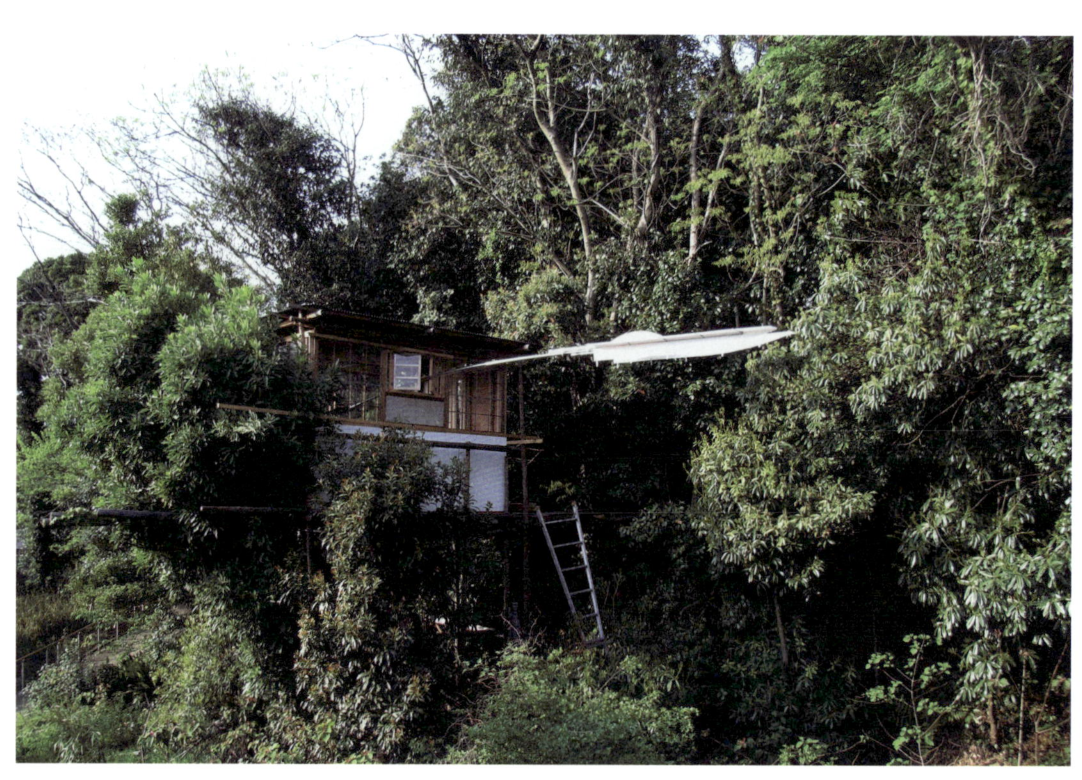

Rikuo Ueda, **House in the Sky**, Sennan City, Ōsaka, 2010

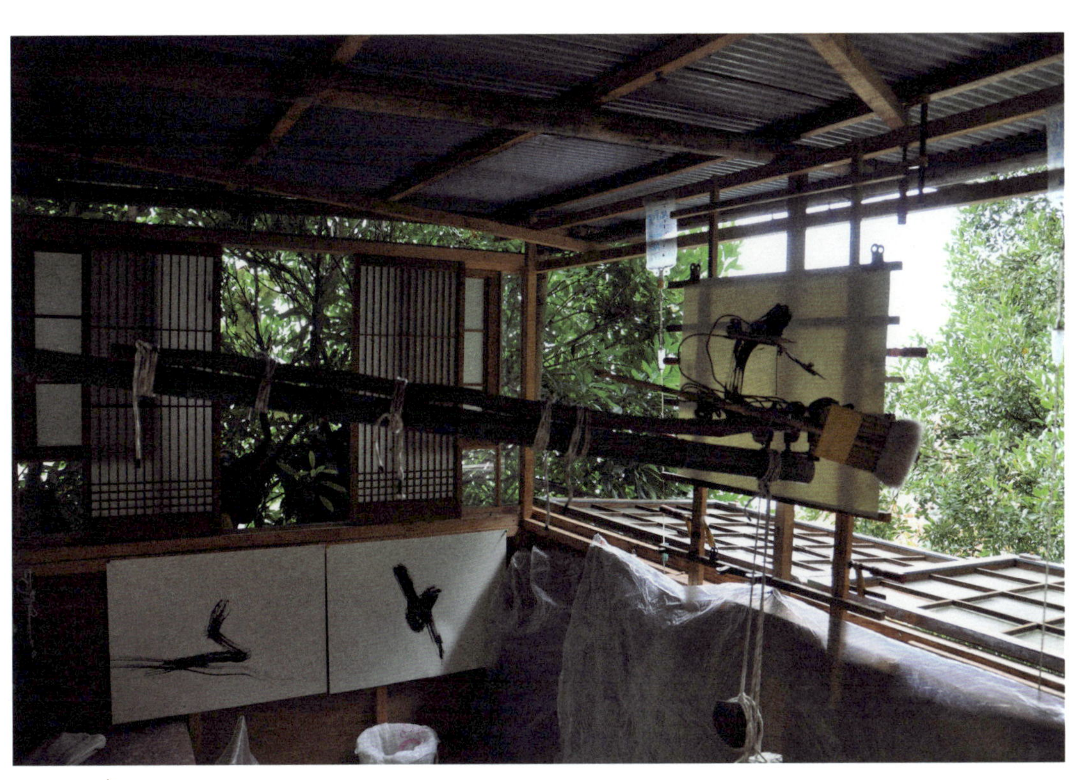

Rikuo Ueda, **House in the Sky**, Sennan City, Ōsaka, 2010

Hide Nasu (b. 1950)
Cloud Portrait, Shaei 写影 222
Encaustic on wood
H 20, W 20, D 3 cm
Atelier Hide Nasu, Frankfurt am Main, 2024

On loan from the artist

The art of Hide Nasu (b. 1950) seems to exist out of time. He uses visual stimuli sparingly, foregrounding shades of grey and black. Nasu uses a limited number of colour pigments, often working only with ink, as well as with wax, to which he applies washi paper. He uses the technique of encaustic painting as per antique mummy portraits, to conjure up colours and shapes on the picture surface using heat.

When showing his work, Hide Nasu finds it important to ensure a lively interaction between the works but also with the viewer. Here, reflections play an important role. This thought began in 1990 with an exhibition of his art in the cloister and inner courtyard of the medieval Carmelite monastery in Frankfurt. Back then, it was a challenge to imagine his abstract, minimalist panels holding their own directly alongside Gothic stone tracery and baroque tombstones set into the walls. Yet the reflective bodies of water he installed on the ground opened up surprising possibilities. Using skewed perspectives and disrupted visual axes, the artist succeeded in achieving harmonies that would otherwise have remained impossible. The outcome was an ensemble in which interstitial spaces and the dialogue formed by the individual elements of the work became an essential element of the artist's statement. In Japan, one refers to 間 *ma* in this context. This difficult-to-translate term is used in architecture as well as in aesthetic discourse more largely to indicate space, period, gap, pause, beat, interval, as well as harmony.

His reflecting ponds integrate the transient moment in time where the process of evaporation becomes visible. The water recedes with infinite slowness, leaving behind its delicate traces, which form an invitation for the "waterer" and observer to submit to a unique aesthetic adventure and experience the comfort to be gained from a continual process of change.

Born in Tōkyō in 1950, the artist joined Kunstakademie Stuttgart in 1977, then the Städelschule in Frankfurt. He taught graphic design at the latter from 1982 to 1987. Since then he has lived and worked in Frankfurt as an independent artist.

On his life, see Frankfurt 2020 as well as https://www.hide-nasu.net/biography.html (accessed 27.6.2024).

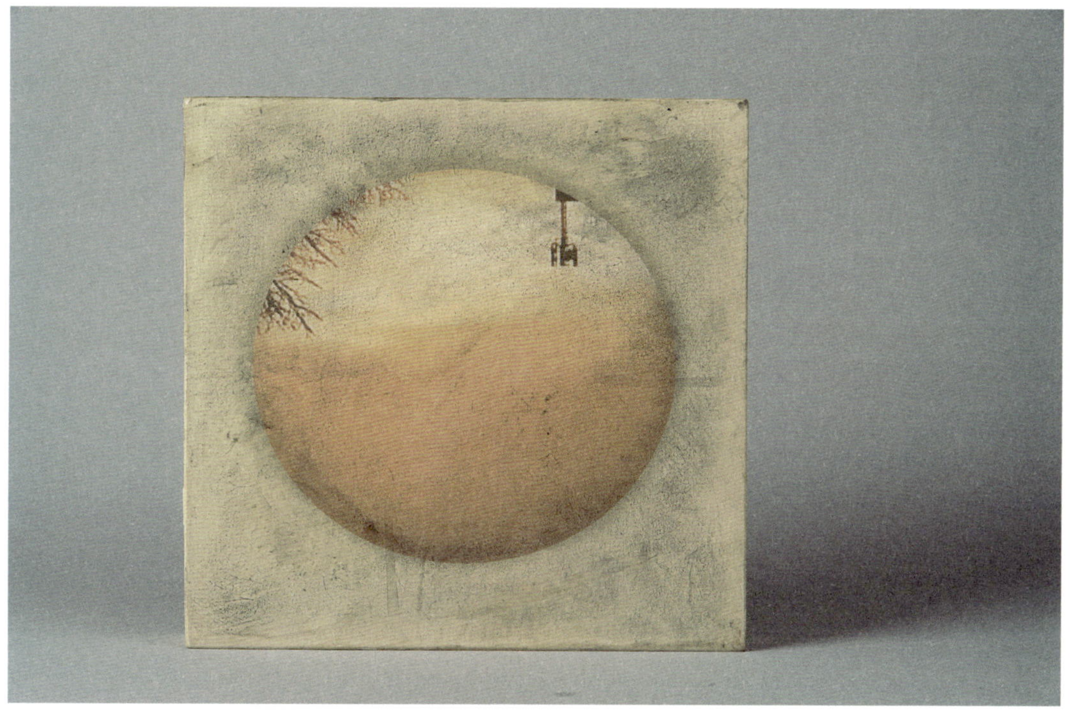

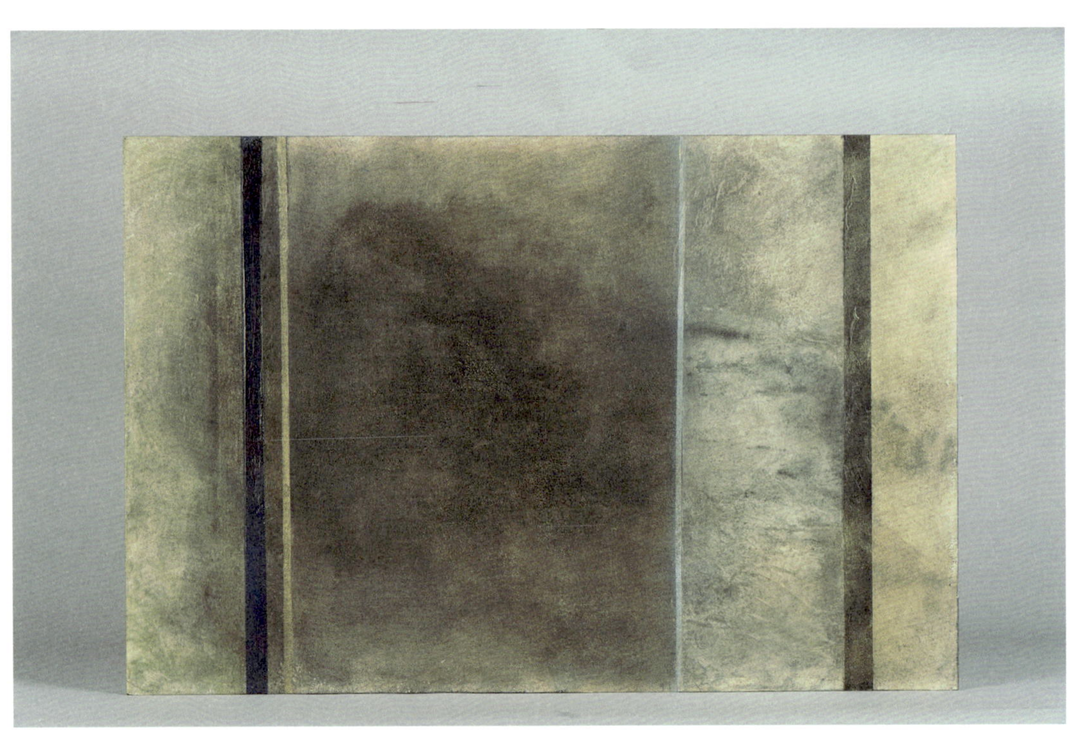

Hide Nasu, 間 *Ma* - **01**, encaustic on wood, H 60, W 90, D 4 cm, Atelier Hide Nasu, Frankfurt am Main, 2024

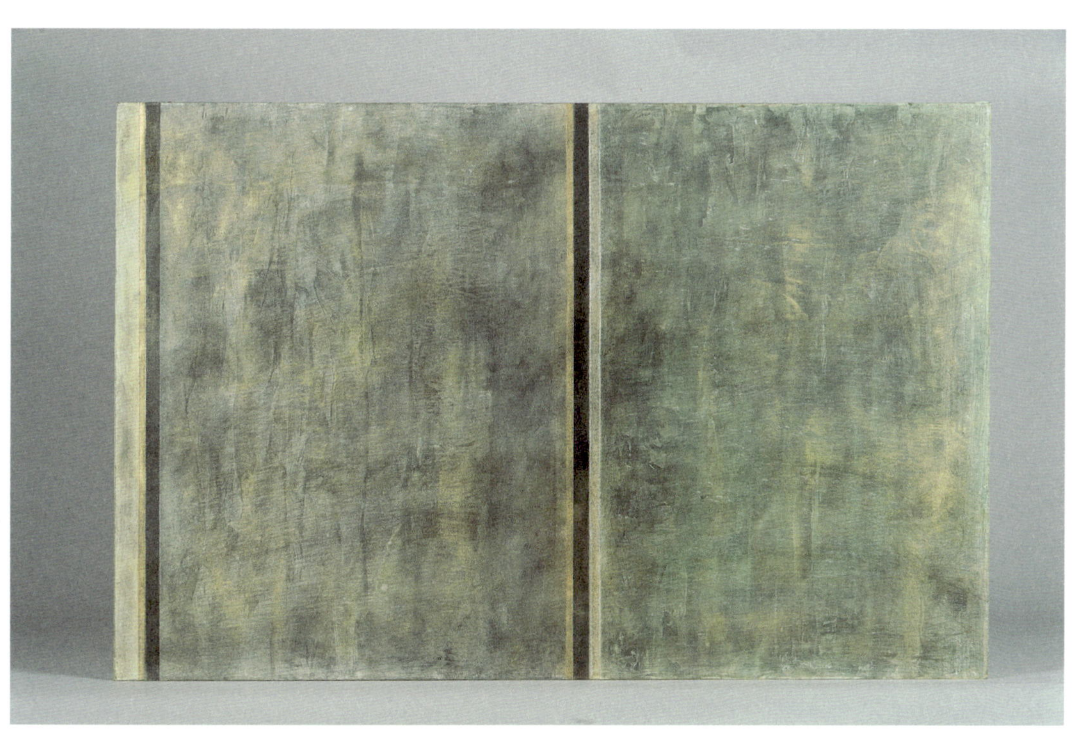

Hide Nasu, 間 *Ma* - **02**, encaustic on wood, H 60, W 90, D 4 cm, Atelier Hide Nasu, Frankfurt am Main, 2024

Shiriagari Kotobuki (b. 1958)
台風中継 **Television Coverage of a Typhoon**
C-print in variable size
2024

Parody on Katsushika Hokusai's woodblock print "Ejiri in Sunshû (Suruga Province)" (c.f. cat.no. 58, p. 172f.)

Shiriagari Kotobuki already came to Frankfurt with his team once in 2008 in order to construct his impressive paper kingdom at Museum für Angewandte Kunst over a series of a few days for the Mangamania exhibition.[1] In his installation, he created a kind of live manga. One could wander on shaky wooden planks through this seemingly meaningless, intentionally fantastical landscape. Within this haunted scene summoned through ink on paper is a small, old-fashioned cathode TV set showing a minimalist animated film, itself a work by the artist.

In the exhibition *A Floating World*, we show an intimate homage by Shiriagari Kotobuki to the internationally acclaimed Japanese artist Katsushika Hokusai (1760–1849).[2] The artist had already interviewed Nagata Seiji, the curator of the major Hokusai exhibition in Berlin in 2011.[3] Even then, Shiriagari Kotobuki evidently saw Hokusai as a major source of inspiration for manga artists. When the discussion turned to Hokusai's rendition of a samurai who emits gas to blow out a candle, Shiriagari explained: "I love the way in which Hokusai is obsessed with depicting something so trivial. His spirit is close to that of a contemporary manga artist who takes pleasure in artistic expression. We are amused by things that people generally consider trivial or beside the point, not worthy of our attention. Our work is different from the paintings that decorate major temples and mansions."

The series "Nearly Thirty-Six Mischiefs of Shiriagari Kotobuki" ironically nods to the Great Wave master and has acquired special meaning at Museum Angewandte Kunst. Many of the works by Hokusai interpreted anew here are part of the *ukiyo-e* collection belonging to Otto Riese, which the museum only acquired in 2012.[4] Thus the exhibition places one of the most innovative manga artists of our time in direct dialogue with a person probably regarded as Japan's greatest *ukiyo-e* masters.

1   C.f. the exhibition catalogue of the Deutsches Filmmuseum/Museum für Angewandte Kunst 2008.

2   C.f. the exhibition Hommage à Hokusai: Nearly Thirty-Six Mischiefs of Shiriagari Kotobuki at the Sumida Hokusai Museum, Tōkyō, 2018, https://hokusai-museum.jp/modules/Exhibition/exhibitions/view/491?lang=en (accessed 27.6.2024).

3   C.f. https://www.wochikochi.jp/english/topstory/2011/10/hokusai-berlin.php (accessed 28.6.2024).

4   C.f. Schulenburg/Höhn 2009, and http://ukipedia.de/ (accessed 28.6.2024). each no. 178, Museum Angewandte Kunst, Otto Riese collection.

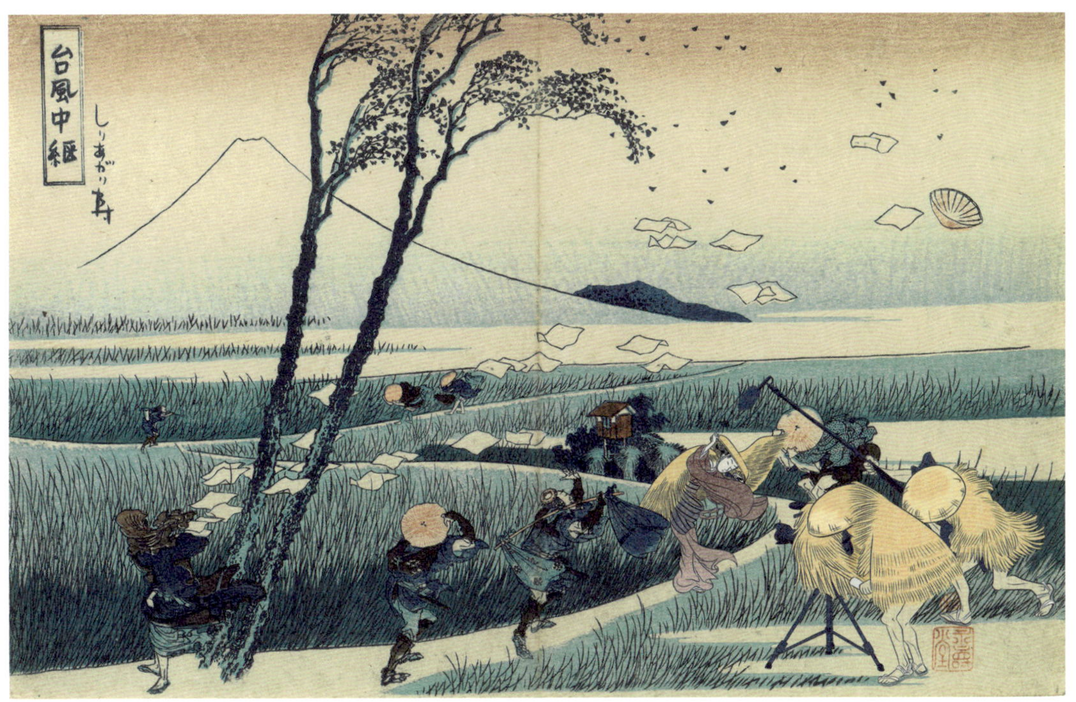

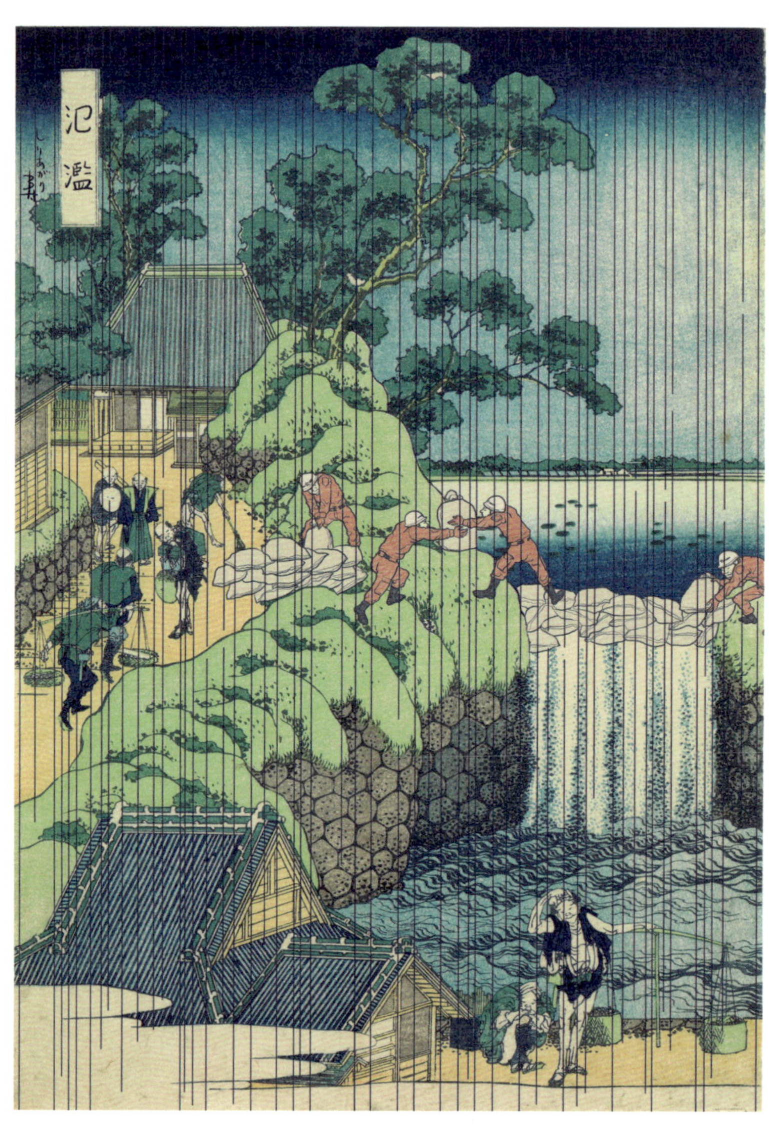

Shiriagari Kotobuki, **諸国瀧廻り 氾濫 Flood**, C-print in varying dimensions, 2024
Parody of Katsushika Hokusai's woodblock print "The Waterfall by Aoigaoka in the Eastern Capital" (c.f. cat. no. 61, p. 178f)

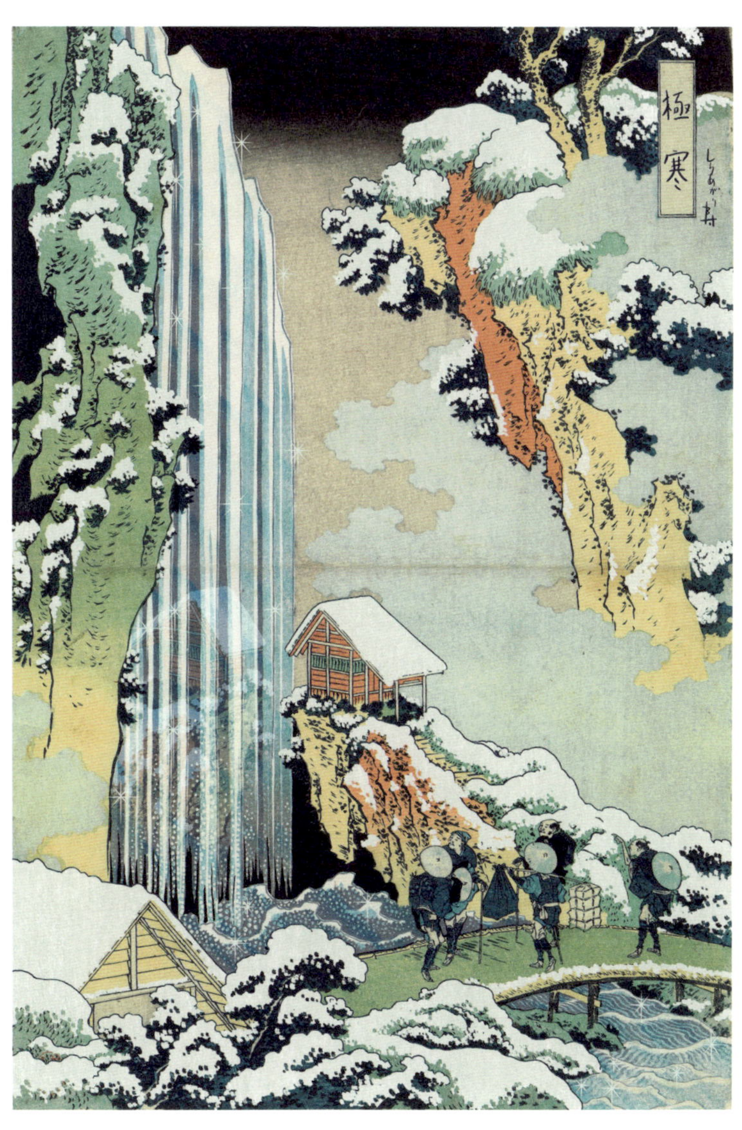

Shiriagari Kotobuki, 諸国瀧廻り 極寒 **Extreme Cold**, C-print in varying dimensions, 2024
Parody of Katsushika Hokusai's woodblock print "The Waterfall by Ono at Kisokaidō" (c.f. cat. no. 60, p. 176f.)

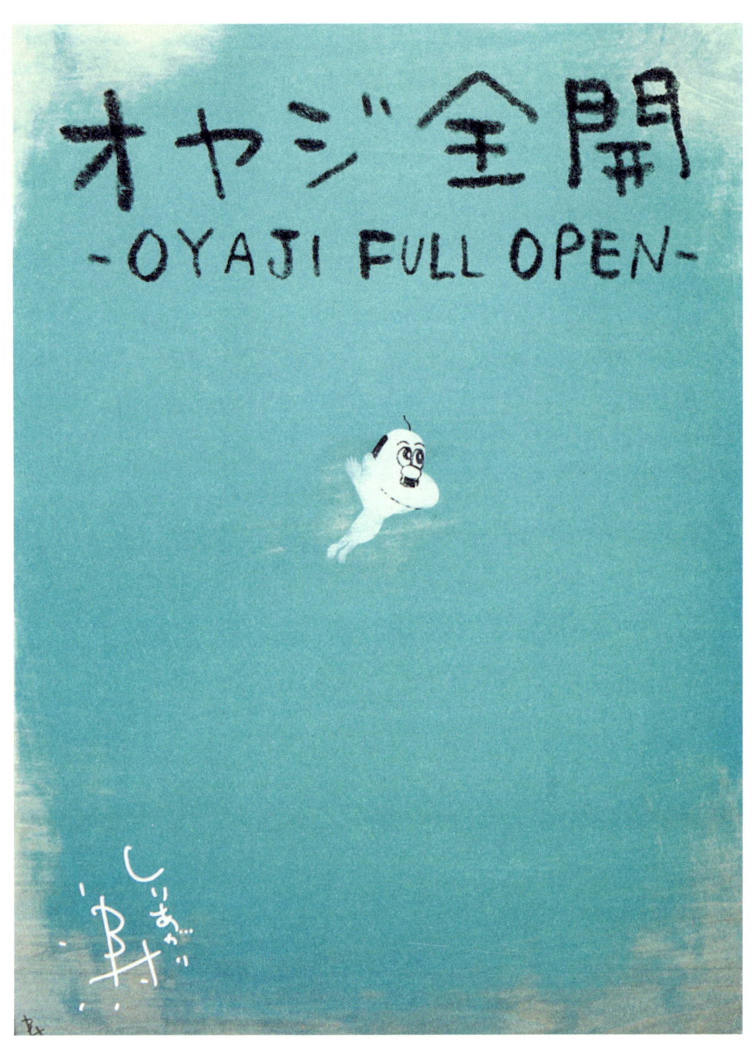

Shiriagari Kotobuki, **オヤジ全開 - OYAJI FULL OPEN** (cover and back page of book), catalogue, Tōkyō: Studio Saruhage, 2023

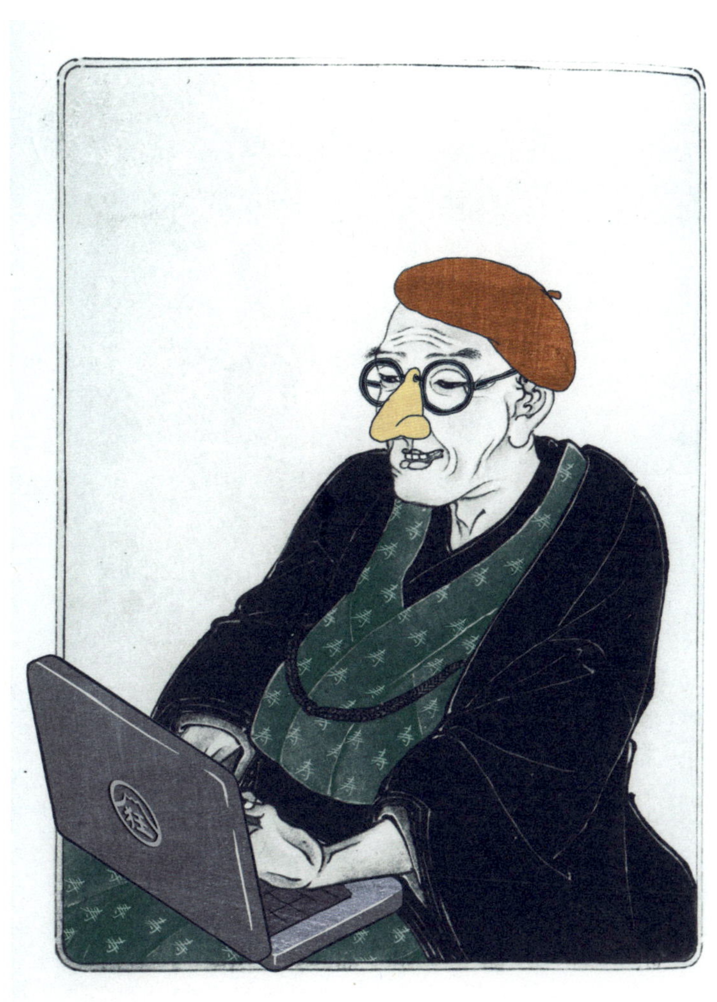

Shiriagari Kotobuki, **Satirical portrait of Katsushika Hokusai with pince-nez and beret at a laptop**, C-print in varying dimensions, 2024
Parody of a Hokusai portrait made by his disciple, Keisai Eisen (1791–1848)

Kengo Kuma (b. 1954)
Teahouse
Double layer of plastic (Tenara 3T40) held in shape through air pressure
L 830, W 440 cm

Museum für Angewandte Kunst, Metzler Park, Frankfurt am Main, 2007

Japanese tea culture has long played a role in the West. Okakura Kakuzō's Book of Tea appeared in English back in 1906.[7] Two years earlier, in 1904, two Raku tea bowls from the Wilhelm Peter Metzler collection (1818–1904) became part of our museum's holdings (cat. no. 14, 15 in the present exhibition).

Over a century later, Kengo Kuma's teahouse in Frankfurt was opened in the garden of the Museum für Angewandte Kunst in 2007. Kuma (b. 1954) is one of Japan's most important contemporary architects. Following his unique understanding of art and architecture, he created a "breathing architecture" constructed from a special plastic and inflated solely by air. This structure was intended to be temporary and could be dismantled or assembled using simple tools at any time.[8]

On p. 210 image of the interior; outside view see p. 48.

7   Okakura Kakuzo, The Book of Tea: *A Japanese Harmony of Art, Culture, and the Simple Life* (New York: Duffield & Company, 1906); first published in German by Insel Verlag in Leipzig in 1919.

8   C.f. Fischer/Schneider 2008. However, this use of the teahouse proved complicated. Major damage was swiftly inflicted on the moveable foundation constructed on a hill and accessible around the clock in Metzler Park by vandals. For some time, the museum heads have sought to protect Metzler Park with a fence that may be locked at night, which would make it possible to use the teahouse in the spot for which it was intended.

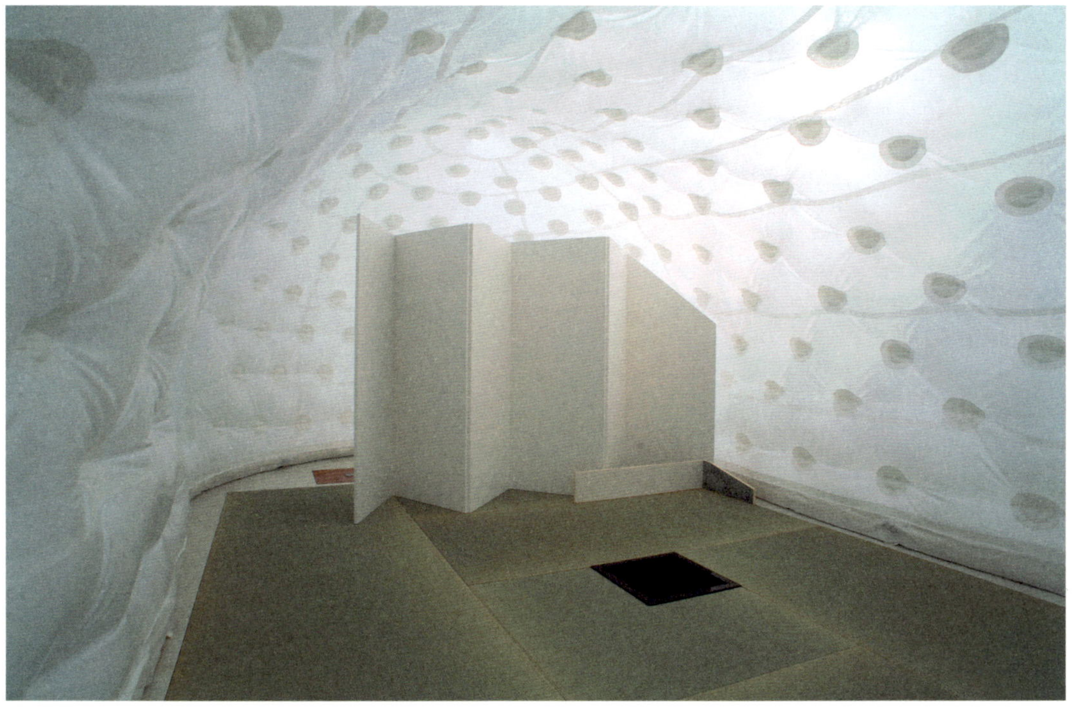

Peter Granser, in collaboration with Mari Kashiwagi
"The Manchurian Crane and the End of the World"
Teahouse installation, scaffolding, C-prints, wood, tea ceremony implements (dimensions variable)
Dimensions of teahouse: L 300, W 300 cm (exterior), L 215, W 215 cm (interior)
Museum für Angewandte Kunst, Frankfurt am Main, 2025

On loan from Stiftung Federkiel, Munich

The project "The Manchurian Crane and the End of the World"
(満州鶴 世界の果て) by Peter Granser finds its place in the
exhibition as a more recent essay on the topic of tea culture.
The indigenous people of northeaster Hokkaidō use the term
"end of the world" to describe a region in which the last of
the Manchurian cranes, which are close to extinction, live.
Granser developed a tearoom on this theme whose rhythmically arranged interior walls evoke ancient Japanese standing
screens and resemble a volcano's clouds of steam. In the
book published on the occasion of the exhibition, they are
accompanied by photographs showing an almost-abstract
black-and-white design formed by cranes in the snow. Granser
was able to collaborate with renowned Japanese poet Mari
Kashiwagi, which has allowed him to place a special emphasis
on the element of poetry, which has always played a key role
in Japanese tea culture.

Granser's art has been strongly influenced by Japanese philosophy and aesthetics for many years now. The artist spent
longer periods of time in Japan, together with his partner
Beatrice Theil, and these decisively influenced his project "The
Manchurian Crane…" The ITO project space that the couple
have run in the Stuttgart district of Bad Cannstatt since 2015
also embodies their aesthetic connection to Japan.

More details on the artistic and literary work of Peter Granser
and Mari Kashiwagi may be found in the introduction to the
present catalogue.[9]

9   C.f. p. 50 ff.; an artist book published by Edition Taube
accompanies the exhibition and is available both at the museum and in
bookshops (Granser/Kashiwagi 2025).

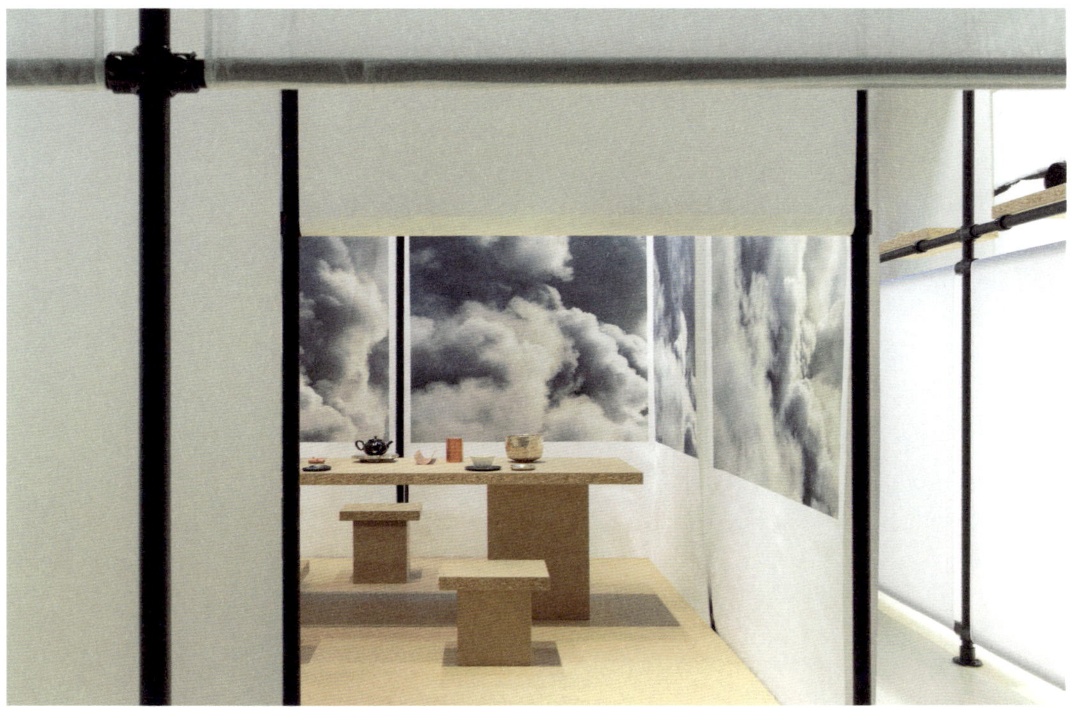

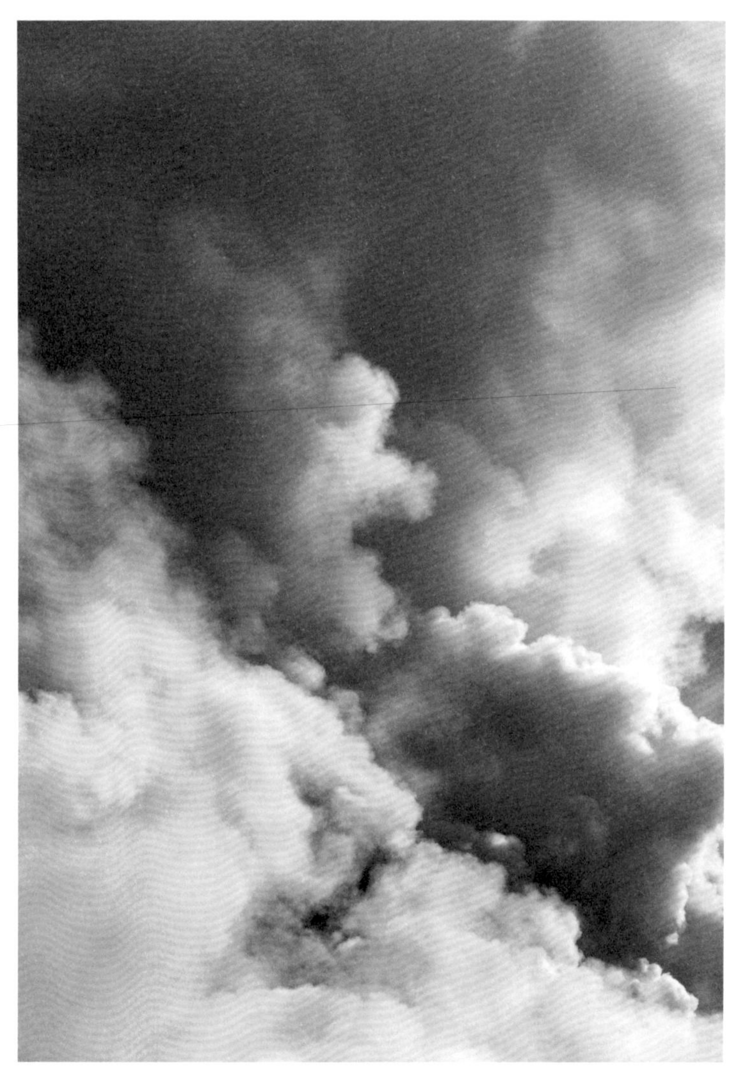

Peter Granser, photograph for the project **"The Manchurian Crane and the End of the World"**, 2025

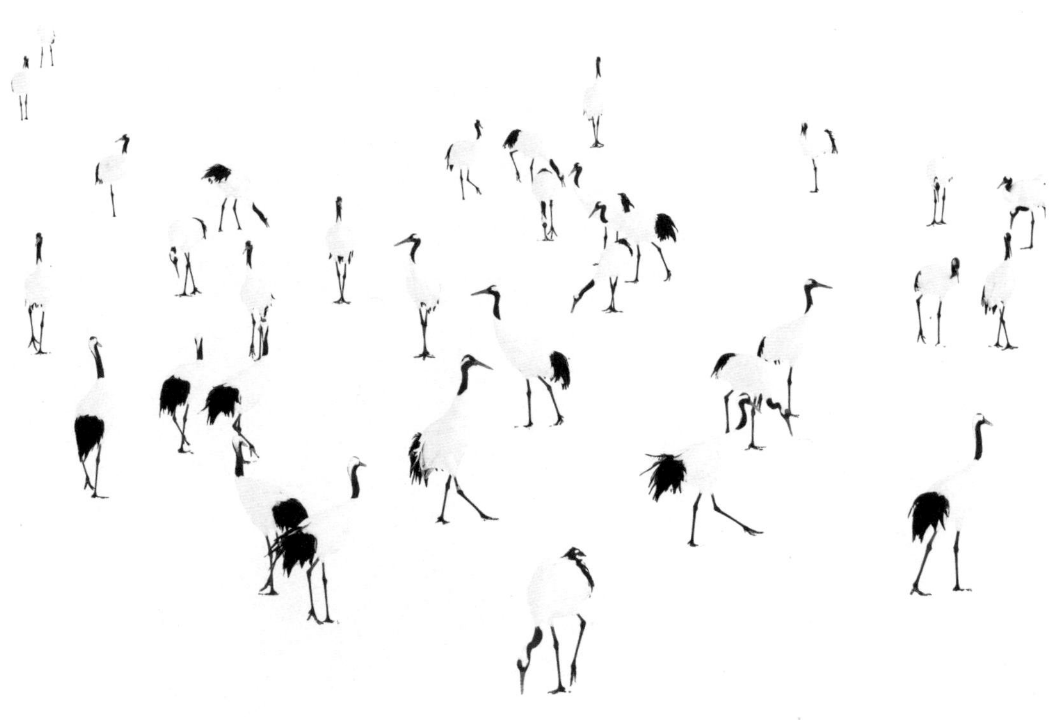

Peter Granser, photograph for the project **"The Manchurian Crane and the End of the World"**, 2025

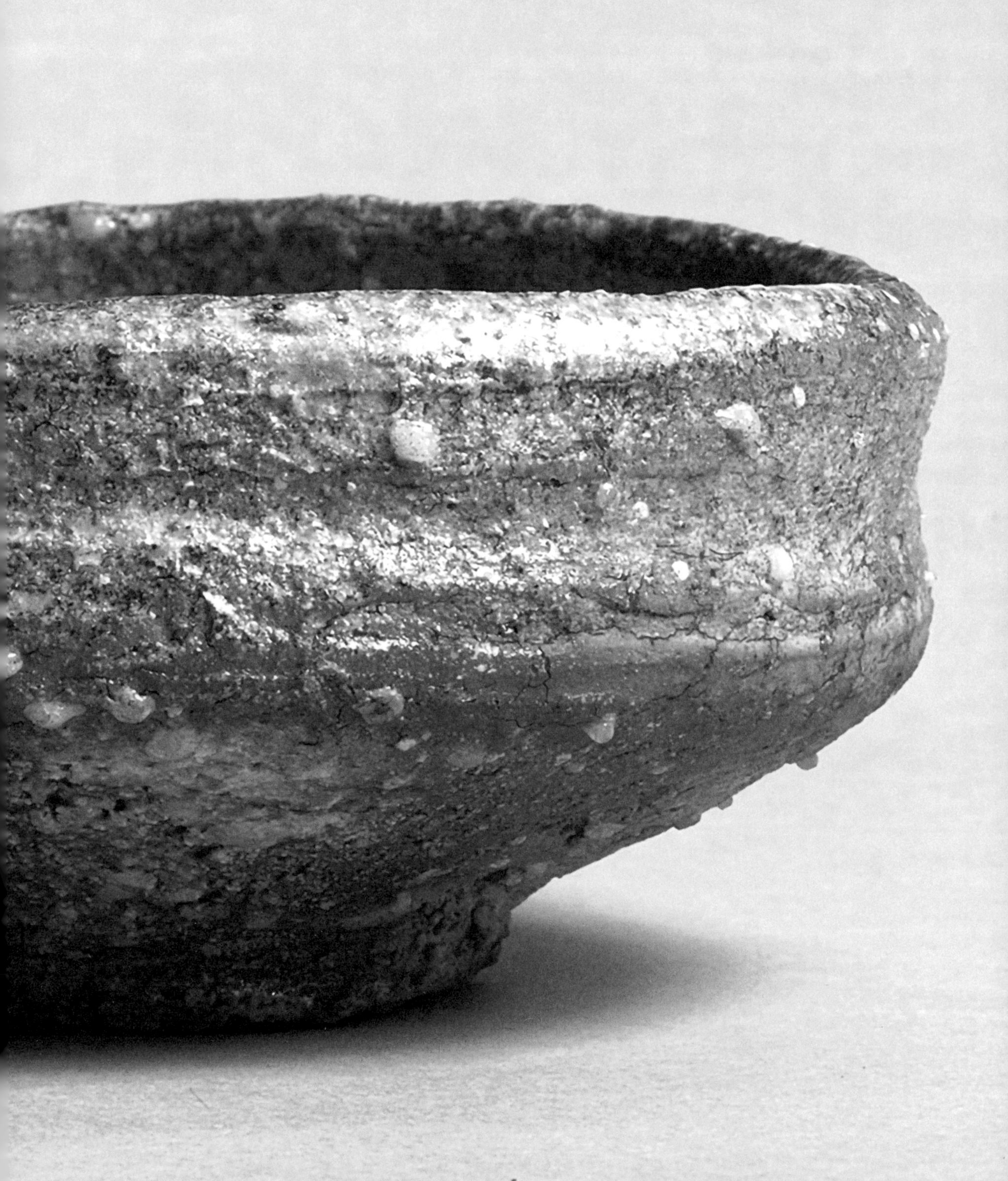

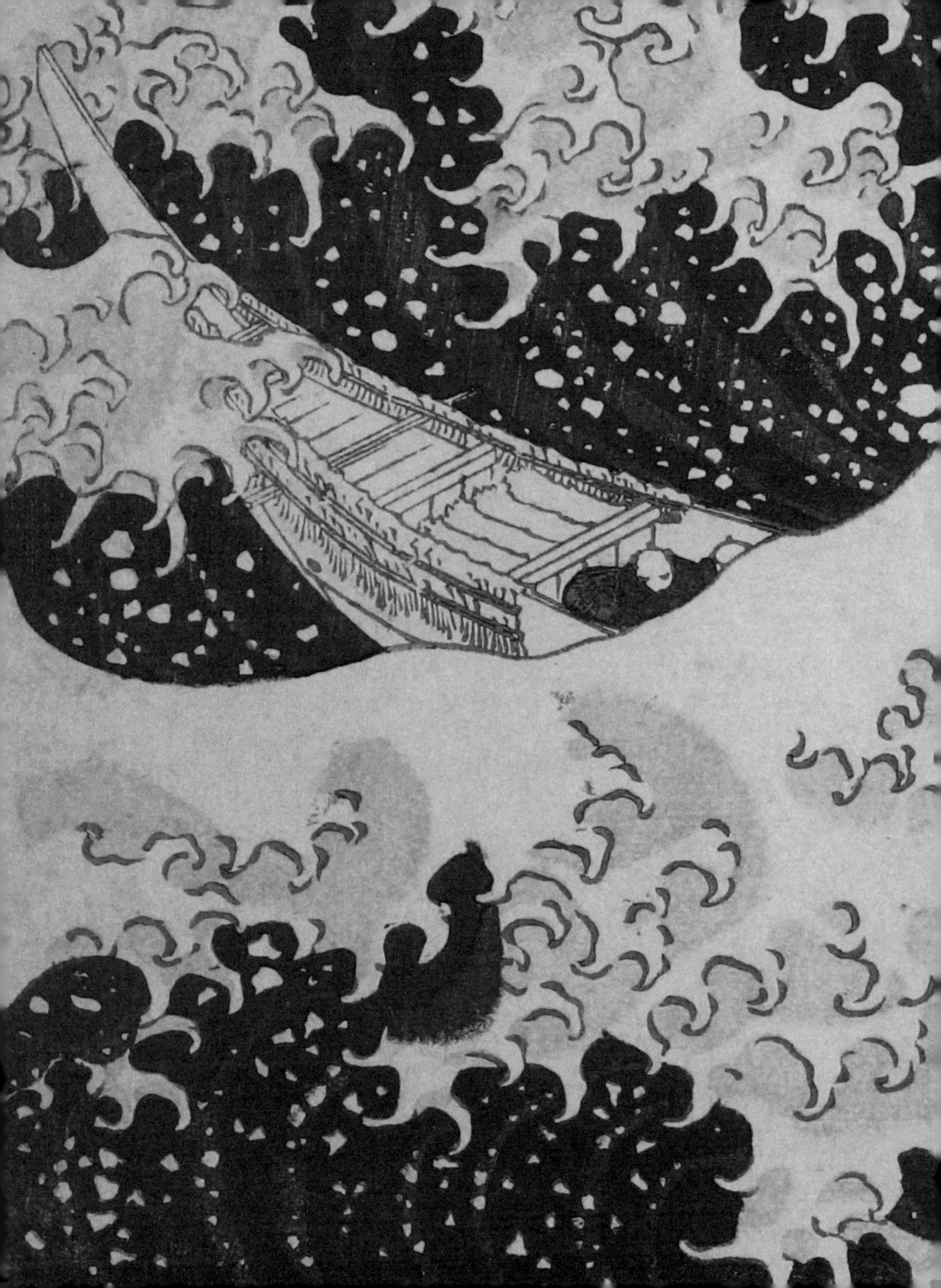

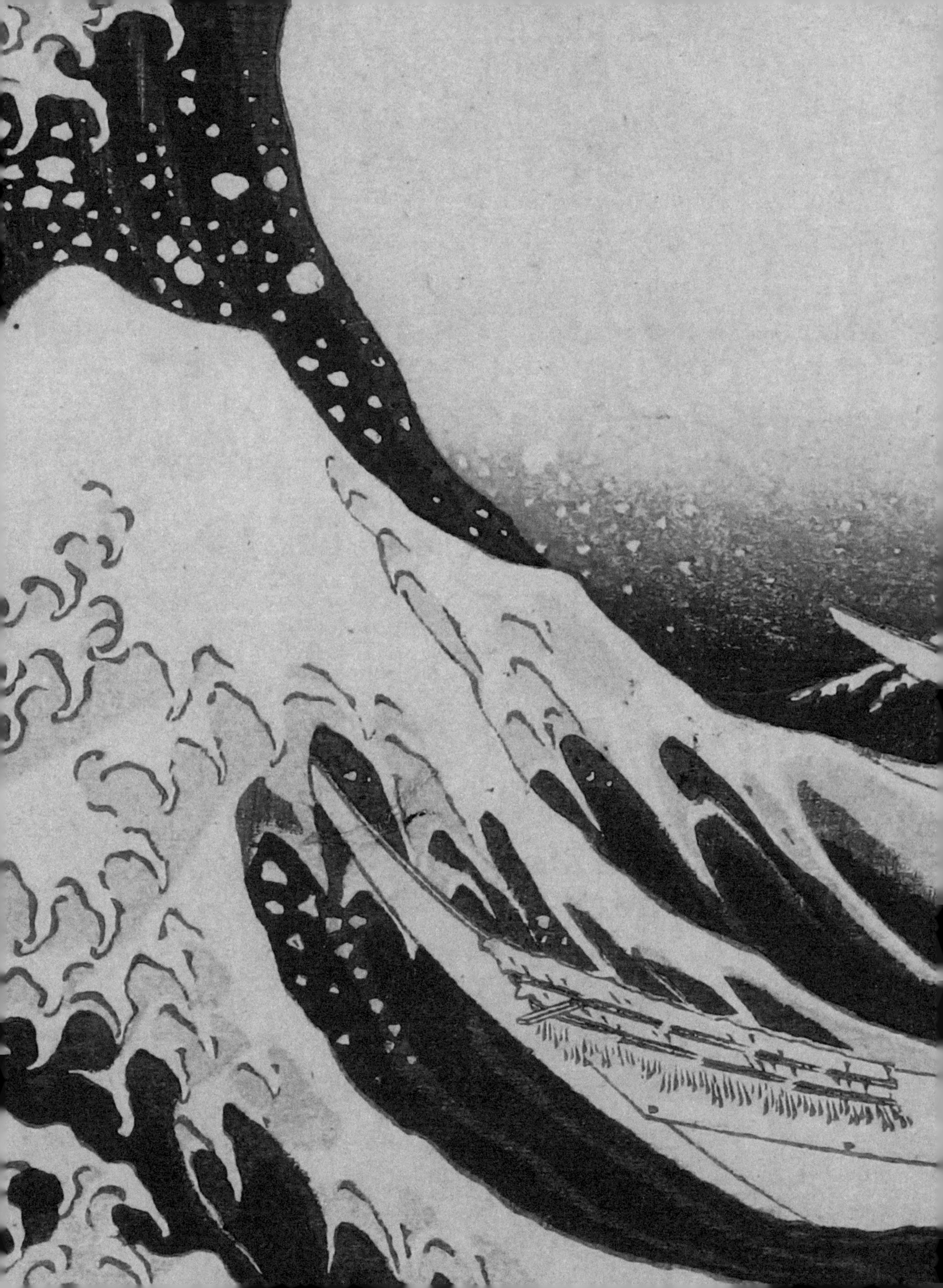

Sources

Bashō 1991
Bashō, Matsuo. *Narrow Road to the Interior*. Translated by Sam Hamill. Boulder: Shambhala
Publications, 1991.

Bauer 1998
*Bürgerliches Mäzenatentum: Die Leihgaben des Kunstgewerbevereins in Frankfurt am Main e.V. an
das Museum für Kunsthandwerk Frankfurt am Main*, edited by Margrit Bauer.
Frankfurt: Museum für Kunsthandwerk, 1998.

Coulmas 2000
Coulmas, Florian. *Japanische Zeiten: Eine Ethnografie der Vergänglichkeit*.
Reinbek: Kindler Verlag, 2000.

Deutsches Filmmuseum/Museum für Angewandte Kunst 2008
Project management: Hans Peter Reichmann and Stephan von der Schulenburg.
Ga-Netchū! Das Manga Anime Syndrom/Ga-Netchū! The Manga Anime Syndrome.
Frankfurt: Deutsches Filmmuseum/Museum für Angewandte Kunst, 2008.

Fischer/Schneider 2008
Kuma, Kengo. *Breathing Architecture: The Teahouse of the Museum of Applied Arts Frankfurt/
Das Teehaus des Museums für Angewandte Kunst Frankfurt*, edited by Volker Fischer and Ulrich
Schneider. Frankfurt: Birkhäuser, 2008.

Frankfurt 2020
Hide Nasu. *Spiegelteich/Mirror Pond/鏡池*, edited by Kulturamt Frankfurt am Main.
Frankfurt: KANN-Verlag, 2020.

Guth 2015
Guth, Christine M.E. *Hokusai's Great Wave: Biography of a Global Icon*.
Honolulu: University of Hawai'i Press, 2015.

Gabbert 1978
Gabbert, Gunhild. *Ostasiatische Lacke*. Frankfurt: Museum für Kunsthandwerk, 1978.

Gabbert Avitabile 1983
Gabbert Avitabile, Gunhild. *Japonica aus der Kunstsammlung des Herrn Wilhelm Peter Metzler
(1818–1904)*. Frankfurt: Museum für Kunsthandwerk, 1983.

Granser/Kashiwagi 2025
Granser, Peter, and Kashiwagi, Mari.
Der Mandschurenkranich & Das Ende der Welt 満州鶴　世界の果て.
Munich, 2025.

Hayashiya 1974
Hayashiya, Tatsusaburō et al. *Japanese Arts and the Tea Ceremony (The Heibonsha Survey of Japanese Art, Vol. 15)*. New York/Tokyo: Weatherhill Inc, 1974.

Murasaki 2002
Murasaki. *The Tales of Genji*. Translated by Royall Tyler. New York: Penguin Classics, 2002.

Ragué 1967
Ragué, Beatrix von. *A History of Japanese Lacquerwork*. Translated by Annie R. de Wassermann. Toronto: University of Toronto Press, 1976. First published in German as Geschichte der japanischen Lackkunst. Berlin, 1967.

Rinne 2015
Raku Kichizaemon XV and Raku Atsundo. *Raku: A Legacy of Japanese Tea Ceramics*. Edited by Melissa M. Rinne. Kyoto: Seigensha, 2015.

Schulenburg/Unagami 1995
Schulenburg, Stephan von der, and Unagami, Masaomi. *YU-ICHI HIN. Werke 1954 bis 1982*. Frankfurt: Schirn-Kunsthalle Frankfurt, 1995.

Schulenburg/Jesse 2000
Mönche, Monster, schöne Damen. Japanische Malerei, Buch- und Holzschnittkunst des 16. bis 18. Jahrhunderts in Frankfurt am Main, edited by Stephan Graf von der Schulenburg. Frankfurt: Museum für Angewandte Kunst, 2000.

Schulenburg/Simon 2002
Schulenburg, Stephan von der and Simon, Rainald. *Feuergeburten. Frühe Chinesische Keramik im mak.frankfurt/The Birth of Form: Early Chinese Ceramics at mak.frankfurt*. Frankfurt: Museum für Angewandte Kunst, 2002.

Schulenburg 2005
Faszination Keramik. Moderne japanische Meisterwerke in Ton aus der Sammlung Gisela Freudenberg/The Fascination of Ceramics: Masterpieces of Modern Japanese Pottery from the Gisela Freudenberg Collection, edited by Stephan von der Schulenburg. Frankfurt: Museum Angewandte Kunst, 2005.

Schulenburg/Höhn 2009
Helden der Bühne und Schönheiten der Nacht: Meisterwerke des japanischen Holzschnitts aus den Sammlungen Otto Riese und Johann Georg Geyger/Heroes of the Stage and Beauties of the Night: Masterpieces of Japanese Woodblock Printing from the Otto Riese and Johann Georg Geyger Collections, edited by Stephan von der Schulenburg. Frankfurt: Museum für Angewandte Kunst, 2009.

Schulenburg 2019
Schulenburg, Stephan von der. *Sieben Schätze: Eine Wunderkammer des japanischen Cloisonnés/ Seven Treasures: A Trove of Japanese Cloisonné*. Frankfurt: Museum für Angewandte Kunst, 2019.

Schulenburg 2023
Schulenburg, Stephan von der. "Kunst als diplomatische Mission: Der Asiatica-Sammler Ernst Arthur Voretzsch (1868–1965)". *Ostasiatische Zeitschrift*, no. 45 (Spring 2023): 32–42.

Soltek 1999
Soltek, Stefan, et al. *Über allen Gipfeln... Naturerfahrung zwischen Goethe und Gegenwart/O'er all the Hill-tops... Experience of Nature from Goethe's Time to the Present*. Frankfurt: Museum für Kunsthandwerk, 1999.

Shiriagari 2023
Kotobuki Shiriagari. *OYAJI FULL OPEN* オヤジ全開. Tokyo: Tokyo Art Beat, 2023.

Trede/Bichler 2007
Trede, Melanie and Bichler, Lorenz. *Meisho Edo hyakkei: One Hundred Famous Views of Edo/ Hundert berühmte Ansichten von Edo/Cent Vues Célèbres d'Edo*. Cologne: Taschen, 2007.

Ueda 2018
Ueda, Rikuo. ウエダ リクオ, edited by Kai Kullen and Guido Schlimbach. Cologne: Kunst-Station Sankt Peter, 2018.

Ueda 2023/2024
Ueda, Rikuo. 手紙 *letter*. Dresden/Hamburg: Sächsische Akademie der Kunst and Mikiko Sato Gallery, 2023/24.

Unagami 2000
Inoue Yūichi shogyō/YU-ICHI. *Catalogue Raisonné of the Works 1949–1985, three volumes*, edited by Masaomi Unagami. Tokyo: UNAC Tokyo, 2000.

Vos/Stiller 2011
Vos, Ken and Stiller, Maya. *Entdeckung Korea! Schätze aus deutschen Museen/Korea Rediscovered: Treasures From German Museums*. Berlin: Korea Foundation, Cologne: Museum für Ostasiatische Kunst, Leipzig: Grassi Museum für Völkerkunde, Frankfurt: Museum für Angewandte Kunst, Stuttgart: Linden-Museum, 2011–13.

Weinmayr 1994
Weinmayr, Elmar. *Kado Isaburō. Lackarbeiten*. Berlin: Museum für Ostasiatische Kunst, Frankfurt: Museum für Kunsthandwerk, Düsseldorf: EKŌ-Haus der Japanischen Kultur, 1994.

Imprint

This publication appears on the occasion of the exhibition

A Floating World
Impermanence and Motion in Japanese Art

Museum Angewandte Kunst, Frankfurt am Main
January 31 – April 27, 2025

Catalogue

© 2025 Museum Angewandte Kunst Frankfurt am Main,
editors, authors, translator and Verlag der Buchhandlung
Walther und Franz König, Köln

Index of Images:
p. 4/5: cat. no 54; p. 8/9: cat. no 9; p.54/55: cat. no 52; p.56:
cat. no 23 ; p. 194/195: cat. no 69; p. 216/217: cat. no 30;
p.218/219: cat. no 56; p. 226: cat. no 19.

Photo and Image Credits:
© 2025 Ueda Rikuo/Mikiko Sato (p. 42f., 196-202), Hide
Nasu (p. 44, 203-205), UNAC TOKYO, Tokio ITO (p. 46f,
207-209), Axel Schneider (p. 46), Shiriagari Kotobuki (p. 46,
208), Shogakukan-Shueisha Productions Co. (p. 47, 207, 209),
Uwe Dettmar (p. 48, 211), Peter Granser (p. 50, 213-215), © VG
Bild-Kunst, Bonn 2024 für [Peter Granser], Stephan von der
Schulenburg (p. 41), Marcus Müller/Japan Art (p. 59), all other
images: Museum Angewandte Kunst Frankfurt am Main

Editors:
Stephan von der Schulenburg, Matthias Wagner K

Author:
Stephan von der Schulenburg

Translator:
Sylee Gore

Designer:
Zarah Landes

Photographers:
Ute Kunze, Franziska Krieg, Rainer Drexel

Lithography:
Lösch GmbH & Co. KG

Printing:
Lösch GmbH & Co. KG

Published by Verlag der Buchhandlung Walther und Franz
König, Ehrenstr. 4, D-50672 Köln

Project Manager:
Nicole Rankers

Bibliographic information published by the Deutsche
Nationalbibliothek

The Deutsche Nationalbibliothek lists this publication in the
Deutsche Nationalbibliografie; detailed bibliographic data is
available on the internet at http://dnb.d-nb.de.

Printed in Germany

Distribution:

Germany, Austria, Switzerland
Buchhandlung Walther König
Ehrenstr. 4,
D – 50672 Köln
Tel +49 (0) 221 / 20 59 6 53
verlag@buchhandlung-walther-koenig.de

Outside the United States and Canada,
Germany, Austria and Switzerland by
Thames & Hudson Ltd., London
www.thamesandhudson.com

United States and Canada
D.A.P. / Distributed Art Publishers, Inc.
75 Broad Street, Suite 630
USA – New York, NY 10004
Tel +1 (0) 212 627 1999
orders@dapinc.com

ISBN 978-3-7533-0714-5

Exhibition

Museum Angewandte Kunst, Frankfurt am Main

Director:
Matthias Wagner K

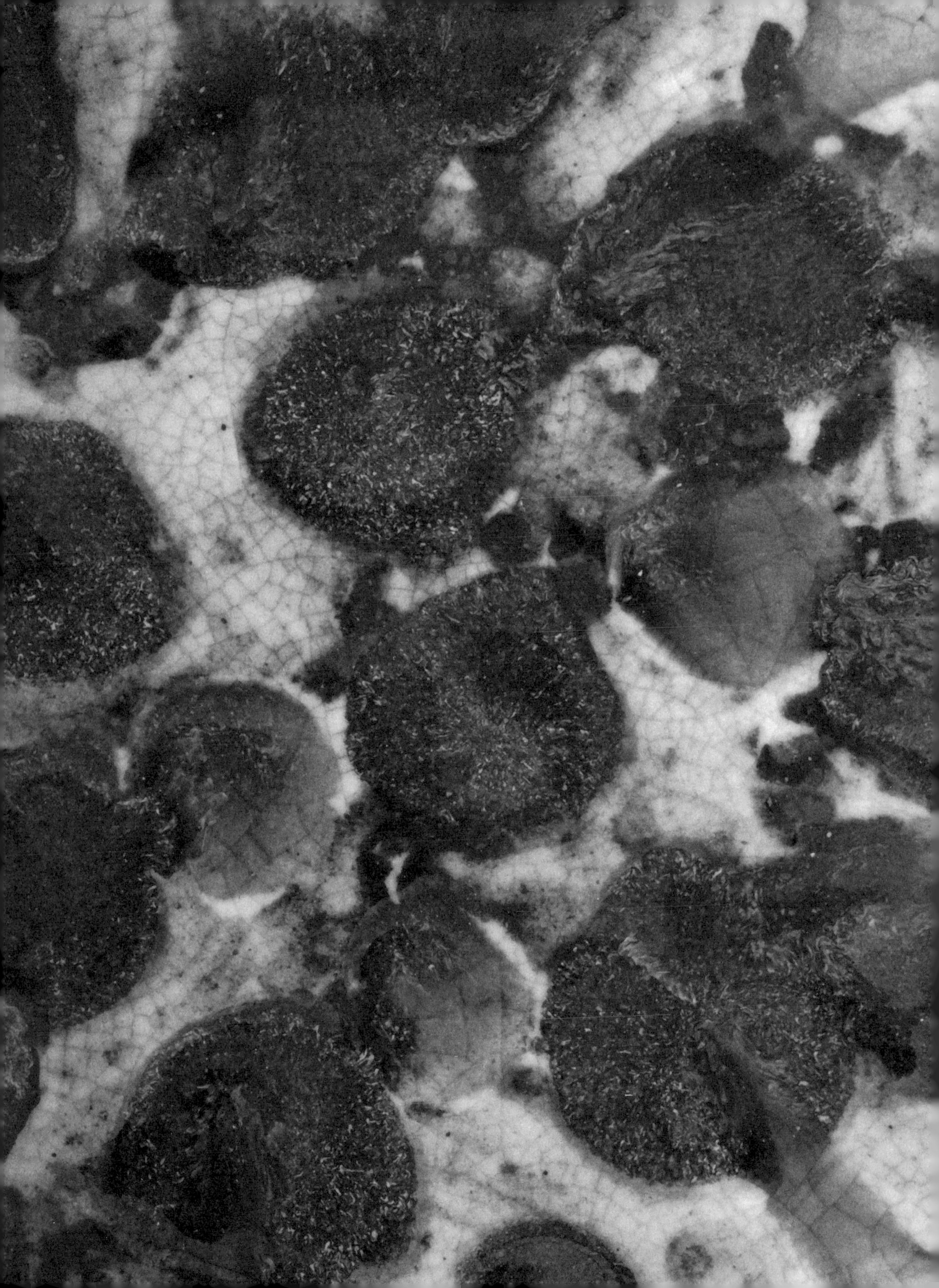